PROPOSAL
SAVVY

In loving memory of my parents
and for

Linda, *Ellen*, and *David*

PROPOSAL SAVVY

Creating Successful Proposals
for Media Projects

Elise K. Parsigian

SAGE Publications
International Educational and Professional Publisher
Thousand Oaks   London   New Delhi

For information address:

 SAGE Publications, Inc.
2455 Teller Road
Thousand Oaks, California 91320
E-mail: order@sagepub.com

SAGE Publications Ltd.
6 Bonhill Street
London EC2A 4PU
United Kingdom

SAGE Publications India Pvt. Ltd.
M-32 Market
Greater Kailash I
New Delhi 110 048 India

Printed in the United States of America

Library of Congress Cataloging-in-Publication Data

Parsigian, Elise K.
    Proposal savvy: Creating successful proposals for media projects /
by Elise K. Parsigian.
        p. cm.
    Includes bibliographical references and index.
    ISBN 0-7619-0026-8 (cloth: acid-free paper). — ISBN 0-7619-0027-6 (pbk.:
acid-free paper)
        1. Mass media—Authorship. 2. Mass media—Research—Methodology.
    3. Proposal writing in business. 4. Business communication.
    I. Title.
    P96.A86P375   1996
    808'.066302—dc20   95-41789

This book is printed on acid-free paper.

96 97 98 99   10 9 8 7 6 5 4 3 2 1

Sage Production Editor: Astrid Virding
Sage Copy Editor: Joyce Kuhn
Sage Typesetter: Janelle LeMaster

Contents

Foreword

Proposal Savvy presents a valuable guide to proposal thinking and proposal writing for anyone in the field of communication. As the author notes, there are many similarities in today's marketplace among the field generally thought of as communication — journalism, both print and broadcast, advertising, and public relations. There are also many differences in these fields, particularly between the traditional role of journalism and the more commercial ventures of advertising and public relations. One of the many things that binds them together is the need for creative thinking, creative problem solving, and creative presentations. The book serves as an introduction to those activities, asks pertinent questions about the work, and provides a plan for proposal writing that is easily adapted to most situations.

There is a need for this kind of book. In an era where clever ideas need the backup of a strong sell and solid documentation, it offers a rigorous approach that stresses the need for thorough thinking before writing. It warns against the easy, quick, or predetermined solution. It makes those who would jump to obvious conclusions realize the necessity for logical progression and the importance of evidence to back up all ideas. The book stresses the importance of defining and understanding client and audience needs and of structuring the proposal in ways that show the ideas fulfill and extend these needs. Using it should lead the proposal writer to workable and winning proposals that can lead to the successful completion of any task.

Tapping into the creative and critical approaches to problem solving, the author stresses the importance of the homework before the writing. She also stresses the need for rethinking, checking, and asking questions about the work at every stage along the way. Proposal writing, as the book states, is a process. Structure, rigor, evaluation, organization, and review are a part of the process. Creative people routinely reject structure as too confining and too time-consuming; this book points out its importance and presents the process as enhancing, not inhibiting, the creative process. From this problem-solving process comes the implementation strategy. It is only after all that thinking and evaluation that the proposal may be written. The author's approach leads to the customized proposal. Closely tied to the specific problem at hand, this kind of proposal has the greatest odds for success.

Although the process is rigorous and although the book gives lists of questions to ask oneself and checklists to review, this book on proposal writing goes far beyond the common cookbook approach to communications. Because it stresses the creative involvement of the proposal writer and because it demands rigorous thinking, it is a catalyst for generating on-target work that is customized to the task at hand and that challenges the writer to ferret out hidden pitfalls before they become traps that inhibit success.

For the uninitiated, the examples and cases provide a good feel for both the scope and the importance of the proposal process in getting ideas articulated and accepted so that the work may proceed. Examples are given both from journalistic story ideas and from advertising and public relations. It goes further in suggesting ways to write proposals for fund-raising, a valuable skill in today's competitive and entrepreneurial environment. A section of practical tips from professionals in funding organizations is filled with hard-hitting advice that works.

It may surprise the novice that fully one half of the book is devoted to activities in the prewriting stage. But the stress on successfully underpinning the ideas and testing them for validity makes the proposal writing process easier and ensures a far greater than average likelihood for success. Brilliant writing, after all, is not at all useful if the real problem has not been identified, scrutinized, and made the subject of a great deal of thought.

The chapters dealing with the writing stage of the task outline key components and pose key questions along with real-life examples and tactics. The distinction between internal and external proposals clarifies the level of detail needed for these differing kinds of work. Cautioning that there is no standard format for proposal work, the book goes on to give the reader a comprehensive set of key components that can be adapted to individual situations. Checklists and examples enhance the material here. By following the ideas and considering the questions, the would-be writer is led to produce a solid proposal that includes all the essential information and at the same time interests the reader. Relevant questions on the inclusion of graphics and other illustrations enable the proposal writer to choose areas that enhance the presentation in a constructive way. When organized effectively, ideas, words, and graphics push the proposal forward smoothly.

The chapter on proposal delivery is filled with practical ideas and enhanced with examples to show effective presentation techniques. There is an excellent section on challenges and questions to help prepare for audience reaction. Timing, style, and nonverbal messages are all discussed. The stress here is on presenting and performing a solid proposal effort. Any reader can benefit from the suggestions given here.

The final chapter on the book gives clear suggestions for the preparation and use of visual aids, always an important element in the actual presentation.

This is a well-organized book. It is straightforward and comprehensive and reads well. It moves easily from the crucial challenges of creativity and critical thinking right through to information gathering and other research, audience and competitive analysis, and then to writing and presenting the proposal itself. The emphasis throughout is on thoroughness, evaluation, and problem-solving techniques. It is a book that should be read in its entirety for the greatest advantage and then placed on an easily accessible reference shelf. Subsequent readings should lead to additional insights.

Experienced proposal writers should not be misled into thinking this book is for the novice alone. Everyone who has an idea or project to sell in any communication venue can gain a competitive edge and profit well from the ideas presented here.

–Mary Alice Shaver
Associate Professor
University of North Carolina at Chapel Hill

Preface

I t's not widely known, but mass media communicators write *proposals*. Knocking out assignments on demand is only one dimension of media work. Writing proposals is another. The ability to produce an idea for a proposal, either as an enterprise project or in response to a client need, speaks to the diverse skills expected of problem solvers in media, especially the writers. Ideation also responds to the needs of a media house dependent on staff initiative to help sustain its competitive edge. The trick is to convince usually resistant decision makers that your proposed ideas serve their purpose. As difficult as that may be at times, today's media climate demands such duty. Media employers expect it.

In the real world of mass media, news and broadcast journalists initiate proposals for projects they believe offer something of value to an audience. Public relations and advertising writers become members of a proposal team organized to resolve a client's problem. Freelance media writers prepare proposals seeking funds to support production of their project idea. In each case, a proposal is prepared not only to describe its purpose and method of implementation but also to convince decision makers that the proposed project merits their support and that the petitioner is capable of getting the job done.

Although personnel in various areas of mass media refer to proposal preparation by different names (memorandum, outline, recommendation, plan, strategy, opportunity), media pros know what the word *proposal* means. They also know that a diverse vocabulary doesn't mean the absence of a common discipline. Media pros are becoming more and more aware that, although differences exist between their divisions, their personal habits of research and report are more similar than they are different. Those habits make up a step-by-step, problem-solving process and the critical-creative thinking technique the process requires.

They apply that discipline to all areas of their work, including proposal preparation and presentation. This book describes and details the process as it applies to producing a proposal whether it's for a print or broadcast, public relations, or advertising project.

The pattern of practitioners' activity and thought became evident following several surveys I conducted with over 90 volunteer professionals. Participants included research, creative, and executive personnel at major newspaper and broadcast houses and public relations and advertising agencies located throughout the country. Their numbers included both male and female respondents and their terms of experience ranged from two to twenty-plus years. An overwhelming majority of them displayed the disciplined practices described in this book. Selected comments from nearly half of the respondents appear in these pages.

Until recently, professionals' habits of work and thought, seen only as "higher-order skills,"[1] had not been identified or described for application to general copy[2] and not until now for proposal writing. Yet media pros and novices in every division of mass communication (print and broadcast journalism, public relations, and advertising) are expected to either produce proposals independently or participate in their preparation as members of a team. The void is there, therefore this book.

There are other reasons for this book. It's no secret that global changes have altered the face of American business. Nor is it a secret that those changes have altered the ways of creative operation in mass media.[3] Like any other business, the mass media industry is dominated by competition, economic pressures, discriminating consumers, and the complications any one or a combination of those forces generally breed.

We're put on notice almost every day that advances up the corporate ladder are won by those who know how to solve problems, produce ideas, and sell solutions. In fact, those are the very qualities that P. Roy Vagelos, retiring president and CEO of Merck & Co., saw in Richard J. Markham, 42, then senior vice president in charge of the drug company's worldwide pharmaceutical businesses. Although more senior officers were expected to succeed Dr. Vagelos, Markham was selected to take the retiring president's position. On the announcement of Markham's appointment, Dr. Vagelos described him as having "all the attributes of a great leader—he's smart, sensitive, perceives problems, and he knows where the industry is going, something that is not true of many people."[4] America's corporate employers want problem solvers, and these days they need them more than ever before.

No less a corporate business than General Motors or IBM, the media industry needs problem solvers as well. Terry LaMarco, associate director for employer relations at the University of Michigan Career Planning and Placement Office, says there are three qualities that prospective employers look for during interviews:

1. Analytical and trouble-shooting skills—that is, the ability to identify a problem situation and do something about it
2. Communication skills, verbal and written
3. The ability to speak and work with clients as well as colleagues and supervisors

LaMarco's observation parallels results of a survey by the American Society of Training and Development, which found a growing number of "projects controlled by teams . . . and a greater need for creative problem-solving" and also that the "top four qualities today's employer wants in its employees are the ability to learn, the ability to listen and convey information, the ability to solve problems in innovative ways, and the knowledge of how to get things done."[5]

Your performance in the '90s and into the 21st century will be measured by the quality of the ideas you generate and the skill with which you present them to decision makers. To develop such propositions, you need to understand the process of problem solving, the innate power you possess to think critically and creatively, and the savvy it takes to compose and present a proposal that will draw approval from decision makers. Making use of those higher-order skills is what this book is all about.

Although the need for higher-order skills in mass media has been known for some time, the effort to train students to become problem solvers and critical-creative thinkers is only now taking hold at universities. This book is written in the interest of that trend.

Chapter 1 puts you in touch with your critical-creative abilities, and Chapter 2 demonstrates that problem solving is far less a mysterious process than you may have imagined. Chapter 3 introduces you to the variety of proposal classes and problem types that media personnel in journalism, public relations, and advertising commonly confront. Chapter 4 helps you identify the true problem, understand the audience you want to reach, and deal with other factors that can influence the success or failure of a proposal. Chapter 5 explains how to critically evaluate and manage collected information in order to arrive at an evidence-based solution to the true problem. Chapters 6 and 7 explain what to include in your proposal and how to say it. Chapter 8 focuses on the creative factor of a media proposal and explores the sources of creativity. Chapter 9 explains how to give an effective oral presentation of your proposal, and Chapter 10 tells how to do it with visual tools.

This journey through the problem-solving process is marked by how each one of its procedures is performed in journalism, public relations, and advertising. In addition, Chapters 4 through 9 end with a special section entitled "How the Pros Do It." These sections illustrate how problem-solving procedures and thought processes described in these chapters play out in the real world of work. Anecdotes, examples, and useful references to authority abound to further illustrate and reinforce the nature of proposal preparation and presentation in mass media.

Proposal Savvy should interest all those who must produce ideas, compose implementation plans, and present them to newspaper editors or broadcast producers, public relations or advertising executives, and ultimately the client. It should be of particular interest to media novices who have had little or no training in proposal composition. It should be of interest to media pros as yet unpracticed in proposal preparation but who would like to see a guidebook that reduces the mystery and therefore the stresses of proposal writing. It should be of interest as well to media pros practiced in the science and art of proposal writing but who want to understand the forces that make the difference between a successful and a failed proposal. Freelancers, too, will find this book useful when applying for funds to support their enterprise projects designed for mass media distribution.

Moreover, this book should serve the purpose of mass media educators who realize the need to teach proposal writing but lack a text designed for that purpose. Educators teaching print and broadcast journalism, public relations, and advertising will be able to demonstrate every stage in the development of a proposal from the point of problem appearance through final composition and presentation.

In each instance, the ultimate aim here is to provide a stimulating reference source for the neglected media problem solver and writer—one that instills an appreciation for methodical process and critical-creative thinking and, at the same time, is a natural and proven means of producing an effectively researched, written, and presented proposition for an enterprise project or response to a client need.

NOTES

1. For example, see L. M. Carl, "PR and Creativity," *Journalism Educator* 37, no. 1 (1982): 6-8; G. Grow, "Higher-Order Skills for professional practice and self-direction," *Journalism Educator* 45, no. 4 (1991): 56-65; M. Ryan and I. R. Firstenberg, "Social Science Research, Professionalism and Public Relations Practitioners," *Journalism Educator* 67, no. 2 (1987): 337-90.

2. See E. K. Parsigian, *Mass Media Writing* (Hillsdale, NJ: Lawrence Erlbaum, 1992).

3. For example, see B. D. Bleedorn, "Number One Talent for Global Futures," *Journal of Creative Behavior* 20, no. 4 (1986): 277-82; L. W. Fernald, "A New Trend: Creative and Innovative Corporate Environments," *Journal of Creative Behavior* 28, no. 3 (1989): 208-13.

4. M. Waldholz, "Merck Positions Markam, 42, as Vagelos Heir," *Wall Street Journal*, 17 December 1992, B1.

5. H. Lancaster, "Managing Your Career: A New Year Brings Do's and Don'ts from Career Gurus," *Wall Street Journal*, 10 January 1995, B1.

Acknowledgments

Many good people contributed to the evolution of this book. I am indebted to the media professionals who willingly shared their expertise and lent a real-world voice to its content. Taking time from their harried schedules, they agreed to be interviewed and demonstrated unlimited patience with a probing, often persistent interviewer, selflessly providing extended explanations to describe their work. Some of the participants are featured herein. The names of others are too numerous to list, but they know who they are.

My gratitude extends as well to colleagues who reviewed chapters of this book relevant to their expertise. Already burdened with their own academic or professional responsibilities, none hesitated when asked to offer their comments and criticisms. Those to whom I owe thanks include Seth I. Hirshorn, associate professor, Public Administration, School of Education, University of Michigan, Dearborn; David C. Nelson, professor, Department of Mass Communication, Southwest Texas State University, San Marcos, Texas; Jack C. Nolan, associate professor, Department of Communication, Louisana State University,

Shreveport; Hayg Oshagan, assistant professor, Department of
Communication Studies, University of Michigan, Ann Arbor;
and Vincent Price, associate professor and chair, Department of
Communication Studies, University of Michigan, Ann Arbor;
also, Richard M. Ansell, vice president and group management
supervisor, Young & Rubicam, Detroit; M. Kathleen Donald,
partner and group account supervisor, Ogilvy & Mather, Detroit;
Robert G. McGruder, managing editor, *Detroit Free Press;* Robert
L. Simonson, Detroit bureau chief, *Wall Street Journal;* Robert
Skuggen, executive vice president, Eisbrenner Public Relations,
Troy, Michigan; and Mark S. Zucco, senior vice president, man-
agement supervisor, Direct Marketing and Sales Promotion,
Wunderman Cato Johnson, Detroit.

I also express appreciation to all those who came before me.
Their thoughtful works provided the inspiration and incentive
to shape their discoveries into a much needed reference guide
for media writers, editors, and executives. Their contributions
and the supportive spirit of so many, including my family, helped
make this book possible.

—Elise K. Parsigian

Introduction

New Age Media Enterprise

The business of media is NOT as usual. Producing bright copy on cue is no longer enough. These days much more is expected of those who put words down on a page. Of course fulfilling an assigned project takes skill, but to make headway in the world of media these days the wordsmith will have to demonstrate other levels of performance. For example, whether you're in print or broadcast journalism, public relations or advertising, you're expected to prepare or participate in the preparation of a *proposal;* that is, an idea that delivers a solid message, promises wide audience attention, provides a feasible implementation and cost strategy to carry out the proposed idea, and convinces decision makers that you're capable of getting the proposed job done to their expectations.

The activity of producing ideas and arguing for them persuasively is part of the general course of sustaining your job and establishing yourself as a key figure in your field. Besides, media executives expect such activity from you, mainly because your project can enhance the image of their media house and, at the same time, strengthen the economic base of the corporate unit that pays your salary.

Not surprisingly, the same proficiencies required to produce a well thought-out media assignment apply to composing a proposal—and a little more. The disciplined problem-solving process and critical-creative thinking expected on general assignments[1] are not unlike the process and thinking techniques required in the preparation of a media proposal. But the preparation and presentation of a media proposal requires far more initiative, knowledge, and ideation, including a lot more savvy. That's true of most proposals, but there are certain characteristics about the nature of media proposals that set them apart from other proposals.

One of those characteristics is that no two media proposals are ever alike, which rules out the possibility of formulaic content in their composition. A media proposal has certain features (described in Chapter 6) that appear frequently enough, but even these are subject to inclusion, substitution, or omission depending on the problem at hand and what the petitioner has discovered about it at the time. The one control that media petitioners have over this amorphous, sometimes chaotic uncertainty is the problem-solving process and the critical-creative thinking that drives it.

Those two basic functions lend themselves to identification and description, as this and other chapters will demonstrate. However, a general definition of a media proposal will always fall short of the many subtle influences surrounding it. Even so, you'll find one here because, at the very least, it'll give you a clear view through the fog as to what a media proposal is and what it's designed to do. Just keep in mind that the making of a media proposal is a creative process propelled by the problem at hand. Since no two problems are ever exactly alike, the nature of that process must be tamed by the discipline of its procedures and reliance on your innate critical-creative thinking abilities.

THE PROPOSAL: SOME SIMILARITIES
AND DIFFERENCES

Herman Holtz and Terry Schmidt, writing generally about "proposalmanship" (a term they coined), say a proposal is a bid for a contract which offers some specified goods or services, explains the terms and costs, and is "an attempt, in writing, to *persuade* the customer [or decision maker] to select the proposer for the award—a *sales presentation.*"[2] All proposals reflect these general characteristics, even media proposals. In fact, media proposals share some features common in grant or business proposals.

The one feature that all proposals do share is this: They all begin with a problem or need. For example, a medical scientist may seek federal grant money to test a vaccine against a crippling disease. An auto parts manufacturer may propose a special device to correct a flaw in a passenger car produced by a company serviced by the parts manufacturer. A nutritionist may propose a special ingredient to a food products company that would improve the taste of their fat-free mayonnaise. However, the problems in media have little to do with discovering a protective vaccine, offering an improved manufacturing device, or upgrading a food product.

Rather, news and broadcast writers report these types of events to a mass audience. The auto manufacturer's public relations department informs print and broadcast editors, trade journal editors, and plant managers about the new manufacturing device. The department also informs consumers about the improvement through various media channels—direct mail, pickup brochures, dealership literature, and the like. The food manufacturer's ad agency introduces the client's "new, improved" product via every communication channel currently available and as a predetermined budget allows.

Like the proposal to test a vaccine, correct a manufacturing flaw, or improve a food product, a media proposal sells something. But one of the things that places the media proposal in a class by itself is its primary audience—the mass market.

Still another difference is the period of personal contact with decision makers during the course of proposal preparation. The petitioner for grant money mails the proposal to the appropriate funding source and may never see decision makers face-to-face. The auto parts manufacturer may have one or two sessions with the auto manufacturer, but the rest is up to the parts manufacturer. It's pretty much the same for the nutritionist.

In media, however, a single conference with decision makers is rarely the case. More often, a number of contacts take place over a period of weeks, sometimes months, until there's a meeting of the minds concerning the *real* problem and before decision makers reach a determination on whether the proposed strategy deals with the problem effectively. In many cases, only then is the ultimate award bestowed on the winning petitioner—the signal to start the recommended project.

Differences aside and no matter what the context, proposals come into play because a problem or need presents the petitioner with a creative opportunity to examine the issue and/or respond with a solution. Moreover, savvy petitioners recognize that proposal preparation is, in fact, a problem-solving function, a critical-creative thinking process that must be carried out before a single line of the proposal can be written.[3]

THE MEDIA PROPOSAL:
A DEFINITION

What follows is a general definition of a media proposal, then two specific ones that take into account each media division's reason for producing proposals.

A media proposal is a creative opportunity to sell a media project that responds to a problem or need and fulfills a decision maker's purpose or goal. It exhibits a plan that promises successful execution to that end, an evidence-based idea that communicates the intended message to the decision maker's publics and demonstrates that the petitioner has the resources, knowledge, and ability to do the job within boundaries set by either the decision maker and/or the petitioner.

- In *print and broadcast* work, the definition applies specifically to a writer's idea or recommendation for a story or series of stories concerning a problem/need that affects the consumer audience and, at the same time, promises to raise circulation numbers or improve station ratings.
- In *public relations and advertising*, the definition applies specifically to an innovative or proven plan that promises to resolve the client's problem or need and, at the same time, promotes the client's company and/or product through various channels of public communication, the result of which may either win the acting agency a new account or sustain a standing one.

The suggestion here is that the content of a media proposal is, in fact, free of formulaic constraints and, therefore, imposes different, sometimes greater demands on one's own critical judgment and creative abilities. Although this book describes the common components and content of a media proposal in all divisions of mass media, it focuses more on the process of fulfilling a decision maker's specific needs in those environments while helping you get in touch with your critical and creative powers.

The precepts you'll find in this book rise out of a proven process and technique of critical/creative thinking long practiced by creative people in such diversified fields as engineering, mathematics, physics, social studies, the arts, and other areas of human activity.[4] The presence of that discipline in mass media has been noted for some time. However, its specific procedures and techniques are only now being articulated, principally through the voices of media pros, some of whom you'll hear from in the chapters that follow. Those voices belong to writers, editors, producers, and executives on staff at prominent newspaper and broadcast houses and public relations and advertising agencies located in 22 major cities from coast to coast. Watch for their comments at the end of each chapter, beginning with Chapter 3.

"BUT I'M NOT A CREATIVE PERSON!"

Yes, you are. Creativity is a natural, human attribute. If you think you are incapable of initiating ideas, it's only because you have not yet found the method and the means of awakening your innate creative powers. Creativity is not a gift. It is earned. Nor is creative problem solution associated with a high I.Q.[5] In fact, many researchers have found that creative problem solution can be taught.[6]

Make no mistake, the journey to creative discovery is not an easy road. It's a tough one and takes perseverance. Few who have traveled that distance would disagree.[7] Yet, calling on your creative ability opens the door as much to self-discovery as it initiates the leap from hard work to creative solution, provided you know the basic process and how that process borrows snippets from the mind's rich bank of information to trigger creative possibilities.[8]

In the next chapters, you will learn more about the proposal writing process, the thinking it requires, and how the two go hand in hand to design the creative proposals you're expected to produce and present. The purpose here is to show you how to tap into what are commonly referred to as your "higher-order" skills, that is, your innate ability to perform a task systematically and to think critically and creatively in the process, and as importantly, to help you become *self-reliant.*

NOTES

1. For a detailed account of the process and critical and creative techniques for general assignments, see E. K. Parsigian, *Mass Media Writing* (Hillsdale, NJ: Lawrence Erlbaum, 1992).

2. H. Holtz and T. Schmidt, *The Winning Proposal: How to Write It* (New York: McGraw-Hill, 1989), 9.

3. Ibid. Also R. D. Stewart and A. L. Stewart, *Proposal Preparation* (New York: John Wiley, 1984); and R. Loring and H. Kerzner, *Proposal Preparation and Management Handbook* (Scarborough, Ontario, Canada: Van Nostrand Reinhold, 1982).

4. For example, see R. Arnheim, *Visual Thinking* (Berkeley: University of California Press, 1969); A. Kaplan, *The Conduct of Inquiry: Methodology for Behavioral Science* (San Francisco: Chandler, 1964); and S. H. Kim, *Essence of Creativity: A Guide to Tackling Difficult Problems* (New York: Oxford University Press, 1990).

5. For example, see J. P. Guilford, "Creativity: Its Measurement and Development," in S. J. Parnes and H. F. Harding, eds., *A Source Book for Creative Thinking* (New York: Scribner's, 1962), 151-68; H. A. Rowe, *Problem Solving and Intelligence* (Hillsdale, NJ: Lawrence Erlbaum, 1984); and R. W. Weisberg, *Creativity: Beyond the Myth of Genius* (New York: Freeman, 1993).

6. M. R. Edwards and J. R. Sproull, "Creativity: Productivity Gold Mine?" *Journal of Creative Behavior* 18, no. 3 (1984): 175-84; Guilford, "Creativity"; R. E. Nisbett, G. T. Fong, D. R. Lehman, and P. W. Cheng, "Teaching Science," *Science* 238 (1987): 625-31; A. F. Osborne, *Applied Imagination* (New York: Scribner's, 1963); and R. Schank, *The Creative Attitude* (New York: Macmillan, 1988).

7. P. Feyerabend, *Farewell to Reason* (New York: Verso, 1987); R. Grudin, *The Grace of Great Things* (New York: Ticknor & Fields, 1990); and C. E. Moustakas, *Heuristic Research* (Newbury Park, CA: Sage, 1990).

8. For example, see F. C. Barlett, *Thinking: An Experimental and Social Study* (London: Allen & Unwin, 1958); J. S. Bruner, "On Perceptual Readiness," in J. C. Harper, C. C. Anderson, C. M. Christensen, and S. M. Hunka, eds., *The Cognitive Processes* (Englewood Cliffs, NJ: Prentice Hall, 1964), 225-57; and Parsigian, *Mass Media Writing.*

2

Media Proposals as
Creative Problem Solving

A s suggested earlier, the art of proposal preparation is essentially a problem-solving function, a
process made up of a sequence of preparatory steps. That is, the
next step cannot be managed and carried out successfully without first having completed the previous step. In fact, writing
cannot begin without your first having completed all steps in the
preparatory process.[1]

Preparation begins with identification of the problem—the
true problem, not the one you or the one with the problem think
it is. To guard against possible misjudgments and to make an
informed assessment, conduct a thorough exploration of the
problem. The information you collect for analysis will not only
reveal the true problem, it will also suggest an appropriate
solution.

Those practiced in producing proposals agree that preparation begins with recognition of the true problem. Too many
proposal writers make the mistake of grinding out solution ideas
before they understand the realities of the situation. Such haste

will, without a doubt, head up a faulty process toward a questionable solution doomed for rejection. It's an expensive waste of time, energy, and money.

Instead, take time to carefully research and study the stated problem. Practiced proposal writers have found that the realities of any problem and the clues to appropriate solutions quickly rise to the surface after a thorough investigation.[2] The time given to careful, disciplined research is, in fact, a time-saver. What's more, decision makers take proposals more seriously when judgments are supported by solid evidence and solution ideas are logical outcomes of what the research suggests.

THE POWER BEHIND THE PROCESS

Before continuing with other fine points in the process of creative problem solving, take notice of an intervening caveat that has long been ignored as the fuel that drives the engine from problem identification to solution—*critical thinking,* the habit of raising questions in situations of uncertainty. Critical thinking is a natural ability of yours, a human attribute you already possess. If you don't use it, no process, model, system, methodology, or whatever, will work for you. Your preparatory progress, judgmental success, and *creative thinking* depend on it. Moreover, you'll need that discriminating power to sense the subtle forces that could negatively influence even the most expertly prepared proposal.

Observe and open your senses to the environment in which those around you operate. That includes executives and co-workers as well as decision makers. Account for their position, responsibility, and motivations in that environment, the extent of their resources and limitations. Notice what they like and dislike, things that interest them, their associations, stresses and pressures, how they interact in various settings. Listen for assumptions, also for what is not said. Records will tell you about a person's position in a company and other background facts, but the rest you'll have to pick up during personal encounters. Above all, listen, listen, listen.

The following chapters will help you call up your critical thinking and discriminating abilities and show you how to pick up interpersonal cues. A good way to start is to first examine some key terms—*problem, solution, problem solving, problem-solving process, creative problem solving, creative knowledge base, critical-creative thinking, the proposal process,* and *creativity.*

THE MEDIA PROBLEM AND SOLUTION: A DEFINITION

Problem solving in mass media is not much different from problem solving in many areas of human activity. First of all, the problem or need is a matter of considerable concern to the one with the problem or need (from this point on, the reference to "problem" will also carry the concept of "need"). It must be a matter of concern; otherwise, the search for a solution would lack the drive and passion required to reach a satisfactory end point.

The proposal *problem* in media may be a question or issue or involve a situation(s) or person(s). The problem in any case presents a difficulty, desire, anomaly, discrepancy, doubt, uncertainty, mystery, or discomforting condition, any of which demand a response that will address the condition by casting light on the source of the problem and drawing attention to a likely solution.

A *solution* becomes apparent as knowledge about the problem accumulates and reveals a strategy aimed at correcting the problem, fulfilling a need, or effecting resolution of a troublesome situation. Chapter 3 reviews some types of problems that journalists, public relations, and advertising pros have worked on. The rundown will give you a better idea of what constitutes a media proposal problem and what stands as its solution.

PROBLEM-SOLVING: THE INNATE DRIVE TO KNOW

Cognitive scientist Jerome Bruner long ago found that problematic situations challenge the human mind and stimulate a purposive drive to know. Many before and since have agreed that within the bounds of a well-thought-out plan, *problem solving* is an engrossing activity that can lead to a creative idea or a new combination of existing ideas.[3]

The term problem solving also sounded a familiar chord in the minds of media pros interviewed for this book. In fact, a number of them described problem solving as a "creative opportunity," naming general assignments as well as proposal projects as problem-solving tasks. All agreed that proposal preparation began with a problem brought to them for resolution by decision makers or recognized by the petitioner who then called it to the attention of decision makers.

However, it is one thing to be aware of a problem and yet another to grapple with it, not knowing where to begin or end. Understanding how to conduct the process involved diminishes much of that anxiety.

THE PROBLEM-SOLVING PROCESS: BACKGROUND

Modern literature concerned with describing the problem-solving process dates back to 1894 when German mathematician and physicist Hermann von Helmholtz identified the presence of process in problem solving. Since then, others have expanded and enlarged upon his three-step model: (1) investigation of the problem in all directions, (2) thinking about it at the subconscious level, and (3) appearance of a "happy idea."

As many as six to ten procedures have been identified and added to those three stages over the years. For example, in 1910, American philosopher John Dewey identified two additional preconditions to ideation; in 1954, mathematician George Polya opted for three; then in 1963, Alex Osborn, founder and former president of the now worldwide advertising agency BBD&O, found a total of ten; in 1980, Robert J. Sternberg, a Yale University professor of psychology, reduced the number to six,[4] and in 1992, a communications educator identified eight basic steps that applied across the four main divisions of mass media.[5] In all these models, Helmholtz's first two preconditions to ideation are phrased differently, but their meaning remains the same.

Three things are important to note in this evolutionary ebb and flow. First, since Helmholtz recognized the necessity for systematic process and that existence of a problem generated a natural drive toward solution, dozens of others have reaffirmed that theory. Second, notice the range of disciplines represented here—subjects from science to the creative arts lay claim to systematic process as a passageway to ideation. Despite their many differences, the presence of each on the same continuum suggests that the precept of systematic discipline leading to ideation applies universally across the range of human activity. Third, each refinement indicates modification of the original in order to fit the needs of a particular discipline at a certain point of time in its evolutionary history. Still, the first two preconditions in the Helmholtz model appear repeatedly in each refinement.

The problem-solving model for media proposals you'll find at the end of this chapter reflects that characteristic; that is, it keeps faith with essential procedures—identification and exploration of the problem, reasoning about the findings, subconsciously thinking about them until a "happy idea" appears—and other precepts necessary in today's integrated work of media communication including those related to proposal preparation and presentation.

The process is there, but it's no easy journey in a direct line to an end. Returns to a previous stage to review a task or make changes and modifications necessarily occur along the way. That flexibility in the process may be why some choose to deny that creative outcomes rise out of a rational or "scientific" mode, that is, a systematic process, and argue instead for their origin in nonrational domains.[6] Others, however, accept the flexibility as part of the nature of problem solving and abide by the guidance that a particular problem-solving schema may offer in order to keep the mass of collected information, creative extravagance, and even personal bias in check.[7]

The point is to have a disciplined process at the outset in order to develop a reliable and substantiated knowledge base in preparation for other tasks in the process. That preparation then permits the problem solver to think critically through the chaos of stored information for a creative yet defensible solution. Yes, the mind wanders through the information maze randomly and subconsciouly, but the seemingly random, irrational journey to discovery begins and ends under the control of systematic process and rational thinking habits.

CREATIVE PROBLEM SOLVING

Like others in media, this author chooses to characterize problem solving as a creative activity because the research function to find the real problem is, in itself, a creative process, the results of which are then pondered, doubted, checked, and verified and then shared, questioned, filtered, and validated again through the informed minds of more than one person. It is the researched and substantiated knowledge base that stimulates creative thinking and becomes the fountain source of creative ideas.[8]

Finding the real problem is only part of the game in mass media. Once the real problem is known, the object is to hit the audience with a creative idea and a strategy that intrigues the decision maker. The recommended strategy may be an attention-getting format for presenting a print news series, a unique subject for a broadcast feature, a bright idea to renew a company's image and logo, a novel campaign idea to promote a product. Or it can be a twist on or an extension of a proven means of public presentation or even a creative combination of several proven strategies put together in an innovative manner for a single project.

Ideas for public messages do not develop in a vacuum. An idea may seem to occur spontaneously, as Helmholtz suggests, but there is nothing magical about it. Make no mistake, spontaneous ideation evolves out of the hard work it takes to accumulate, evaluate, and separate fact from fiction. Then this body of substantiated knowledge is studied and mulled over until the mind bubbles up evidence-based conclusions and ideas. The basic fuel that fires this kind of activity is, again, critical thinking; that is, your natural ability to raise questions about the knowledge you've collected, studied, and thought about.

Critical thinking not only means raising questions, it also means carrying on an internal dialogue, asking yourself questions throughout the process. Ultimately, critical thinking acts as its own creative wellspring. The breakthrough is sometimes so sudden that all too often past hard work is forgotten and attributed, instead, to "talent" or an "extraordinary" mind rather than to diligence, self-discipline, and the naturally endowed ability to think critically and creatively.

In truth, and not unlike the processes in the arts and sciences,[9] the whole of problem solving in mass media, including proposal preparation and presentation, is as much a creative process as it is a disciplined one.

THE CREATIVE KNOWLEDGE BASE

Knowledge, according to Harold Larrabee, is "any founded intellectual acquaintance with a fact or matter, ranging all the way from the simplest perception to the most profound understanding of a complex theory."[10] Acquisition of reliable knowledge, Larrabee goes on to explain, can be distinguished from acquisition of general knowledge because the former represents knowledge that can be substantiated and is therefore, in large part, trustworthy and defensible—an apt description of how knowledge is regarded in this text.

That knowledge serves the creative impulse is graphically described by French chemist Louis Pasteur: "Chance favors only those minds which are prepared."[11] Or, as American poet Robert Frost put it, "The fact is the sweetest dream that labor knows."[12]

Of course, there are as many precautions against the blindness and arrogance that knowledge can induce as there are sentiments about knowledge as a creative source. Oscar Wilde, the Irish wit and writer, had an antidote for erratic expanses of the human mind. In *Intentions*, his collection of essays, he argues that while the imagination imitates, it is the critical spirit that creates.[13] Therein lies the key to knowledge-based spontaneity, or what is gradually being recognized as *critical-creative thinking.*[14]

CRITICAL-CREATIVE THINKING:
A HUMAN ATTRIBUTE

Critical thinking as the essential yeast that activates the solution process is a fairly new concept. Only recently have scholars and practitioners looked at critical thinking and its cognitive role in problem solving.[15] In a 1990 study of 40 college students, a researcher found that the more time students spent on self-inquiry activity the more likely they were to produce substantially accurate conclusions than students who spent less time on questioning activities.[16]

As significantly, those who study this phenomenon have found that the habit of questioning is a gift of nature, a talent of the human mind endowed on all; in fact, they've found that questioning is a natural tendency one cannot avoid.[17] Even more interesting, and as pointed out in Chapter 1, others have found that this natural endowment holds little relationship to intelligence or to "extraordinary" minds.[18] In short, anyone can be a critical-creative thinker simply by exercising their natural tendency to raise and ask questions of others, of themselves, and about what they see, smell, taste, feel, hear, or read. Children do it all the time to understand the world around them, often taxing adult patience.

But what triggers this tendency to question? Some say it is no more than the *need* to know and that asking a question is a means of obtaining the required information. Indeed, it is. However, in the context of mass media work, the questioning attitude involves much more. It entails knowing enough about the problem at hand so that one asks the "right" questions.[19] That's the key.

Begin by carrying on an internal dialogue. Ask yourself questions about what you need to know about the problem. The question itself will suggest where to look for answers. Once you know something about the problem, you'll be able to see the

gaps, anomalies, agreements, contradictions, assumptions, biases, and the like in the information you've collected. All these
conditions provide the content for questions you can investigate
further and put to authorities knowledgeable about the problem.

Ensure against unfair judgments. Ask the right question of
the right source.[20] Make sure you've investigated all sides of the
problem and listened to more than one side of the issue. Ask
yourself questions that inquire into issues like those mentioned
above—gaps, anomalies, agreements, and so on. Include self-
inquiries about your own assumptions, biases, and motivations.
Do your homework. Then the necessary and "right" questions at
each stage of the process will suggest themselves to you.

Morris Stein writes that creative individuals play two finely
balanced roles during the problem-solving process: "They are
both creators and audience. They communicate both with themselves and their work." He sees this as "a dialogue between the
creator and the work."[21] No surprise, really. Carrying on an
internal dialogue is the characteristic stamp of the professional
media writer. The habit of self-inquiry automatically turns on
whether the problem solver has to produce a news report,
broadcast feature, public relations piece, advertising theme, or
proposal.

THE MEDIA PROPOSAL:
PROCESS AND INQUIRY

As indicated earlier, the proposal process in media sustains the basic features of others in its class but necessarily
attends to certain complexities that are exclusively its own. The
process outlined below reflects that predisposition; so do its
self-inquiries.

The overview of the process and its self-inquiries are presented here to stimulate your own thinking about your particular
problem. The pattern of activities outlined typifies the problem-
solving process that pros practice and the kinds of self-inquiries
they raise when preparing a media proposal. Use these brain

ticklers or "starter" questions to generate other questions that apply specifically to your situation because certain aspects of even similar problems can differ and will require questions specific to your problem. However, the ones offered here will help direct formulation of those problem-specific questions.

Many of the questions presented in the overview are repeated in subsequent chapters. Others you'll see in the text apply to a particular problem. Pros regularly perform the procedures outlined below. Novices need a guided tour. The chapters that follow describe the landscape encountered along the way.

AN OVERVIEW: THE
PROBLEM-SOLVING PROCESS

1. Identify the problem (Chapter 4). Articulate and write out a statement of the issue believed to be the problem. Then ask yourself these questions:

- *Is the stated problem the real, the true problem? If not, what do I think may be the problem?*
- *What does the stated problem itself suggest must be questioned? What is missing? What is the anomaly here that raises doubt about the stated problem?*
- *What do I need to know to determine the facts in this case? What questions must be asked concerning the stated problem? Where and in what records, documents will I find answers? What substantiates those records, documents as sources of information, expertise concerning this problem? Who has information on the issue? What are this person's qualifications as a source of information, expertise concerning this problem?*

2a. Conduct preliminary research in order to understand all aspects of the situation; identify and understand not only the real problem but also the specific needs of the audience related to the problem and the purpose and objectives to be achieved (Chapter 4).

- *What are the specific goals, objectives involved?*
- *What questions must I carry to documented sources?*

- *What is known in documented sources and by whom about the problem? What are their assumptions, biases, motives? What questions do these sources fail to answer? Where can I get this information or from whom? What qualifies these persons, records, documents as sources of information?*
- *What questions must be raised to learn the specific needs, problems, preferences, characteristics of this audience? Where can I get this information or from whom? What qualifies these persons, records, documents as sources of information? If such sources are unavailable, would a poll, survey, and the like produce that information? What would it cost? Will the budget allow it? What questions need to be asked of survey subjects?*
- *What other limitations must I consider?*
- *What are decision makers' preferences, resources, pressures, limitations? Where can I get this information or from whom? Why would these be reliable sources of information?*

2b. Conduct primary research in order to obtain current information not yet published, to verify documented data, and/ or to obtain a reality check on the nature of the perceived problem via such means as field observations, one-on-one interviews, surveys, focus groups, and the like (Chapter 4).

- *What questions are still left unanswered? What do I have to do to get these answers? What additional documents, records would be useful? Who could provide those answers? What are their qualifications, biases, motives? Would an on-scene observation and/or survey do it? If not, or neither is possible, what alternative sources of information are suggested by the problem itself?*
- *What do I need to find out from what documents and from whom in order to substantiate information obtained thus far?* When in doubt about sources of information, rely on librarians at a local university, public library, your in-house research library, or, after obtaining permission, a corporate research library.

3. Review, evaluate, organize, and analyze the accumulated information in order to draw a well-reasoned, justifiable, and creative solution to the problem (Chapter 5).

Review: Read the collected body of information as many times as necessary to secure the whole in memory and to evaluate it.

Evaluate: This term suggests that bias could tilt the balance of fair judgment. Control that tendency with questions concerning the possibility of others' and your own assumptions, biases, and motivations tilting the scale. Use the following self-starters:

- *What documented and other collected information indicate confirmation of a particular issue? In what periods of time do these confirmations occur? Are they outdated or current? Do any of these affect a confirmation? If so, how or why?*

- *What information contradicts or modifies a confirmation(s)? How so or why? How many of these in contrast to the confirmations? Have I reviewed and included all contradictory material currently available? In what periods of time do the contradictions occur? Do any of these conditions diminish the agreements? If so, how or why?*

- *What anomalies and differences concerning the problem play into it? Do these change the original perception of the problem? If so, how or why?*

- *What anomalies, differences, or new information concerning the problem would serve the solution, planning strategy, or creative need? If so, which ones and why?*

- *What personal biases, motives, assumptions may be coloring my judgment? Have any of these interfered with a true representation of the facts pro and con? What modifications are, therefore, necessary in my evaluation?*

Organize: Categorize or arrange the most relevant, informative, interesting, and previously unknown points of information under topic headings so that each set of information may be reviewed, compared, and analyzed against other sets of information to determine the overall meaning of the whole. To do this, ask yourself these questions:

- *What information stands up to question? What doesn't?*

- *What information can be defended as substantial, relevant, informative, interesting, previously unknown, and a fair representation of the facts?* "Relevant" refers to both the pros and cons in information related to the problem, also to confirmations and contradictions, differences and similarities, even anomalies that may contribute to the final problem statement or conclusion statement.

- *What reviewed and evaluated information seems to fall together to form a unit or category of knowledge?*

- *What are the appropriate headings for each of these?*
- *What personal biases, motives, assumptions may be coloring my judgment in the categorizing procedure? Have any of these biases, motives, assumptions interfered with a true representation of all the relevant facts? What modifications are therefore necessary in my organization of the facts?*

Analyze: Compare and contrast items of information within a set of related items in a category and draw a conclusion about these. Then do the same between differing sets of categorized information. Review all points of information in each set, consider the conclusion drawn about each set and the conclusion drawn from your comparison and contrast of all sets. To effect this cognitive exercise, ask yourself these questions:

- *What points stand out in terms of relevancy, are most informative, interesting, unique, and previously unknown?*
- *Where are the similarities, differences, anomalies, unknowns in this body of evaluated information? Where are the agreements, disagreements, conflicts, contradictions? Where are the relationships, correlations, patterns, trends?*
- *What personal biases, motives, or assumptions may be coloring my judgment? Have any of these interfered with a true representation of all the facts? What modifications are, therefore, necessary in my categorization or table of facts?*
- *Where does the weight of the evidence fall and why? What does that balance of the evidence say about the originally stated problem? Is that initial perception of the problem correct? If not, why not?*

4. Draw an evidence-based conclusion(s) (Chapter 5). This is your moment of insight. It's the "Aha!" moment when all things fall into place and synthesize into a unity and when articulation of an evidence-based conclusion statement becomes possible. That moment is rarely spontaneous. It more often follows a good deal of self-directed thinking, mainly at the subconscious level in isolation or during group discussions. Now that you've reassured yourself about the true face of the problem, that is, whether it's the originally stated or different problem, you can move on. Express your conclusion in a written statement by asking yourself these questions:

- *What is the final conclusion inherent in and manifested by the body of evaluated and analyzed data?* Articulate that and then write out a conclusion statement. If you have trouble writing it down, refer back to your answer to the question: *Where does the the weight of the evidence fall and why?* Then write the statement. Edit it over and over until it clearly, concisely, and fairly represents the facts concerning the true problem.

- *What is the evidence that substantiates that conclusion?* Either include its most outstanding features in the statement or become well versed in its content because you'll be asked to support your conclusion.

- *Based on what I now know about the problem and the evidence concerning it, are changes in the intended goals/objectives necessary? If so, what?*

5. Test the outcome (Chapter 5). Pass the problem statement and the evidence that substantiates it through an internal review (depending on the structure of your organization, this may mean going through more than one or two levels of authority). Answers to the above questions usually provide the support base necessary to defend against challenges you can expect from internal sources. However, any questions raised by internal sources should be taken seriously and followed through with additional research, if necessary. That attitude should hold even when it's necessary to present the problem statement to outside sources or a client group for they, too, will raise questions you may or may not have answers for at the moment and that need investigation. In preparation for any type of review, anticipate the challenges. Begin by asking yourself these questions:

- *What challenges, questions may be raised concerning any aspect of the conclusion statement, the evidence, or its relationship to the problem?*

- *What information in the body of knowledge must I review in order to respond effectively?*

- *Can the conclusion be stated more clearly, succinctly, effectively?*

- *Who internally must review this statement before passing it along to others?*

6. Design an implementation strategy based on the substantiated problem statement, one that responds pragmatically as well as creatively to the situation at hand (Chapters 6 through 8). This assumes you have the information you need that tells you about the true problem, the needs of your audience, and the requirements of decision makers. It also assumes that you have either researched this on your own or research specialists have provided you with points of necessary information covered in Items 2a and 2b above. To stimulate ideas about an appropriate solution strategy, raise these self-inquiries:

- *Based on the conclusion statement what objectives, goals must be met to resolve the identified problem, develop a solution, and create an implementation strategy?*
- *Based on the result of these considerations, what recommendations for an implementation plan or strategy can be made to meet recognized goals, objectives?* If your plan differs from original expectations, prepare an explanation as to why this is the case.
- *Do the recommendations respond fully and effectively to the problem?*
- *What evidence justifies making the proposed recommendations?*
- *What does the evidence suggest would be the most productive means of implementing or executing the recommendations?*
- *What evidence justifies use of those means?*
- *In similar cases, what means have been used in the past?*
- *What were the weaknesses, strengths of those methods?*
- *What can be added, changed, or modified to strengthen a weakness or capitalize on a tested and proven plan?*
- *Why would the modified plan be better?*
- *Is the implementation plan feasible? How so?*
- *What are the costs for what services and what is the justification for each?*
- *Is the cost of implementation within budget boundaries? If outside the budget, what justification can be made to support the extra cost? If within and even less than the known budget, how and why can the job be done so economically?* Have ready answers to these questions. They serve as a test of your recommendations, but they also protect your recommendations against challenges that decision makers will surely make. Your specific problem and its creative strategy will suggest even more challenges you may encounter. Anticipate them and be prepared to respond with solid evidence.

7. Test the creative strategy internally and/or externally to assess its effectiveness.

Print and broadcast journalism. Discussions are more likely at this stage than any form of "testing." That is, discussions with artists, photographers, editors, producers, and other decision makers on how a story should be presented—for example, whether it will be a single story, series, or supplement; what graphics, tables, sidebars will be used for what; the amount of print or air space that will be needed; what format design would be most attractive, and so on.

Public relations and advertising. "Testing" is a more appropriate term in this context. Such a function could include a variety of activities—for example, testing the creative outcome on agency executives, team members, or relevant personnel, obtaining an opinion from a group of experts representative of a particular public, or obtaining a reaction from a group of consumers representative of the target audience. A test of the creative outcome is not always a consistent part of every agency's process. Whether it's done or omitted depends on the agency's confidence in the evidence that generated the creative outcome.

8. Write and present the proposal (Chapters 6 through 10). You'll see many of these self-inquiries later in the text, but here's a preview:

- *What components will be necessary for inclusion in this particular proposal in addition to the ones commonly included?*
- *What information must be included in anticipation of questions raised by decision makers?*
- *What will the decision maker expect to see first, second, third, and so on so that the proposal can be read in an easy and facilitating manner?*
- *What parts can be eliminated?*
- *What challenges, objections can I anticipate?*
- *Do I have the answers?* If not, better get them.
- *Should these be included in the proposal or held in reserve in case these issues come up at the time the proposal is delivered?*
- *Are all proposal parts clearly written, easily read, neatly and succinctly presented?*

• *Does this proposal call for a rehearsal in preparation for the oral presentation?*

Following a structured process like the one outlined above is not to everyone's liking, but research studies and the experience of many give credence to the fact that some guiding framework is crucial in the development of any creative project.[22] It's a sentiment shared equally by members of such diverse groups as researchers, creatives, and business leaders. Here's what Mortimer Feinberg, chairman of a Manhattan consulting group, learned:

> Bright people may resist structure, but they need it. Suspending the rules for your top brains is no favor to them. Apart from the fact that it makes them the target of resentment by their colleagues, it may encourage their most self-destructive, loose-cannon tendencies. When smart people are supported by sound structure and candid comment, they are, in effect, even smarter.[23]

Among the seasoned media pros interviewed by this author, an overwhelming majority demonstrated systematic process in the effort to produce proposals even in the face of varied settings and differing problems. For example, journalists were sometimes given a proposal assignment, but more often journalists perceived a problem that needed exploration, which then led them to editors with suggestions for an enterprise project. Public relations and advertising personnel make it their business to identify clients' operational needs before a problem leads to serious consequences, but clients frequently come to an agency with a problem (not always the real one, as agency personnel often discover after testing the waters).

The situations that pros face across all divisions of mass media vary widely from case to case. Aside from problem variety, the sources of information to be explored change with the needs of the problem, as do the types of field research. In addition, one implementation plan may not work for more than one solution strategy, and testing methods, too, vary according to the problem at hand and its purpose for resolution. Still, the problem-solving process remains the same; it just flexes to the needs of a particular problem. And, based on results of the evidence, the implementation design must fit the ultimate purpose intended. The efficacy of the choices you make depends in large part on the critically driven judgments you make at each step of the process. Together process and questioning reflect the holistic operation that must be applied in the pragmatics of producing a creative media proposal.

Also keep in mind that hitting upon a creative solution is just one of many creative opportunities open to you in the preparation of a proposal—for example, locating the sources of information to research the problem, finding the means of implementing the solution strategy, designing the proposal in a manner you believe would best serve the recommended ideas for a print or broadcast story, public relations or advertising campaign.

The sky's the limit for creativity in the mass media, but only if that creativity responds to the verified problem at hand, is based on substantiated evidence, and meets decision makers' identified needs. Unlimited opportunities for creative discovery in mass media may be one of many reasons why the term "creativity" in this realm, perhaps in any realm, may be indefinable.

CREATIVITY: AN ELUSIVE CONCEPT

Creativity escapes definitive description, partly because its meaning is altered by the many areas of work it serves, and partly because those contexts act on one's creative resources in different ways. The issue is introduced here only in response to the likely question, "But what exactly does creativity mean?" Generally speaking, most definitions incorporate the sense that creativity is the discovery of something new, something never done before. For example, in the literature of creative problem solving, James Adams, who takes a "particularly pragmatic view of creativity," defines creativity as "something without precedent" which carries impact only in its implementation and when that implementation is "intrinsically motivated."[24] Robert Kuhn, editor of a text on ideation and innovative practices in business management, defines creativity as the discovery of a new concept, idea, method, or mode of operation.[25] However, neither one of these explanations adequately defines "new," "innovative," "something without precedent." What do these terms mean? How are those intended meanings achieved? They leave the meaning of "creativity" open to question. Here's another view, from best-selling author Harold Kushner:

> In the beginning, the Bible tells us, God created the heaven and the earth. The earth was formless and chaotic, with darkness covering everything. Then God began to work His creative magic on the chaos, sorting things out, imposing order where there had been randomness before. He separated the light from the darkness, the earth from the sky, the dry land from the sea. This is what it means to create: not to make something out of nothing, but to make order out of chaos. A creative scientist or historian does not make up facts but orders facts; he sees connections between them rather than seeing them as random data. A creative writer does not make up new words but arranges familiar words in patterns which say something to us.[26]

Kushner's definition throws new light on the meaning of creativity and rings true with the meaning of creativity in this text. By introducing the concept of "order," Kushner also introduces the imperative of seeing "connections" between items in the chaos of "random data," which then lead to an "order" and creation of a "new" idea. That ability marks the creative person and the result of that ability as "creativity."

One must keep in mind, however, that the "new, "original," or "innovative" usually means no more than a rearrangement or reconstruction of a previously ordered body of elements. Most things dubbed "creative" are often discoveries built on the ideas and discoveries developed by others who, in turn, have produced "new" ideas built on the work developed by those who preceded them, "and so it goes," as television producer Linda Ellerbee might say. Creating "something without precedent" is a rarity, if not unlikely.

Furthermore, and in media work particularly, one cannot always be "intrinsically motivated" to produce "something without precedent." It is the job of mass media communicators to produce on demand. So initially there is extrinsic pressure to come up with a new idea.

The saving grace here is that extrinsic pressures can lead to intrinsic motivation. Once involvement with a problem begins and immersion in its study becomes intense, curiosity mounts and excitement builds with each incremental addition to or modification of the creative knowledge base. Within the boundaries of unbiased and sound critical judgment, the mind becomes hostage to the evidence and its creative opportunities. That's intrinsic motivation and it's available to anyone who choses to labor through the chaos in order to find its particular order.

If creativity were to be defined specifically within the context of print and broadcast media, perhaps one could describe it as drawing order from a mass of unrelated but substantiated data and creating a proposal in such an engaging and fulfilling manner that the reader or listener turns full attention to, becomes engrossed in, perhaps even motivated by its content.

In public relations, creativity may be described as bringing about order from a mass of unrelated but substantiated data and creating a solution strategy in response to a specific problem, one that sells the client and produces the desired effect on the intended audience. And in advertising, creativity may be described as bringing about order based on a mass of unrelated but substantiated data and developing and implementing a solution plan that wins client approval and promises to favorably motivate the audience the client hopes to win.

You've learned that the road to discovery, solution, and ideation follows a systematic but often recursive course. You've learned that all of us are naturally endowed with a questioning habit of mind and the resources to solve problems, produce a creative idea, write a proposal. Attention, then, should fall on *how* order and unity evolve out of chaos through disciplined process and critical-creative questioning. That's the essence and focus of creativity in this book, not the *what*. As you read through the chapters that follow, you'll see some of the mysteries of the process unfold and begin to understand how creativity develops in mass media work and how you can be as productive as other members of that select group known as creative.

Considerable attention has been given to examining terms in this chapter because even though these terms pass through the language of mass media communication, few practitioners have a clear or uniform idea of their meaning or impact. Understanding the language of problem solving and critical-creative thinking is important, but so is knowing something about the classes of proposals and types of problems media pros frequently encounter. The next chapter provides the necessary backgrounding in classes and types before getting into the nitty-gritty of proposal preparation and writing.

NOTES

1. For example, see D. M. Johnson, *Systematic Introduction to the Psychology of Thinking* (New York: Harper Row, 1972); and G. Nadler and W. C. Bozeman, "Relationship of Planning and Knowledge Synthesis," in S. Ward and L. J. Reed, eds., *Knowledge Structure and Use* (Philadelphia: Temple University Press, 1983), 515-50.

2. J. L. Adams, *Conceptual Blockbusting* (San Francisco: Freeman, 1974); J. Lefferts, *Getting a Grant in the 1990s* (New York: Prentice Hall, 1990); R. J. Loring and H. Kerzner, *Proposal Preparation and Management Handbook* (Scarborough, Ontario, Canada: Van Nostrand Reinhold, 1982); C. E. Moustakas, *Heuristic Research* (Newbury Park, CA: Sage, 1990); R. D. Stewart and A. L. Stewart, *Proposal Preparation* (New York: John Wiley, 1984); and E. Tepper, *How to Write Winning Proposals* (New York: John Wiley, 1989).

3. J. S. Bruner, *Toward a Theory of Instruction* (Cambridge, MA: Harvard University Press, 1966); H. A. Larrabee, *Reliable Knowledge: Scientific Methods in the Social Sciences* (Boston: Houghton Mifflin, 1964); and Moustakas, *Heuristic Research.*

4. H. A. Rowe, *Problem Solving and Intelligence* (Hillsdale, NJ: Lawrence Erlbaum, 1984).

5. In E. K. Parsigian, *Mass Media Writing* (Hillsdale, NJ: Lawrence Erlbaum, 1992), 7-8.

6. For example, P. Feyerabend, *Against Method* (New York: Verso, 1988); and A. Koestler, "The Art of Creation," in D. Dutton and M. Krauz, eds., *The Concept of Creativity in Science and Art* (Hingham, MA: Martinus Nijhoff, 1981), 1-18.

7. J. L. Adams, *The Care and Feeding of Ideas* (Reading, MA: Addison-Wesley, 1986); M. Antebi, *The Art of Creative Advertising* (New York: Reinhold, 1968); Larrabee, *Reliable Knowledge;* Moustakas, *Heuristic Research;* Parsigian, *Mass Media Writing;* and J. M. Ziman, *Reliable Knowledge* (New York: Cambridge University Press, 1978).

8. For example, see S. H. Kim, *Essence of Creativity: A Guide to Tackling Difficult Problems* (New York: Oxford University Press, 1990); Parsigian, *Mass Media Writing;* and R. W. Weisberg, *Creativity: Beyond the Myth of Genius* (New York: Freeman, 1993).

136408

9. See J. W. Getzels and M. Csikszentmihalyi, *The Creative Vision* (New York: John Wiley, 1976); W. R. Shea and A. Spadafora, *Creativity in the Arts and Science* (Canton, MA: Science History Publications/USA, 1990); and Weisberg, *Creativity*.

10. H. A. Larrabee, *Reliable Knowledge: Scientific Methods in the Social Sciences* (Boston: Houghton Mifflin, 1964, rev. ed.), 3-4.

11. From Louis Pasteur's inaugural lecture on his appointment as professor and dean at the University of Lille, Lille, France, 7 December 1854.

12. From Robert Frost's poem, "Mowing," in his *A Boy's Will* (London: David Nutt, 1913).

13. Oscar Wilde, *Intentions* (Leipzig, Germany: Heinemann & Balester, 1891).

14. See S. J. Parnes and H. F. Harding, *A Source Book for Creative Thinking* (New York: Scribner's, 1962); R. Schank, *The Creative Attitude* (New York: Macmillan, 1988); and Weisberg, *Creativity*.

15. S. D. Brookfield, *Developing Critical Thinkers* (San Francisco: Jossey-Bass, 1987); M. Bryson, C. Bereiter, M. Scardamalia, and E. Joram, "Going Beyond the Problem as Given: Problem Solving in Expert and Novice Writers," in R. J. Sternberg and P. A. Frensch, eds., *Complex Problem Solving* (Hillsdale, NJ: Lawrence Erlbaum, 1991), 61-84; U. S. Chaudari, "Questioning and Creative Thinking: A Research Perspective," *Journal of Creative Behavior* 9, no. 1 (1975): 30-4; and Schank, *The Creative Attitude*.

16. C. Shiang, "The Effects of Self-Questioning on Thinking Processes" (Ph.D. diss., Purdue University, 1990).

17. Adams, *Care and Feeding;* Brookfield, *Developing;* Bruner, *Toward a Theory;* and Sternberg and Frensch, eds., *Complex Problem Solving.*

18. Studies show that those with a high intelligence metric may reach solutions faster than those with an average or lower IQ but that both groups not only are capable of raising questions about the problem but are likely to produce original and creative solutions. See J. W. Getzels, "Creativity: Prospects and Issues," in I. A. Taylor and J. W. Getzels, eds., *Perspectives in Creativity* (Chicago: Aldine, 1962), 90-116; also, J. P. Guilford, "Creativity: Its Measurement and Development," in Parnes and Harding, eds., *A Source Book,* 151-68; and Rowe, *Problem Solving.*

19. N. Miyake and D. Norman, "To Ask a Question, One Must Know Enough to Know What Is Not Known," *Journal of Verbal Learning and Verbal Behavior* 18 (1987): 357-64; and M. F. Rubenstein and I. R. Firstenberg, "Tools for Thinking, in J. E. Stice, ed., *Developing Critical Thinking and Problem Solving Abilities* (San Francisco: Jossey-Bass, 1987), 23-36.

20. For a guide on identifying reliable sources and formulating productive questions, see Parsigian, *Mass Media Writing.*

21. M. I. Stein, "The Creative Process and the Synthesis and Dissemination of Knowledge," in Ward and Reed, eds., *Knowledge Structure,* 383.

22. R. Arnheim, *Visual Thinking* (Berkeley: University of California Press, 1969); G. Nadler and W. C. Bozeman, "Relationship of Plan and Knowledge Synthesis," in Ward and Reed, eds., *Knowledge Structure;* and Stein, "The Creative Process."

23. M. R. Feinberg, "Why Smart People Do Dumb Things," *Wall Street Journal,*" 21 December 1990, A10.

24. Adams, *Care and Feeding,* xiii, 6, 7.

25. R. L. Kuhn, *Frontiers in Creative and Innovative Management* (Cambridge, MA: Ballinger, 1985).

26. H. S. Kushner, *When Bad Things Happen to Good People* (New York: Avon, 1981), 51-2.

3

Media Proposal Classes and Types

Unlike other proposals, media proposals do not lend themselves to well-defined classifications. That's because categorization depends on the presence of similarity among a group of items. In media, problems and their objectives are never similar enough to merit hard and fast categorization. The rule, therefore, is flexibility. For example, problems showing a few shared characteristics but different objectives may be seen as a single class. Then, a single class may pair off with another to make up still another proposal class. So names for proposal classes and types remain subject to choice and the petitioner's experience with the specific problem at hand and its objectives.

On the other hand, it's important to look at examples of proposals that are produced by media pros so that you have an idea of the more common classes, combinations, and problem types that do exist in each of the four divisions of mass media. The examples given in the following pages are taken from interviews held with media pros experienced in proposal writing and represent some of the types of problems these pros either chose to examine or were asked to explore.[1]

Note particularly that in these cases some of the problem statements are framed as questions. Note, too, how starter questions given in Chapter 2 lead to problem-specific questions and objectives. Keep in mind, however, that initial objectives often change as more about the problem is learned. But even at this opening phase of the process, you can see how the problem statement influences initial questions and first approaches to problem management. Don't look for specific criteria to identify each problem type. The variety of problem types rules out such standardization. On the other hand, there are some basic standards in terms of writing the proposal, and you'll find these in Chapter 7.

PRINT AND BROADCAST JOURNALISM

Most of the problems encountered in journalism deal with social, economic, political, ethical, or environmental issues or with health care, home maintenance, lifestyles, educational, and humanor general-interest topics. Proposed stories in any of these types may fall into classifications known as investigative, exposé, exploratory, explanatory, and descriptive, but they can also represent combinations of these. Space prohibits listing all possible classes and combinations that emerged from interviews with journalists, but the ones listed here are indicative of media proposals most frequently produced. In the examples below, journalists first articulate the problem they want to pursue and then explain what they hope to accomplish (the objective) in the process of bringing attention to the problem and often motivating correction of it.

Investigative/Explanatory

☐ One reporter proposed a story that had never been done before—a look at investigations of aircraft crashes conducted by the National Transportation Safety Board (NTSB).

Problem: What procedure does the National Transportation Safety Board (NTSB) follow in its investigation of commercial aircraft crashes?

Objective: To examine findings of past air crash investigations and to find out how regulatory and bureaucratic aspects of the NTSB affect the safety of airborne travelers.

David Hanners, special projects writer,
Dallas Morning News, Dallas, Texas

Uncertain that Hanners could obtain the cooperation of government officials, editors nevertheless felt confident that his preliminary research demonstrated promise of a unique story. Before drawing up his formal proposal, Hanners had studied clip files and other documented sources on past aircraft crashes. He wanted to find out why these crashes occurred, the part that regulatory agencies played in crash prevention and investigation, and how forces such as meteorology, metallurgy, and audio technology fit into the picture.

Because he had done his homework on these and other issues concerning the problem, Hanners won his editors' approval to proceed and, eventually, earned the cooperation of government inspectors and science experts. Government agents made their files available to him, agency personnel charged with investigating aircraft disasters invited him to join their investigations as an observer, and scientists and government officials, aside from those at NTSB, agreed to be interviewed.

After nearly two years researching aircraft disasters and writing a number of proposals summarizing his findings, Hanners was able to formalize his proposal and present his ideas on how the story should be presented, including the use of appropriate graphics, artwork, tables, sidebars, and the like.

The *Dallas Morning News* accepted his proposal and published his story, a 12-page special insert entitled, "The Anatomy of an Air Crash." It won the 1989 Pulitzer prize for excellence in investigative reporting.

☐ A Seattle TV writer wanted to know why one of the West's prized natural resources was approaching extinction, so he proposed an investigation and explanation of an issue that no one had thus far questioned.

> *Problem:* At one time the Columbia River was abundant with its most popular fish resource—salmon. That is no longer true. Why?

> *Objective:* To find out and explain what factors are contributing to the demise of Columbia River salmon and to make known the impending consequences to an audience generally unaware of the threat to its most marketable natural resource.

Ben Saboonchian,
documentary writer and producer,
KIRO-TV, Seattle, Washington

Saboonchian earned quick approval for his proposal because he brought attention to a problem of current concern and demonstrated that most area residents weren't even aware of its threat to them. He had spent about five months researching the decline of Columbia River salmon while working on other assignments, first looking into government records to determine the rate of decline over time and then reviewing other records such as stats on market sales, fishery closings, and unemployed fishermen.

He queried a number of area residents to assess their awareness of the problem. He interviewed fishery owners, wholesalers, and consumers. He talked to members of Indian tribes whose religious ceremonies centered on appreciative reverence for this natural resource and the nourishment and employment it provided. Indian tribes in this northwest area had never allowed photographers to film their sacred ceremonies, but Saboonchian was successful in obtaining their permission in the interest of bringing public attention to the problem.

Saboonchian's prime-time production, an hour-long documentary entitled "When the Salmon Runs Dry," won the 1992

Peabody award for "a timely and important documentation of the environmental situation in the station's [KIRO-TV] service area—a compelling local documentary."

Investigative/Exposé

☐ Sometimes, solid enterprise ideas are rejected simply because the project would call for more dollar investment than a newspaper usually cares to invest. That was not the case here. Decision makers at this Florida newspaper equipped its offices with an updated computer system and agreed to underwrite all other expenses involved in a project proposed by this seasoned journalist.

> *Problem:* Few knew that the justice system made a practice of erasing from the record second and third offenses committed by known criminals deliberately engaged in unlawful acts. This practice endangered public safety and needed to be exposed.

> *Objective:* To build a sound evidentiary base exposing this practice, call citizen attention to the abuse, and encourage correction of the problem.

John A. Costa, deputy managing editor,
St. Petersburg Times, St. Petersburg, Florida

Management endorsed Costa's project and its cost budget so that he and his team of reporters could carry out the extensive investigation this problem required. Part of their research effort included examining local court records to verify the suspected problem, collecting stats on repeat criminals in other Florida communities, checking erasure and release policies in other states, and then setting up a system of comparative charts to analyze how all this measured up against Florida's records.

The team also interviewed judges and lawyers, crime victims, and paroled repeat criminals and worked with paid legal counsel at every step to guard against libel or any other violation of the law. Aside from documented facts, the team also sought opinions from lawyers about the state's practice of erasure and release and the comments of victims and criminals regarding this policy.

Costa gave editors periodic reports on the progress of the team, always including a plan of what he felt should follow in the next stage of the research process. After a year and a half of investigation, Costa and his team submitted a proposal suggesting that the story be told in a series of features and recommended the graphics, artwork, and other visuals to accompany the copy.

Costa and his team won the 1992 Sigma Delta XI Merit Award for their effort. As significantly, the exposé so affected the citizenry that the Florida legislature passed a law making the practice of erasure an illegal act.

☐ Beyond a cost investment to get an important job done, a media house will often take significant risks to air a story. In this case, the risk involved possible loss of supporting advertisers.

> *Problem:* There were some indications that retail store security officers indiscriminately targeted minorities in their surveillance of shoplifters. The practice violates state and retail store security laws which prohibit undue retention of suspects based on age, sex, or race. So the question was: Are retailers violating these security laws?
>
> *Objective:* To find out through local sources if this is indeed the case, to find out how prevalent this is in other public places, and to conduct a surveillance task force in several stores to learn more definitively about this problem.
>
> **Joel Grover,** investigative reporter,
> KSTP-TV, St. Paul-Minneapolis, Minnesota

At the risk of losing valued advertisers, Grover's editors encouraged him to follow through on his belief that major retail stores were in violation of the law. The idea to propose the project came after Grover noticed reports in local and out-of-state newspapers about minority arrests in public places. Given the signal to pursue his investigation, Grover sought answers to questions concerning biased surveillance policies in area stores by researching stats on minority group arrests made at these stores. He also interviewed former security officers to learn about arrest policy in the stores they had worked for, asking this question: *What was the store's surveillance practice, their attitude toward minorities, and their retention customs?*

To verify his preliminary data, editors approved Grover's plan to have members of the station's staff, plus some of their friends, hired as security officers in stores suspected of violating the law. Grover talked to experts on discrimination in public places, and he also wanted to know the extent of minority arrests across the nation (statistics on these may be found in a document called the *Uniform Crime Reports,* available on request from the FBI).

All this went into a formal written proposal, including recommendations for visuals that had been secretly shot by team members while observing surveillance practices of store security officers. Production of the project soon followed and was made ready for airing in 10-, 8-, and 5-minute segments over three nights during the late evening news hour. The documentary won the 1991 Peabody award for "the best kind of investigative reporting in its identification of an important problem."

Exploratory/Explanatory

☐ As you've probably noticed, several forces direct journalists into a pursuit that ends in a proposal. The first is being aware of and then exploring what's happening in one's environment or its place in history. The second is an absorbing curiosity about the "whys" and "hows" of a prevailing situation and exposing it. Another is the drive, and in some cases the courage, to bring it to the attention of others. This case displays all those characteristics.

   Problem: Are traditional civil rights groups really reflective of the black population's wants and desires?

   Objective: To find out how black Americans feel about the effectiveness of these groups and why they feel the way they do; to report findings and explain each group's representative strengths and/or weaknesses.

                              Everett J. Mitchell II, assistant city editor,
                                   The Detroit News, Detroit, Michigan

Mitchell first became aware of this problem when he was a reporter in Louisville, Kentucky, where he detected dissatisfaction among African American members and nonmembers of the local NAACP. Although his observations of similar incidents elsewhere continued for a few years, earnest study of minority group leadership came after he joined the staff at *The Detroit News*. The NAACP enjoyed wide national respect. Yet the incidents he had seen and read about seemed to contradict the prevailing belief.

Among other questions, Mitchell couldn't help asking: *Does the NAACP mean something different to me than it did to my parents? Are there generational differences in the perspectives of others? Are these groups meeting the needs of their African American constituency?* He drafted a preliminary rationale, giving reasons why the issue should be explored, but then set the proposal aside because he felt the time for telling the story was not yet right. Winning approval of a proposal in journalism depends a great deal on whether editors agree that their audience is ready to learn about it.

The right time came, Mitchell said, with the nomination of Clarence Thomas to the U.S. Supreme Court. News stories carried the reactions of African Americans to Thomas's nomination, some violently opposed, others not so volatile. Mitchell then wrote his proposal, complete with his past and current observations of African American disillusionment with their leadership. He also suggested that *The Detroit News* undertake a nationwide opinion poll of African Americans using questions that Mitchell had formulated and that stories could be built around results of the poll, which would either confirm or disconfirm the disillusionment he suspected. Editors supported the suggestion and Mitchell's suspicion proved to be true. In the meanwhile, Mitchell interviewed African American activists, sociologists, and other experts that he had named in his proposal. The project was approved, and final stages in the process were completed.

Early in 1992, Mitchell and his team saw their efforts published in *The Detroit News*. Their story appeared over a period of three days in a series of special sections totaling 16 pages of newsprint. Because the story drew wide national as well as local attention, the pages were consolidated into one special section in response to nationwide requests for copies from various groups and individuals.

Educational/General Interest

☐ Not all proposals are the watchdog type. Some need only appeal to a public interest such as this one.

> *Problem:* We needed to fill about a dozen 2- to 3-minute features to air between breaks during coverage of the 1992 Olympic Games at Barcelona, Spain.
>
> *Objective:* To provide the American public with information about the culture, landscape, businesses, and people of Barcelona and to show the impact of the games on the economy of Barcelona and its people.
>
> **Victor D. Solis,** producer,
> NBC News, Europe

Solis, who covers the international scene, explained that he's constantly sending proposals with ideas for mini and major TV features to his home station in New York and that the proposals for minifeatures composed for the Barcelona games were no exception. Having covered the Olympic Games in 1986 and 1988 and the World Cup soccer games in Mexico City, Solis knew what the network expected to see in these proposals for minifeatures, designed mainly for viewers during breaks in the coverage of the 1992 Olympic Games.

For this project, Solis researched the sounds and sights of Barcelona. He spent nearly three weeks talking to and locating Barcelona's architects and historical experts. Solis wanted to know: *Which are the most interesting buildings? What is the history behind them? Were any persons related to persons associated with Barcelona's history and still living that he could talk to?* He then scouted these locations and mapped out some visual possibilities and who he would interview against these settings.

Solis's purpose was to give American audiences a visual sense of this ancient European city as he captured its citizens' reactions to the presence of the Olympics in their historic city and also how their economic well-being had been affected by that presence. His editor's only question was: *Can this be done in less time?* It's not an unusual question for print and TV editors because less time spent means less overhead.

Before submitting a proposal to his editors, Solis knew precisely what structures he was going to shoot, the history behind them, the facts about the architects and artists who put them together, the city and rural folk he had lined up for interviews, and what he would ask them. The 4-minute piece Solis proposed was produced and ran with NBC's reportage of the Olympic Games.

☐ The following also represents a public-interest-type proposal, but in this case the project began as the result of an RFP, that is, a "request for a proposal" from a source outside the media house.

> *Problem:* It was the 75th anniversary of the Shubert Theater [located in New Haven, Connecticut], and they wanted us to do a program in honor of that event. The usual practice is to call on performers of past plays held at the Shubert or other stage artists.
>
> *Objective:* I felt we should do something different. So what we did was to give members of the audience an opportunity to recall and relive experiences about their attendance at this famous theater because most of the stage performances that went on to long-term Broadway successes originated here. Those experiences remained alive in the minds of Shubert's patrons.
>
> **Faith Middleton,** manager and executive producer, WPKT, National Public Radio, New Haven, Connecticut

Middleton had produced many programs featuring authorities responding to questions she and her viewers raised about various topics of current interest. This time, she thought: *Why not bring in those who actually have experienced the events we talk about?* Station producers liked the new approach and suggested she follow through with her idea. For the anniversary program, Middleton was successful in locating and gathering theater patrons who had seen plays at the Shubert in past years.

Middleton said most were able and more than willing to share their personal experiences and anecdotes about the plays and the players. In fact, Middleton added, their remembrances about the plays, particularly those that later became Broadway hits, captured an excitement that was far more contagious on radio than it would have been on video. The production was broadcast under the title "The Shubert Theater: 75 Years of Memories" and won the 1990 Peabody award for "an invaluable historic record of a lost era, as well as a delightful hour of radio listening."

PUBLIC RELATIONS AND ADVERTISING

As in journalism, there are certain PR and advertising problems that crop up more often than others. The most common classes include proposals designed to obtain new business or retain a house account, to launch a media or community awareness program, manage a crisis situation, introduce a new product campaign, increase the market share of an established product, or conduct a "repositioning" program, that is, readjustment of the company's publicly perceived "image." Other problems can create still other proposal classifications and combinations, but the ones described below are the ones you're most likely to confront.

One note of caution: Expect peripheral problems that may have contributed to the predominating problem, some known to the client while others usually remain undetected. These peripheral problems may be traced to any number of situations— for example, inefficient production operations, a weak sales force, misinformed company representatives, employee dissatisfaction, misplaced marketing efforts, and the like. Probing questions and careful research usually uncover associated problems.

The examples below serve only as an introduction to classes and types of predominating problems and first questions raised to begin the problem-solving process. Although some of the descriptions suggest peripheral problems, the focus in most of these examples is on the major problem.

Crisis Management

☐ A client facing a crisis always calls for very thorough and cautious managment by whomever they appeal to for assistance. The cause of the crisis could lie hidden in a dozen different sources, which was the case in this example. Like the preceding example, this too was an RFP. Notice all the preliminary explorations conducted by this public relations executive before running willy-nilly into ideas for a solution.

> *Problem:* The company had a hot product [women's western jeans], but they could not fill orders fast enough and were therefore rationing the product to retailers, which made the retailers very unhappy. So they had to win a very different type of audience that included the retailers and several other publics of which they were unaware. Attention to those audiences called for a higher company profile which the company resisted and that was an overriding problem for us.
>
> *Objective:* To identify weaknesses and develop strengths in the production, distribution, and sales force operations in order to restore the manufacturer's reliability factor with retailers and retailers' customers.
>
> **Gwin Johnston,** CEO,
> JohnstonWells, Denver, Colorado

The client had invited JohnstonWells to compete with several other agencies for this new business. To prepare their presentation, Johnston and her team conducted a six-month preliminary study of the problem. They began by asking the client questions about what ongoing programs they had with retailers and other groups related to the product. Johnston's queries soon revealed a lack of communication between the company and its employees, sales force, retailers, or industry partners. At their first meeting, Johnston advised the client that the problem called for a research plan that would assess the company's communication problems.

Following that first meeting, the agency sent the client a letter in which it proposed a research strategy that would identify the needs of key audiences in order to shape the most appropriate means of reaching them. The letter also contained a brief description of each phase of activity the agency felt it had to complete for a successful public relations program and an estimate of what the client would be charged for these services.

The client approved the initial "letter" proposal, and several other formal proposals followed. These contained plans to explore the situation separately with each product-related group. Johnston's team then conducted extensive interviews with company executives, plant managers, employees, the sales staff, distributors, retailers, and their customers. Once the reasons for sluggish production and distribution were uncovered, Johnston presented the client with the results of their research. She also included recommendations that would improve communications with the company's key publics and provided the means of correcting the weaknesses found in their production and distribution operations.

JohnstonWells won the contract to carry out the rest of their proposed public relations program.

Community Awareness Program

☐ You may be dealing with institutional as well as product manufacturing problems. The institution may be a public service agency, a university, a charity, or a hospital, as it is in this example.

> *Problem:* A local hospital had moved its location and changed its name and wanted to make its new location and new identity known in order to dispense its services to a community in need of health care and social services.

Objective: To define the institution and its services to community groups, area churches, business organizations, block
clubs, and political leaders and through them provide the
community with ongoing health care information and the
social service facilities available to them at the hospital and
in the community.

Gerald Lundy, executive vice president,
Southfield, Michigan

A specialist in hospital community-reach programs, Lundy
was the client's exclusive choice for this public relations project.
Before meeting with the client, Lundy had obtained some background information about the hospital (Mercy Hospital) and the
community surrounding it (inner-city Detroit). Then he raised
questions about what the client was willing to do to be perceived
as a contributing presence in the community, how familiar they
were with their new community, what they had in place currently,
and so on.

To get answers to a question he raised for himself—*What's
out there?*—Lundy studied the structure of the community, obtained the names of officials, identified the locations of citizens'
groups, block clubs, schools, churches, recreation halls, businesses, and the like. He identified key groups whose cooperation
he could muster to help launch the hospital's programs for
community health care and prevention—all this in the interest of
developing the "good neighbor" image the hospital hoped to
create.

Among other unique moves, Lundy and his team also researched ZIP codes located within the hospital's primary and
secondary service areas and compiled mailing lists in order to
reach residents and inform them about the hospital's services.
The press was notified only after hospital programs were
launched, and awareness of the hospital's educational programs
motivated community participation in its services.

Local and community newspapers and hospital journals
picked up on the story and Mercy's health care services stood as
a model for programs that could be developed at other hospitals.

Media Awareness Program/Repositioning

☐ Here's another awareness program, but with a different public—educating the media so that the client's product receives accurate representation in the press and on the air. This was not a new business venture, a crisis situation, or an RFP but an example of how an agency looks after the best interests of a valued and established client. In this case, the agency brought client attention to a problem requiring correction.

> *Problem:* We had reason to believe that many automotive writers did not understand the anti-lock braking system (ABS), why it is a valuable safety system in an automobile, and why the Bosch system is different from other similar systems. The media was also unaware that Bosch provides auto manufacturers and its customers with products other than the ABS. We needed to re-establish the Bosch identity not as a single-product automotive parts manufacturer but as a multiproduct, multiparts manufacturer.
>
> *Objective:* To educate the media so that automotive writers communicate knowledgeable information about the Bosch ABS and to re-educate the media so that news reporters and automotive editors communicate the true identity of Bosch.
>
> **James A. Bianchi,** vice president,
> Eisbrenner Public Relations, Troy, Michigan[2]

In the general course of serving their clients, public relations agencies monitor all published reports concerning clients' products. In this case, agency staff noticed that trade journal writers and newspaper writers displayed a lack of knowledge, even misconceptions about the company's product and its diverse manufacturing capabilities.

When this was brought to the attention of the client, the client agreed that the agency should research the problem further in order to learn, for example, *Who besides Bosch is getting press coverage? What are they saying? Who are the people writing these stories? How much do they know and not know about Bosch, its product, and manufacturing diversity? Is there some kind of consistent message coming through? Exactly what misconceptions must be corrected?*

Bianchi and his team wanted to be sure they were making the right assessment of press knowledge before delving into what might be a costly investment for the client. They explained that such an investment would include, among other elements, the cost of developing a reeducation program for their primary audience (the media), creating a new company logo, and organizing an ongoing press campaign. In his proposal, Bianchi presented evidence that convinced the client that the projected expenditure was justified. The client then asked the agency to resolve the problem and to present strategies to resolve still other problems that had emerged due to a recent merger.

Consumer Awareness Program/ Market Share Increase

☐ Like public relations agencies, advertising houses handle a variety of problems. Yet they share many types of proposals that are similar in kind. For example, this problem belongs to the class of proposals competing for new business, but the problem itself bears little resemblance to the one the Denver public relations agency had to resolve.

> *Problem:* An urban center shopping complex wanted to increase its market share of potential customers working in office buildings near the mall and to attract suburban shoppers to the center of town.

> *Objective:* To provide key audiences with information via multimedia about the mall's ambiance and conveniences, including the ample parking space available close to the mall, best shopping hours, and most efficient shopping patterns.

> **Philip Smith,** creative director,
> NKH&W, Kansas City, Missouri

The potential client invited NKH&W to a preliminary meeting, and Smith knew his agency had to compete with other agencies for this account. He said there was no written request for a proposal, nothing on paper that clued them in on the problem, so it was up to his group to raise the necessary research questions.

The shopping mall, not the typical suburban mall, was located in the downtown area where the community used to shop before suburban malls drew shoppers away. So the "brand," as Smith called it, that is, the shopping mall, was unique in its class and specific information about it was needed—for example, *Where is the brand in the market today? Comparatively, is it a growing or declining share? Is the brand being supported with dollars at a rate above or below previous standards? Where is the competition currently? Who's spending, and how much is being spent on your audience? Where do you want to be in this market? How do you want to get there?* The client had conducted research on all these issues and so had ready answers for the asking.

The agency then returned with a proposal suggesting a research program in order to obtain a current profile of the brand's audience, customer perceptions of downtown shopping, attitudes about parking availability, best shopping hours, and the like. The client approved the plan and the cost estimates for these and other research activities.

Research results then suggested the design for an implementation strategy. This and the research justifying it were presented to the client in a formal proposal along with recommendations for a creative campaign informing shoppers about the conveniences offered by this downtown shopping mall. NKH&W won the opportunity to implement its plan, to develop its creative recommendations, and to distribute them.

Repositioning/Market Share Increase

☐ Typically, four or five other ad agencies had been invited along with Crispin & Porter to present for this new business opportunity. Crispin had some advantage over the others. It knew the resort trade, knew about travel patterns, had done similar work for the government of Jamaica, and understood vacationers' perceptions of Jamaica as a country.

   Problem: A new Jamaican resort, not a hotel but a complex of private villas, was dissatisfied with its occupancy performance and sought repositioning in order to win a larger share of the tourist trade.

Objective: To reposition the resort not as an all-inclusive [a way of low pricing, that is, paying one price for room, food, drinks, recreational facilities, and the like] but as the finest private resort complex in the Caribbean and to reeducate travel agents that this villa resort should not be compared on the same scale with hotel resorts and other all-inclusives.

Charles Crispin, president,
Crispin & Porter, Miami, Florida

At their first meeting, Crispin's questions quickly revealed that the client's average daily rate charges were out of sync with the occupancy and profits they hoped to achieve, and also that their all-inclusive marketing campaign was self-defeating and misdirected to the general population rather than to affluent travelers. But before Crispin got involved in the project he said he had to find out if the client was willing to undertake the development, marketing, and sales reeducation that this project required and, in fact, if the client had the resources to support agency recommendations—not an unusual precaution for agencies these days.

The client provided information indicating they had the resources, but Crispin needed additional background information. So he talked to people he knew in Jamaica and who also knew the client. These contacts included members of the Tourist Board involved in the economic development of the island, persons in Jamaica's economic development agency, and the like. Crispin and his team then did some basic research that included a look at the travel trade in key gateway markets. They asked travel agents about their awareness of the product (the client's resort), their perception of it, where they would place it in relationship to other resort products on the island, the level of popularity of this and other resorts, and so on.

Results of this and other research went into a proposal of some length. Crispin and his team proposed a new image for the resort, a marketing strategy that promoted that image, a media campaign plan to support the strategy, and the dollars it would take to do it. The proposal also recommended, among other suggestions, a sales training program for members of the client's sales force (one of the peripheral problems that needed correction) and production of literature informing travel agents about the resort's new face, facilities, services, and occupancy policy.

The quality of Crispin & Porter's research and proposed recommendations earned client approval, and the agency was awarded the account.

New Product Campaign

☐ It's a common occurrence—the need to change a product in response to consumer demand or a competitive market. But the problem in this case was multidimensional. The client, a long-time account with this agency, was interested in regaining Jeep leadership in the sports utility category. Chrysler had created the category with the introduction of the Cherokee model some years earlier, and competitors had flooded the field with new entries in the years that followed. The goal was to reestablish Jeep's position with an updated and innovative model, the Grand Cherokee, one that had the appearance of a passenger car but behaved like a sports utility vehicle. By doing so, Chrysler would be able to create still another category within the class of sports utility vehicles and once again lead the field.

> *Problem:*   Chrysler came out with a new Jeep vehicle, the Grand Cherokee. The old Cherokee had been a very successful product. So the question was: *How can we employ that popularity, yet differentiate the Grand Cherokee from the old model?*

> *Objective:*   To reestablish the Jeep Cherokee image by focusing on the new style-oriented and technologically improved Grand Cherokee model.

> **Thomas J. Deska,** managing partner,
> Chrysler Corporation,
> Bozell Worldwide, Inc., Southfield, Michigan

A series of discussions with the client took place over the course of several years during which Chrysler's researchers surveyed consumer needs for a new design, studied engineering and safety requirements, designed and developed the new vehicle, and conducted field and consumer tests. The agency team knew the product well, but the Grand Cherokee was a new offering in the Jeep line of vehicles—a whole new story.

The Jeep line of vehicles had been on the market for the past eight years and was extremely successful; over three million had been sold up to 1992. But it was time for a new model. As Chrysler researchers studied current market needs and engineers re-designed the new product, Deska and his research team spent a good portion of their time observing the development of the new model and reviewing the results of market studies. In the interim, Chrysler executives kept Deska informed about the technological improvements in the new model, improvements not found in competitors' products.

Additional feedback came from results obtained at product research clinics the client had conducted with consumers and which Deska and his team had observed. Other necessary information came from additional studies the agency's research department conducted, including market and media research, cost studies, and input from personnel at Chrysler dealerships.

All along, Deska said, he and his team had to think about getting answers to mounting questions, not the least of which were: *How are we going to market this product? How does the new model fit current consumer expectations of the Jeep? Is it rugged, durable enough for tough use and, at the same time, does it render the appeal of a passenger car?*

The agency submitted several communications regarding its findings and prepared a number of preliminary proposals, but a final proposal, including the creative strategy, was presented only after all the facts were in from all departments, the data analyzed, and agreements on judgments reached, including the agency's recommendations on how to market the new product.

Aside from the problems, objectives, and management features these examples display, note this characteristic feature—

proposals are not composed overnight. They take considerable time to research and prepare. Some do take less time than others, sometimes just a few weeks; some take months, others a number of years. The determinant is the problem itself and the dollar expenditure that editors, producers, and clients are willing to invest on what activities. Just don't expect to get by with clever ideas and snappy presentations. It doesn't work. Proposals require due process, substantial evidence, and solid, critical-creative thinking at every step.

THE FUNDED MEDIA PROJECT

Not all media proposals develop within the corporate enclave of print and broadcast houses and public relations and advertising agencies. Freelance writers and independent broadcast producers also write proposals. Without the financial base of a corporate network to assist them, however, these independents are obliged to seek public or private funding to support an enterprise project they feel is worthy of delivery to a mass audience. Some of these appeals are free-form proposals, much like the ones prepared in the private sector. Some follow guidelines set down by the funding group. Other funding sources want only the information they expect to see on standard forms they've designed.

Those who sell their work to print media houses do not ordinarily have the high production costs incurred by broadcast journalists and so have less reason to appeal for dollars. But if you're in telecommunications, at some time during your career you may have to seek funding from corporations, private foundations, or government agencies for a project you want to produce. For example, if you work at a public broadcasting station (PBS), writing proposals becomes a routine part of your job. Many PBS stations plan projects they would like to produce, but their limited resources force them to seek additional funding from several sources for a single project.

If you want to sell a proposed project to a privately owned broadcasting station or a PBS station, it'll be up to you to obtain all or part of the funds to produce it. PBS stations, independent producers, and telecommunication freelancers rarely have enough money to implement their projects. Nevertheless, they're in the business of creating programs that serve the public good. To obtain funding, however, they need to be certain that their purpose also fits the goals of the funding group they plan to touch for dollars.

Whether you write a proposal as an employee of a PBS station, as an independent producer, or as a freelancer you will find that such proposals are not too dissimilar from those prepared in the private sector. The process and purpose of proposal preparation described in Chapter 2 remain the same, as does attentiveness to decision makers' needs, in this case, the funding group. For that reason, it's up to the proposer to find out what kinds of issues occupy the funder's area of concern.

But it's also imperative that the funder learn precisely what the support group expects to see in proposals—that is, whether they want a free-form proposal prepared according to their guidelines or if they want the proposal issued on one of their standard forms. In the private sector, editors, producers, and clients expect the proposal writer to show them what they need to know without being told about a specific format.

Most of the following examples deal with seeking grants from private foundations and government agencies, but don't overlook the corporations. They often fund projects that give the corporation an opportunity to associate its name with a worthy social, educational, or cultural enterprise. You just need to find out where the corporation is willing to put its money. A call to its public relations office will give you a lead on this and whether they are open to free-form proposals or have their own proposal guidelines or standard forms.

Where to Find the $$$

Media independents search through reference directories at public libraries to find out what funding agencies support what kinds of projects. Ask the reference librarian for directories on private, public, and corporate groups that have support money available for social or cultural projects. Some of those titles might include *Foundation Grants to Individuals, Annual Register of Grant Support, Foundation Directory,* and *Grants Register.* There are others. If you are near a major university, ask its Division of Research and Development for assistance. They usually keep records on source groups for their own personnel but are often willing to assist outsiders.

Most directories list the name of the funding group, who to contact, the cause or goal to which the group is dedicated, and where to write for guidelines or an application form.[3] At this point, there is no need to inform the funding group—government, private, or corporate—about your project idea. Disclosure can wait until after you see the group's literature and know precisely what they're looking for and how they wish to be informed about your project.

Ten Tips from the Pros

Without any texts to guide them, these enterprising writers learned their lessons the hard way—trial and error. Here they give you the benefit of their experience. There are no guarantees, of course, but these precautions can help you avoid receiving rejection slips from funders.

1. Identify the funder's goals, objectives, or purpose. Make sure your particular project meets that purpose; otherwise, you'll just be spinning your wheels. Take this precaution seriously. Without knowledge about the kinds of programs the resource group is willing to support, you risk having your proposal tossed into the nearest circular file. Independents, any pro, will tell you that ignoring this important research task invites not only rejection and disappointment but loss of precious time and energy as well.

Here's what one radio producer advises about learning early on what federal funding agencies are willing to support:

The Corporation for Public Broadcasting (CPB) is one of the primary funders for large radio projects. They give out roughly a dozen grants a year and they're very difficult to get. It's very competitive. Half of the grants go to radio stations for productions made in-house, half go to independent producers. It's extremely important to meet the funder's criteria, including their level of audience appeal need. For instance, the CPB wants to improve public broadcasting and they look for programs that will be heard by large audiences. In comparison, the National Endowment for the Arts (NEA) is interested in developing artistic integrity and furthering artistic vision and they'd be much more willing to fund an arts proposal of an experimental type that appeals to a very limited audience.

Steve Rowland, producer,
SR Productions, Philadelphia, Pennsylvania

Rowland created a radio documentary featuring jazz trumpet artist Miles Davis. Davis had always shunned publicity in the past, so very little was on record about this gifted artist. Davis finally consented to participate because Rowland convinced him that, far from being a personal promotion, Davis would be making a valuable contribution to radio history and that the project had been endorsed for funding not by private investors but by a public service agency, the Corporation for Public Broadcasting (CPB).

Rowland's radio documentary on Miles Davis won the 1991 Peabody award for producing "a milestone in radio biography destined to become the official record of the career of this important musician."

Another pro voices sentiments similar to Rowland's:

If you want to make points with a sponsor, make points that prove to them that what you propose is going to benefit them, and if there's a bureaucratic process you have to follow, do it. It's just the game you have to play to let everyone know they're going to get what they're looking for.

Max Horowitz, staff writer,
WNCN-FM, New York City

2. Write and request literature concerning the funder's proposal requirements. If your project answers more than one funder's needs, request information about grant applications from each one. After seeing these and before submitting a proposal application, pros send letters of inquiry explaining briefly what they have in mind and why they're qualified to do the job. It's possible to receive a letter of interest in return, but such a response does not mean you will receive dollar support. It's just an indication that a submitted proposal may generate a grant.

Whether you're required to write a free-form proposal, prepare one according to their guidelines, or fill out an application form, follow whatever directions you're given. The criteria for submission vary widely among funding groups and corporations, so follow any given criteria to the letter. In some cases, particularly with corporate funding, you may have to either write a free-form proposal or a proposal prescribed by the corporation and fill out a form as well. Here's an example of how much variation there can be among funding agencies alone:

> CPB is different from other agencies. They require a very detailed and specific plan of exactly what you intend to do. Many agencies, like the NEA, require much less of a description of your plan. Often it's just a one-page description of the project and a one-page budget, a very common scenario for an NEA application. CPB requires an extremely detailed written narrative proposal and an extremely detailed budget as well as a work sample or demo. CPB tells you exactly what they want and you have to fill in those requirements accordingly.
>
> **Steve Rowland,** producer,
> SR Productions, Philadelphia, Pennsylvania

Another independent producer affiliated with a privately owned TV station believes that attention to funders' requirements sends reassuring signals to the funding group:

Follow their [the funding agencies] prescribed format because that tells them you know how to follow guidelines, that
you can perform in whatever format they prescribe. It's like
doing any production. If PBS says, "This program should be
an hour-and-so-many minutes, we need this and that element
within that time," you give them what they need. That's being
professional. It's an indication of your expertise.

Larry Walsh, freelance producer,
KNME-TV, Albuquerque, New Mexico

Walsh received the 1992 Peabody award for his production
chronicling the untold story of Columbus's relationship with
various American Indian tribes encountered on his several voy-
ages from Spain trying to find a westward sea route to the Orient.
The documentary was cited for creating "simultaneously an
important local document and an instructional film for future
generations."

3. Try to secure a support group. Contact personnel in
various departments related to your project at a university,
institute, association, or state agency. Consult government directories and/or *The Encyclopedia of Associations* for groups that may
be interested in your project. An alliance with a credible group
could prove to be a strong selling point in your appeal for
funding. If the group shows interest in your project, ask for a
statement of confidence in your work. That will give your grant
appeal additional power. Furthermore, ask these groups for
names of other persons who might provide certain resources or
information you need. In fact, getting experts on board as
project advisors or in some other official capacity reassures the
funder that your proposed project has the authoritative endorsement of more than a party of one. That was this television
director's experience:

We knew Dr. Elders at the State Health Dept. had been
working on the state's teenage pregnancy problem for years,
so we knew we had a natural ally in her. You need to have

someone in that position on your side. You need to have
them in your playing field before you go before a body like
the State Legislature. Our partnership with Dr. Elders carried a lot of weight. That is, her saying "I believe in these
people. I think they can pull it off. I know they're dedicated
to helping us resolve our teenage pregnancy problem." That
lent a great deal of importance to our proposal presentation.
In the end, our relationship with the State Health Department proved to be a very happy marriage.

> **Anne Wright,** director, community relations,
> KARK-TV, Little Rock, Arkansas

KARK-TV is a PBS station that needed to augment its financial resources with funds from the state for a proposed multi-
media educational program designed to prevent teenage pregnancy, part of which included a series of TV programs, handouts,
seminars, billboards, a hotline, personal counseling, and other
communication devices. The project won the 1991 Peabody
award for "addressing a critical local problem with an agenda for
action and remediation."

Here's another viewpoint on securing a support group:

If you're working for a small station, it's really a good idea
to make an alliance and open your project to co-production
because you have much more fundability if you're working
with other institutions. A lot of people, particularly in journalism and television, have sort of an anti-intellectual men-
tality. They want to control the production themselves. I can
understand that because the academics they may be working
with are so stuck on the facts, which is as it should be, but
then they forget or don't understand that you have to tell a
story. So you have to work with them to establish the facts so
you can tell the story.

> **Larry Walsh,** freelance producer,
> KNME-TV, Albuquerque, New Mexico

Walsh had reviewed the bios of Native American directors
listed in a directory of TV directors and found one at the Institute
of American Indian Arts in nearby Santa Fe. The Institute opted

to act as a project support group and suggested still other sources of support and authoritative information.

4. Know exactly what tasks need to be done. As importantly, know precisely the cost of setting up and completing each single task. Remember, your proposal is also a contract. You cannot go back to the funder after the fact and say that you forgot to list this or that service, and therefore you now need this much more money to get the job done. You must say up front exactly what you intend to do and how much each operation and service will cost. It's possible to obtain cost estimates of certain types of operations and services from network stations or independent producers in your area. Compare the estimates. Then decide how much you would charge for similar services to do the kind of quality production you want to do.

Don't overcharge or undercharge because proposal reviewers know the general cost of operations and services listed. If you undercharge, you risk reducing the quality of your production or facing unpaid bills. If the charges seem high, explain why. Perhaps labor in your area is costly, perhaps you want top-notch people, or perhaps you need high-quality equipment to do a first-rate production. The cost of a radio or television production can run anywhere from five to six figures. In any case, give the review committee honest reasons for the expenses you expect to incur. Be prepared to provide documentation to justify those charges—for example, a cost estimate of services and equipment from several sources that shows your quote is fair and reasonable.

As this practiced producer knows, there are no formulas for estimating production costs. Each production will be different from the last and will require careful consideration of all its specific requirements. No matter how many times you do a cost estimate, you're likely to learn something new the next time.

> I had never produced a project of this magnitude [his radio series on the jazz musician Miles Davis] and I really didn't know how much it was going to cost. I had to provide CPB with a very detailed budget, broken down into every conceiv-

able part, about five pages of financial information. I spent weeks talking to other producers, recording studios, editors, and writers to find out exactly what everything was going to cost, being very accurate about the numbers I put into the budget—salaries, daily cost use of a sound truck, a 24-track sound truck, every and any possible detail. [Although NEA prefers a one-page budget, it should be no less accurate than a detailed budget plan.]

With CPB, especially, your application becomes a binding contract in which CPB says, "Yes, we'll give this amount of money that you asked for and you have promised to do this, this, and this in your proposal. We want a quality series of so many hours worthy of national exposure which will include these details for exactly this amount of money." And you have to sign that.

The proposal process is preparation a lot of novices try to avoid, but actually it's the key to laying the road map for your production work. Without it, you won't have a structure to work from and will most likely face very serious production problems later on, particularly if you've underestimated your costs, or worse, lied about what you intend to do.

Steve Rowland, producer,
SR Productions, Philadelphia, Pennsylvania

5. Prepare a sample segment of the proposed project. It's a good idea to send the sample along with your application form or proposal. The sample, also called a "demo," may be a 10- to 30-minute sound or video pilot that introduces the spirit and essence of the overall project. In the course of researching their projects, writers tape the events and people they plan to use in their final production, and these sections become part of the demo.

The cost of producing a demo for a quality program is high but not as high as the actual production. Sometimes, the cost necessarily comes from out-of-pocket capital, but these expenses are often recovered if the demo can be sold to stations or marketed along with the major program. Because most independents have limited capital to produce a demo, they apply for funds from groups other than the one they hope will underwrite their major production. Often, funds to produce a demo can be obtained more easily than the amount of money required for a major production. These pros know that preparing a demo pays off in the end and in more ways than one.

> In the world of radio and television, you almost always are expected to produce a work sample and present it along with your proposal to a committee. I've learned from my experience as a reviewer for NEA that the sample work tape is critical to the success or failure of a grant. That's the window evaluators use to see whether you're capable of doing what you say you are.
>
> Actually, before we had any funding at all, we recorded one of Miles Davis's rehearsals. That allowed us to capture these jazz musicians at work, to watch their creative process, find out what language they used to communicate musical ideas. As importantly, we were able to get tapes of Miles working with musicians that no one had ever seen or heard before. That helped our credibility with the funders tremendously because Miles had a reputation for avoiding the media.
>
> **Steve Rowland,** producer,
> SR Productions, Philadelphia, Pennsylvania

The pilot became part of Rowland's 8-hour radio series which was presented in six 1-hour programs and a 2-hour concert program over PBS stations.

As this freelancer points out, providing a sample gives the funding group a chance to hold, see, and react to the project requiring big bucks from their treasury. It can be the key to winning approval of your application.

> As a funding strategy, you really need to have something that the funding agencies can see, how you're going to treat it, what type of quality you're bringing to the production, what type of scholarship, the authenticity of the voice. A lot of the time you get a brilliant idea, and you can't get the money to put it together, but if you put together a pilot, which is a lot simpler, then you get money to do it. Then they can see it and say, "Ah, you've really got a valid point. You can really execute it well." The pilot for our 2-hour program ["Surviving

Columbus"] got reedited and was broadcast nationally as the "Pueblo People" on PBS.

Larry Walsh, freelance producer,
KNME-TV, Albuquerque, New Mexico

Besides winning the 1992 Peabody for his 2-hour program, Walsh also won the Ohio State University award for his pilot production.

6. Use demographic data as evidence where necessary. If you need demographic data to support an argument in your proposal, don't overlook the ready data available at CPB. Their surveys are available to you for the asking and requesting them is far less expensive than conducting your own market survey. Rowland and other independents have found CPB data useful on more than one occasion.

> In the past five or so years, there's been a tremendous emphasis on market research in public radio that wasn't there before and many proposal writers, producers and stations are doing market research and using the results of their research as a basis for arguments in their proposals. The CPB has an ongoing demographic survey project, and they publish booklets with the results of these surveys and people often refer to these publications for basic stats. You can get the listening patterns of public radio—that is, who listens to what on public radio, the level of listeners' classes and incomes, where they spend their money, how many books and records they buy, how many hours per week they listen, how many hours they listen to jazz, how many hours to classical music, and so on.
>
> So if you go to a corporation, Pepsi-Cola, let's say, and you ask them for money, you could use that information to support an argument or position—for instance, what group in the population of audiences your program would appeal to, that sort of thing. It just gives your project a reason for being, an evidentiary base for being. If you've got capital to spare, you do your own research or hire an expert.

Steve Rowland, producer,
SR Productions, Philadelphia, Pennsylvania

7. Request help in preparing your proposal from the government agency. Many of these agencies are usually staffed by people who will help you assemble a proposal that meets their established requirements. Ask about this when you call to request information about their grant application procedure.

8. Include your vita. At the very least, construct a brief biographical synopsis of your background demonstrating the experience that qualifies you to execute the proposed project. If application directions fail to indicate how the vita or synopsis should be submitted, enclose it as a separate document or make it part of your free-form proposal. Include the titles of other relevant projects you have produced, the results of same in terms of audience response, and the awards they may have earned. If you have none you can name, use any ammunition that reassures the funder that if you are given the grant you are qualified to see the job through. Above all, be honest. Anything less than honesty could mean rejection of your project, personal embarrassment, and loss of your time and energy.

9. Appeal to more than one source for funds. When you do, count on completing an application form for each one. Sounds tedious, and it is, but the good news is this: If you fill out one form, you have a good start on all the others, and if you have written a free-form proposal for one funder, that exercise will make the next proposal easier to do. If you have to do all three types for a number of funders, try to maintain consistency and uniformity in your submissions. The best of all worlds is to get one proposal out to all funding groups, but that's not always possible.

10. Don't overlook the corporations. If you begin with a private foundation or government funding agency, supplement your needs with an appeal to a corporation—better yet, target all three. In fact, if you're able to win one over, that endorsement is likely to attract the support of other funding groups, but only if your project fits their aims and purpose. Meeting funders' aims and goals is the overriding determinant. Also, having more than one support group is a good strategy, especially when it comes down to finding buyers for your funded program.

Filling out applications for grants or writing proposals according to funders' specifications requires the ability to follow directions, give clear and concise explanations, and provide a neat presentation. Writing the free-form proposal requires all this and more. Chapter 6 explains the components of a free-form proposal and how it should be presented, but don't skip to Chapter 6 just yet. It bears repeating —proposal writing begins only after the hard work of researching the problem has been completed. The latter is what the next two chapters are all about.

NOTES

1. Titles and affiliations of interviewees named throughout this text represent those given at the time the respondent was interviewed. Changes that may have occurred since then are noted wherever the author received knowledge of same.

2. Mr. Bianchi is now president of his own company, Bianchi Public Relations, Inc., which is located in Bloomfield Hills, Michigan.

3. For their *Guide to the National Endowment for the Arts* and their *Application Guidelines*, write or call NEA, Nancy Hanks Center, Public Information Office, Room 803, 1100 Pennsylvania Avenue, NW, Washington, DC 20506; 202-682-5452. For their *Overview of Endowment Programs*, write or call the National Endowment for the Humanities, Public Information Office, Room 407, 1100 Pennsylvania Avenue, NW, Washington, DC 20506; 202-606-8438. To receive their brochure *Who Funds PTV? Producer's Guide to Public Television Funding*, write or call the Corporation for Public Broadcasting, 901 E Street, NW, Washington, DC 20004-2037; 202-879-9600. In each case, ask if you need to send a self-addressed, stamped return envelope and the size required. Federal and state aid has always been in short supply and may soon become extinct. Nevertheless, ask for the literature. The material will give you a good idea of the expectations of funding groups, government or otherwise.

4

Pre-Proposal Activity I

Key Functions

Editors and clients buy solutions to problems. That's why isolation of the true problem is the most essential function in the whole problem-solving process. Without an accurate assessment of the problem, any argument, strategy, or presentation scheme is rendered either false or unconvincing. In Chapter 3, you were introduced to some common types of problems media writers encounter, but the purpose here is to describe how one identifies the real problem, which may not necessarily be the one perceived by the problem carrier and is, very often, concealed from view.

IDENTIFY THE PROBLEM

In his classic text, *Personal Knowledge: Towards a Post-Critical Philosophy,* Michael Polanyi observed that identity of the problem is a means to knowledge and that the ability to recognize a problem worth solving is an essential ingredient in the discovery process.[1] Physicists Albert Einstein and Leopold Infeld held a similar view. In fact, they regarded the problem more essential than its solution because problems provided opportunities to raise questions, new possibilities, and to regard old questions from a new angle, all of which called on one's creative imagination and led to real advances.[2]

Although politicians and business leaders cut paths through different forests than philosophers and scientists, they have much in common with Polanyi, Einstein, and Infeld. This suggests that passage through the density of any forest is achieved by those who recognize problems begging solution.

During the 1992 presidential race, the challenger, Bill Clinton, focused on one of the issues foremost in voters' minds—unemployment—an issue that apparently escaped the concern of incumbent George Bush. Clinton's unemployment issue captured voter attention as did his reminder that "if George Bush doesn't understand the problem, how can he solve it?"

Everyone loves a problem solver, especially employers, including those in mass media. The problem with the problem, however, is that there's more to it than simply noticing it. Awareness must then give way to the more important question of whether it's the perceived problem, an underlying problem causing it, or something else entirely. The bottom-line precaution is to be aware that the perceived problem is not always the true villain.

THE ROLE OF CRITICAL THINKING

Although agreement prevails that productive problem solution depends on an accurate assessment of the situation,[3] no one, as Robert Rich points out, explains how to do it.[4] It's true, few signals are available, particularly in the literature of mass media. However, some clues on disciplined process may be found here and there in the literature of other disciplines.[5] The consensus among these observers is that critical thinking, that is, raising questions, is the most effective cognitive tool in any solution process and particularly so at the point of trying to identify the real problem.

Use this technique to turn on your thinking machine: Once you hear or see a statement of the problem, consider it first as a whole, then consider its several parts. Think about the whole and its parts by asking yourself questions. Flaws in the problem statement rise to the surface with every question; others follow naturally one after the other. If you need a push, try the "starter" questions listed in Chapter 2.

It helps to corroborate your initial understanding of the problem with the problem carrier, perhaps asking the carrier the same questions you asked of yourself. Sometimes, questioning the problem carrier works, sometimes it doesn't. Too often, problem carriers have little notion about their needs and are ill-informed about the problem. All they may know is that something's wrong or urgently needed, but they don't know what it is or what to do about it. That's why they've come to you. You have to show them what's really wrong or needed, why it's so, and what to do about it.

For example, a law firm hoping to increase its clientele approached Kekst & Co., a New York public relations agency that markets the specialized legal skills of law firms. When agency partner Jeffrey Z. Taufield asked, "Well, what's interesting about your practice?" the law firm said they didn't know but "thought hiring a public relations firm would take care of that."[6]

The problem may be just as obscure even when problem carriers have knowledge to communicate. The transferred information often complicates the matter. That usually happens, business writer Dorothy Leeds points out, because people do not readily volunteer information, or they talk in generalities, jump to conclusions, make wrong assumptions, or simply perceive things from motivations you may know nothing about.[7]

THE ROLE OF RESEARCH

Identity of the true problem takes a lot of self-initiated exploration on your part—in short, just plain old hard work, otherwise known as research. It begins by first pondering what is perceived as the problem, then raising self-inquiries about it, looking for answers in relevant materials and documents, and then questioning appropriate sources and making on-scene observations and the like. No big secret here—research work and asking yourself questions are two of several key functions in the problem-solving process.[8]

IS IT THE REAL PROBLEM?
PRELIMINARY RESEARCH

The principal difficulty facing the problem solver, James Adams noted some years ago, is the absence of clues.[9] An obvious observation? Not really. Understandably, uninitiated proposal writers not only ignore their presence, they also fail to recognize their absence. They assume, instead, that they're specialists, so the needed inspiration will suddenly appear of its own accord. No such luck. Such assumptions bring on nothing but disaster.

No practiced media writer dares set out on a proposal venture without first doing a great deal of research. The result may require verification of one's first assessment of a situation, suggest a modification, or completely change one's initial assessment. The research makes the presence of clues more visible, makes their absence more obvious, renders up missing clues, and either corroborates, modifies, or corrects first perceptions.

You may well ask: *If research produces clues to the real problem, what detection device is used and where and on whom does the detective work begin?* As suggested earlier, the most useful detection device is critical thinking, not just at the outset or at this point but throughout the whole process. Self-inquiry is the motor that drives the engine, but you're the one who turns the key. The journey toward solution begins with you.

You believe you're incapable of raising "appropriate" research questions? Set such doubts aside. Look at the process outlined in Chapter 2. Procedures 1 and 2a in the first stages of research are *preliminary* functions, so use the starter questions listed in those procedures to collect initial research. Study the information you've collected. "Appropriate" questions, that is, those specific and relevant to your particular problem, will rise to the surface and prepare you for the next stage of exploration—primary research (Procedure 2b).

If you're new at the research game, begin by studying the perceived problem statement. Trust your innate sense of curiosity. Rely on your natural ability to wonder, to raise questions, any question. Believe it, no question is a dumb question. A problem is a problem because no one concerned with the problem has enough information about it to raise appropriate questions. So, start with the problem statement: Let it tell you what to ask, where to look for answers, and who to talk to for additional information. The more background information you accumulate, the more proficient you become about raising specific and relevant questions about the problem. Still insecure? Read on.

Some of the explorations conducted by media pros shown in the case examples at the end of this chapter will help you understand more about the preliminary steps in the research process. It makes no sense to provide a list of research sources here because, as explained earlier, no two problems are ever exactly alike and the types of resources vary according to the problem at hand. The important act is to ask yourself questions because more often than not those questions hold clues about where to get answers.[10]

If you have difficulty formulating a question, you may be making it harder on yourself than it really is. Begin each question with one of the five Ws—who, what, when, where, and why—and also how and if; for example, "If such-and-such, then how come this?" or "If such-and-such, then why that?" Notice all the W, how, and if questions in Chapter 2's list of starter questions. Use them as a preface to any query you may want to make. The rest of the question will fall into place. Poet Rudyard Kipling regarded the W and how questions as his best friends. So do media writers, and so should you.

Are there "right" specific questions? If there is such a thing as a "right" question, the concept of rightness may be related to results found in a study conducted by two cognitive scientists,

Naomi Miyake and Donald Norman. They found that some learning about the subject at hand must take place before questions can be raised in order to expand the scope of one's knowledge.[11] In other words, to ask "right" questions you must learn something about the problem. After a preliminary study of the problem, you'll find that formulating specific questions concerning your specific situation comes quite naturally. The key test of each question's merit is to critically examine your own formulations:

- *What information am I trying to get at?*
- *Are my questions phrased in a way that will obtain the needed information?*
- *If this is the information I need, what peripheral questions are necessary?*
- *If my questions are not phrased appropriately or for maximum response, what modifications are necessary?*
- *What follow-up questions or probes do I need in anticipation of stonewalling or misleading interviewees?*
- *Are any of my questions biased, unclear, ambiguous?* If they are, redo them to remove bias, clarify them, or make them more specific.

Notice the number of W and how questions that pros raise in the case examples presented at the end of this chapter. Notice, too, the tone of wonder those questions express. As importantly, notice how their questions hold hints of the initial research work that has to be done in order to construct a preliminary knowledge base about the problem.

Those first questions serve as a necessary prelude to more specific questions for primary research and a broader knowledge base about the issue. All this is in the interest of identifying the true problem and becoming, as John Behling says, "a minor expert in the area of concern."[12] If specific questions seem to come too quickly after a pro's first questions, keep in mind that they're practiced in the art of casting questions; they need only a few activators to move them into the specifics.

THE AUDIENCE: THE REASON
FOR MEDIA'S BEING

Understanding your audience is another key function in the preparation of writing a proposal. The rule about audience is simple: Find out who your audience is, what they need, then give 'em what they're asking for. In any case, addressing the audience relevant to the problem at hand is just downright good business sense. The insurance company Liberty Mutual knows the meaning of that basic rule. Their ads tell prospects that Liberty Mutual takes individual concerns seriously because it is a company that is, the slogan goes, "Facing the issues that face our customers."

The rule is simple, but its application is not. It takes methodical research to identify and sketch the profile of an audience, to learn about their reading and listening habits, their preferences and motives, their political leanings, age, areas of employment, annual income, and the like. Newspaper houses, public relations, and advertising agencies often have in-house research groups, but if the project calls for extensive market research, an outside agency is usually called in. For example, the experts may be asked to monitor voter reaction to legislation that would raise taxes to support construction of a new prison within city limits, or they may be asked to explore the possibility of identifying a new consumer market for a product that has always been directed toward a particular segment of the population.

These activities usually lie outside the domain of the writer, but the results of those activities bear heavily on who the writer must address, the focus of the message to be communicated, and what content should be included. Take those results seriously. They're an essential element in your knowledge base and a vital component of your proposal. So is another element.

KNOW YOUR DECISION MAKERS

Getting an inside line on decision makers isn't easy. Usually, writers are one, two, or more times removed from those central players. Still, it's a key function that can and should be done.

Journalists review their own newspapers and broadcasts. They compare them with similar products produced by other media houses. That exercise gives them a fairly good idea of how their house likes things done and how their house measures up against the competition. It tells them what their house is failing to do, where their management stands on the attitude scale concerning any particular issue or policy, and why the competition is so successful. They observe in-house relationships between editors and between editors and staff. They learn about company policy and decision makers' preferences and expectations. In time, a fairly good picture evolves, and you begin to understand your work environment.

Public relations and advertising writers read the client's literature about their product, read the criticisms and praises of the product in other literature, read the literature on products similar to the client's, and observe how the product is produced in the plant and distributed in the marketplace. They talk to people who produce the product or are involved in the company's business. One can learn a lot about the executive branch as well as the work environment just by talking to key personnel and observing them in action. If it's possible, and it often is, a one-to-one contact is the best window on decision makers' personalities. It also gives you a lead on the prevailing climate at the client's workplace—casual or conservative, formal or informal, restrictive or free, warm or cold.

Look and Listen for Clues

Meetings may be arranged or spontaneous. It can be either way for journalists. But in public relations and advertising it's a little different. Meetings with the client are usually arranged with just the executives present. But make no mistake, most account executives want writers in on these sessions. They may begin with a prelude of small talk and questions that indicate *genuine* interest in the other person. The emphasis here falls on genuine because if you're insincere or show a modicum of boredom, don't even try. Clients, everyone, an advertising executive says, like to talk about their business and personal problems. The way to open them up, he says, is to ask questions about their families, what they do to relax, their concerns about the problem at hand, and what's keeping them up at night.

Genuineness also means being a good listener, making keen observations, and being sensitive to even the most subtle clue. All are of equal importance. It also means making prompt responses to phone calls, messages, correspondence, and attending meetings even when you think they're unnecessary. Above all, it means developing an astute sense of what is solid information and what is not, recognizing biases and prejudices, and differentiating genuine messages from phony pronouncements. Bias, prejudice, and impatience say a lot about a person who manifests these signals, characteristics you have to consider when producing something for that person but without compromising the data-driven solution to the problem.

In addition, notice or learn about decision makers' work habits, food preferences, favorite places, leisure activities, special interests, family connections, choice of motor vehicles, mannerisms, style of dress, types of acquaintances, selections in office decor, wall hangings, and even color choices. Each one says a lot about the person.

A cosmetics manufacturer nixed an entire campaign plan because the artist had selected pink as the predominant color in artwork ordered for brochures and ads. The client simply had an aversion to pink. Who would have thought? Pink and its variations are basics in the cosmetic industry. Nevertheless, the question of color should have been raised by someone on the creative team early in the preparation process or picked up from something as simple as a comment during a luncheon engagement about the use of pink tablecloths, a shade of linen frequently used in fine restaurants.

When in Doubt, Ask

But what can one do if contact with decision makers is rarely, if ever, possible? Some journalists work at bureaus distant from the home office of decision makers. A public relations or ad agency may be serving a client miles or an ocean away. Even so, you can work around such barriers. Ask teammates who've had previous encounters with the decision makers. Listen carefully to others at in-house meetings. A great deal can be learned just by listening carefully and observing exchanges during project discussion periods or exchanging ideas with a colleague over coffee at a favorite gathering place.

If nothing turns up, ask questions. Still no clues? Ask the person in charge to find out what needs to be known. Journalists can request permission to attend a management meeting concerning the proposed project; public relations and advertising writers can ask to accompany account executives on their next visit to client location sites. Such requests are rarely rejected, sometimes expected, and in some cases, the person in charge may insist on the writer's presence.

Getting an inside line on decision makers and their world can mean the difference between acceptance or rejection of your proposal—a rejection even for such a seemingly frivolous reason as an artist's choice of colors or because the decision maker doesn't like people who slouch or wear sneakers. Don't laugh, it happens.

The point is, try to learn as much as you can about the people you have to deal with and stand alert to clues that inform. Those clues tell you what to avoid. They also tell you who to avoid and how best to carry out your ideas.

HOW THE PROS DO IT

Print and Broadcast Journalism

Not surprisingly, pros in print and broadcast journalism go about exploring a proposal problem just as they do an assigned project involving a mystery begging for an answer. For example, news director Mort Meisner, WJBK-TV, Detroit, was startled by a CBS feature regarding the growing number of hate groups in America. He raised the issue in a memo to Scott Lewis, one of the station's investigative reporters, and asked: *How much of this is going on in Michigan? If this is going on, what groups are out there in Michigan?*

Recognizing a challenging assignment and intrigued by the unknowns, Lewis felt it necessary to raise still other questions: *How many groups are out there? How many people are involved? What is the organizational nature of the hate movement in Michigan? Who are their leaders? Who would know about what organizations exist in Michigan?*

For answers, Lewis first studied news clips on hate crimes committed in the United States and Michigan and then followed through on Meisner's lead to contact an Alabama group called the Klan Watch. Meisner had read about the organization and its purpose—tracking and recording the hate movement in America.

Lewis realized that if hate groups existed in Michigan they probably received and distributed mail. Preferring anonymity, they most likely used post office box numbers. The post office keeps a record of box renters, so these groups could be identified through those records. The Klan Watch had records on some of the hate groups in Michigan, but Lewis also wanted to know: *What less known and unnamed groups were out there being directed by low-profile, even phantom leaders?*

Results of his three-month research effort led to approval for a 5-part series of 3-minute broadcasts that exposed Michigan hate groups and their leaders and put formerly unknown groups on record along with the knowns.

Is the approach any different for journalists when they propose an enterprise project? Not at all. Take a look at the enterprise projects two journalists undertook, each with a knotty problem the journalists identified themselves. Nevertheless, they felt obliged to verify the problem before proposing coverage of it. Journalism proposals usually begin informally, during meetings, at the water cooler, or just catching the editor's or producer's attention in passing.

Once the nod to proceed is given, a proposal is written to clarify agreement as to the purpose and plan for preliminary research. That initial plan is usually followed by a series of reports to the editor or producer regarding the research and its progress. A final proposal may follow with identification and statement of the real problem, whether it varies and why from the originally perceived problem, and an implementation plan for coverage and presentation of the story.

One should expect changes to any submitted plan. Such amendments can come from editors, producers, or managment and for any reason, or changes may be necessary in the original plan because new information calls for it. In the case studies that follow, notice how journalists' original perceptions of the problem were altered by the data, and how certain implementation plans were adjusted to accommodate a need or limitation.

Notice, too, how journalists find opportunities for enterprise projects. Sometimes it's just being aware of what's going on around you. For example, this journalist knew that local citizens were unhappy about their elected officials. Polls and surveys gave ample evidence of their discontent. So he felt the time was ripe to address the problem. Here's how he started thinking about it:

> I had to ask myself: *What exactly are so many people fed up about? If that's their attitude, how come they don't run for office?* We started with a number of hypotheses, mainly questions about what we thought was the case out there, then turned reporters loose to find out [from the voting public] which one of our hypotheses were true, false, or maybe more true than the others. We're always trying to guess the prevailing conventional wisdom because you have to begin somewhere, but then you need to find out for sure what it is out there in reality. Then you can decide where to focus energy. Once we learned the extent of the apathy, disinterest, anger, and frustration among the body politic, we took up primary research on such questions as: *How do you get your name on the ballot? Who is eligible to run for office? What kind of person would be most likely to succeed? How much money do you actually have to spend to enter your name in a political race?*
>
> **Ronald D. Dzwonkowski,** projects editor,
> *Detroit Free Press*

Execution of the project began after senior editors responded postively to Dzwonkowski's verbal suggestion and then a one-page proposal that included answers to his initial self-inquiries. The projects editor began with a small team of reporters that increased in number as research progressed from preliminary to primary stages of research. In the last analysis, the team's concerted effort helped refine the proposal presented to senior editors.

The team's research strategy included checking records on registration procedures at the state election office and city and county clerks' offices, interviews with the chairpersons of political parties, candidates who had run for office, and public relations and advertising personnel who specialize in promoting candidates for political office.

Previous knowledge of a matter always serves the enterprising media writer. So does an observant eye. This freelancer had been studying materials about Christopher Columbus hoping to hit on a new theme for a TV documentary in recognition of the quincentenary observance of Columbus Day. At the same time, he was helping a group at the Latin-American Institute, University of New Mexico, plan a magazine format in honor of the observance. He quickly noticed a flaw in their initial approach. Because of the preparation the broadcaster had done for his own documentary, he was able to point out that their effort concentrated only on the European perspective of Columbus's discovery and had overlooked the important part that American Indians played in that drama. Their oversight set the theme focus he chose for his documentary (see case introduction, Chapter 3):

> Here we were in the midst of Pueblo Indian country and everyone seemed to have forgotten that these people were the ones who had the longest contact with the Europeans, longer than any existing Indian group in the United States. They [the magazine planners] were focusing on one culture when actually this was a story about two cultures. For my documentary, I read tons and tons of materials; the libraries here are full of Spanish history, not much on the Indians. So

you have to ask: *What are the Indian ways captured in all this?*
What is the Indian perspective? Who made the first contact with
the Pueblo people? When was that? I had done my homework. I
had read the Spanish histories on the discovery of the Americas. So I knew what to ask the experts on Indian culture, and
when they would say "Here's the sense of Pueblo culture," I
could say "Yes, I understand that." I soon realized that the
thing that was missing from the Columbus story in all these
quincentenary observances was the Pueblo factor in the
discovery of the Americas. The impact and consequence of
that cultural encounter between the Spanish and the Indians
became the essence of my video documentary.

Larry Walsh, freelance producer,
KNME-TV, Albuquerque, New Mexico

Understanding one's audience is a significant part of the
research function and, as the next two cases demonstrate, knowing your audience is as important in journalism as it is in any
other division of mass media.

We knew from the start that we had a concerned audience
and a great story [U.S. Department of Agriculture waste of
taxpayer dollars], but we were surprised to learn that readers
not only in Kansas but in other states as well were so interested that they, in fact, ordered and read the whole of a
24-page reprint of our daily series. We got calls from all over
the country requesting the reprint, and that told us that not
just farmers but all taxpayers are eager for information that
has an impact on them, particularly information concerning
our farms and food products. Farmers and taxpayers want us
to look hard at government. We learned that they wanted us
to follow their tax dollars, tell them if their meat is being
inspected properly, if their food is properly labeled. Our
audience was a wide one, but the important thing here was
we gave them answers they needed to hear.

Jeff Taylor, national correspondent,
Kansas City Star, Kansas City, Missouri

Taylor and his teammate, Mike McGraw, worked on this
project together, which was titled "Failing the Grade: Betrayals

and Blunders at the Department of Agriculture." Their series won the 1992 Pulitzer prize for a "distinguished example of reporting on national affairs."

An audience's "need to know" was one of the factors that motivated a Seattle television producer to pursue his enterprise project (see case introduction, Chapter 3). Here he explains how he learned about his audience and their need:

> I was new in the area and knew nothing about the people who lived here or the environment. I believed I had a good subject [extinction of Columbia River salmon], but I wasn't sure I had a listening audience. I read a lot and talked to everyone I could. I soon learned I knew more about this area than the locals. I was at a party once and somebody asked me, "What are you working on now?" I said I was just starting on this show about the demise of the Columbia River salmon. He said, "Oh, yeah? What happened to 'em?" I had to ask how long he had been living in the Northwest and was astounded to learn that he had been here for ten years and didn't know what happened to a delicacy that came only from his area of the country. That scenario repeated itself time and again, so I knew I had found my subject and an audience for it.
>
> **Ben Saboonchian,** documentary writer
> and producer, KIRO-TV, Seattle

Message receivers make up just one of your audiences. You have still another—the decision makers in your media house. They're as much one of your audiences as the general public is your marketplace. That's something this investigative reporter knows something about. Her enterprise project concerned the absence of police enforcement in women's rape cases, particularly minority women's. It was a touchy subject and she realized she might face some resistance from management, so she investigated the issue mainly on her own time and shared her progress only with her immediate supervisor.

> I think there are a lot of variables that go into the sales job that one needs to do when they undertake an enterprise or

investigative story. There are a lot of intangibles that have nothing to do with the quality of the idea or the length of time that it will take or the impact of the story, all the things that you might think would be the essentials of negotiating a proposal like that. There are newsroom politics that are brought to bear on this process that are very powerful, as powerful as the essence of the story. So it's very important in this process—that is, it depends on the people around you, your stature in the newsroom, how they regard you as a person. Although I kept my immediate supervisor aware of what I was on to, I never sent out initial or formal proposals to him or anyone else. I knew there was some disbelief that the police might not be doing their job, perhaps even an attitude about women reporting rape cases. So I worked on it very much in the background, very quietly, over a period of months while I was carrying out my regular assignments. It was only after I had uncovered enough powerful data to carry the idea that anyone beyond my immediate supervisor knew what I was working on.

Candy Cooper, investigative reporter,
San Francisco Examiner

Cooper spent about three months collecting information before going to the editors with her proposal. Because her data, she said, were so "powerful," it was an offer they couldn't refuse. Her published story ranked among the finalists for the 1991 Pulitzer award.

Caution was this radio writer's rule as well. He knew he'd face a cool reception. His project concerned an educational radio program for New York's public schools. Music classes had been canceled due to school budget reductions and he wanted to make up for that by giving primary students a radio series introducing them to all types of music—from the medieval period to Mozart to rap. His station was willing to foot the bill but needed approval from the New York Board of Education to air it to a public school audience. Even so, he knew the Board would balk at even a station-funded project. Like Cooper, he quietly collected proof of the merit of his proposal before submitting it.

The Board's indecision finally gave way under the weight of the writer's data. They approved the proposal for a series of 13 half-hour radio broadcasts.

> The Board of Education, like any other government agency, is a bureaucracy and the review process is always very slow. But this Board was also disenfranchised and, although members never raised questions, the uncertainty surrounding education's future just held things up much longer than usual. So it didn't hurt the process when they learned that the schools we had canvassed—we had a database from over 800—were thrilled to have such a project and that the station would underwrite the cost.
>
> **Max Horowitz,** staff writer,
> WNCN-FM, New York City

Parents, teachers, and students alike called for more of the same after the first program aired. Titled "New York City Musicbox," the Horowitz project won the 1991 Peabody award for "an important program which entertains young people while it simultaneously kindles their interest in music."

Public Relations and Advertising

In most respects, the process in public relations and advertising follows a route similar to the one in journalism, but there are some differences. Once the problem is stated, agency personnel hold discussion sessions both in-house and with the client. They share information about the problem and determine what more must be known to ascertain whether the stated problem is indeed the true one. Preliminary research begins with a study of the company and its product. With the company's permission, agency personnel obtain information about the company and its product from company files and other relevant sources—government documents, magazine and newspaper articles, business and trade journals, and consumer and marketing reports.

They collect other data related to the problem situation by interviewing key company personnel—officers, managers, employees, sales representatives, and the like. They study current and untapped customer markets. They visit the client's plant or place of business and make whatever observations of any setting that relates to the problem. The results of focus group and even more elaborate surveys may help in determining whatever else must be known. It's dangerous to rely solely on a client's view of the problem. As one executive put it, the "voice of the customer" is a critical input and one needs to determine firsthand what that voice is saying.

Client contact is usually the responsibility of account executives, not the writers. If executives fail to raise relevant questions in-house or with the client, the writers are expected to do so, not at client meetings but during in-house sessions, or they may send their questions in a memo to account executives or to the head of research or marketing.

Depending on the size of the project, in-house sessions may be highly structured meetings with a team made up of researchers, marketing personnel, writers, artists, and sometimes even sales personnel, or they may be informal meetings with just the writer, creative director, and account executive or group supervisor present. In large agencies, questions and answers and other information may flow through standard forms completed by account managers, creative directors, and general and market researchers. Although some executives insist on the writer's presence at all client meetings, in other cases writers may have very limited or no contact with the client.

Such formality, however, should never preclude a writer's responsibility to raise a question that could clear some aspect of the issue and lead to validation of the perceived problem or identification of the real one. Don't be shy. Executives appreciate these probing questions. It clarifies things for them, too. Use the direct approach. It will give you an idea of the client's perspective on the problem, and then you can go on from there. The direct approach always works well, even with clients, according to this public relations pro:

> You have to say to your person, whether it's a client or a manager, you have to say, "Look, tell me the problem be-

cause what you're asking for, in fact, could make it a lot worse [the problem situation]." From there, the first step in what we call the "consulting diamond," is the step where you confront the data. What you're doing is deflating the assumptions. All sound public relations begin with research, data you can trust.

Patrick Jackson, senior counsel,
Jackson, Jackson & Wagner,
Exeter, New Hampshire

That research, in fact, might reveal that the client's perceptions of the problem are unrelated to its realities. For example, United Airlines (UA) approached several public relations agencies with their particular problem: a declining level of the market share accompanied by some diminishment in consumer perceptions of UA service. In this case, the agency that had the account, Hill and Knowlton, Chicago, had to compete with three other agencies to maintain its ownership of the account.

All four agencies were given a verbal briefing concerning the situation as well as some supporting documents to substantiate UA's view of the problem. The airline was convinced there was a definite connection between loss of market share and perceived UA service. Nevertheless, this Hill and Knowlton account executive wanted to make sure that UA's assessment was actually the case. He and his team worked two years on the project—from the point of researching the problem to producing a creative solution.

I think, oftentimes, that the greatest hazard in business development is an agency's quick acceptance of an expressed need, which could very well have been ill-perceived by the client, or an agency's misunderstanding of what the client is looking for. The only way to avoid either one of these pitfalls is to go through a process, and that process involves several steps. The first is to ask the client to give us a face-to-face briefing of the problem so that we can hear directly from the client what the issue is. That's much more valuable than just getting it written down on a piece of paper because oftentimes articulation of the problem verbally becomes much more meaningful. This gives one the opportunity to raise questions, have a dialogue, watch reactions, and clarify the given data.

The second thing we do is ask the client to permit us to continue to ask questions even after the briefing has taken place so that we can get clarification either on where our process is taking us or on what the client thinks they said they wanted. In the UA case, we had to know first and foremost: *What evidence did UA have that there was a link between the image change and the market-share change?* As it turned out, they couldn't establish the linkage and after some preliminary research, we couldn't either. The client had made a leap of intellect to say that there *probably* was a need for improvement in the service level. We relied on other sources of research about the airline industry and did some primary research of our own among UA passengers to find out what their perception of service was at that time. Survey results showed diminished perceptions of UA service but for reasons not readily seen originally. We altered our overall approach to the declining market-share problem and our plans included consideration of ways to improve UA customer relations.

> **Hud Englehart,** executive managing director,
> Hill and Knowlton, Chicago

Hill and Knowlton's proposal predominated over presentations made by the other three contenders and the UA account remained with Hill and Knowlton as the agency's account of record.

In the next case, the client again made the initial approach. Again, it was a bid for business, but this time it was a new account opportunity for this agency. Several other advertising agencies also competed for the business offered by American Express and its product, the American Express Gold Card. The company's problem: The Gold Card had failed to meet expectations in the marketplace and the client wanted to know why.

The client gave each competitor a written statement of the problem, but no clues as to possible causes. The account executive and his team had to probe.

It was necessary to ask a lot of questions. What was wrong was clear enough on its face—the product had not received broad market acceptance, but the underlying cause was unknown. *Why was a charge card that already had the mark of prestige not winning the market?* We asked the client: *What's the card's current market position? To whom is the product positioned? What is their expectation in terms of expenditure investment?* [crucial to the agency's investment of time, talent, and depth of research] We asked for their understanding of why this product couldn't coast comfortably with the successful Green Card, which was the standard in the industry.

Their explanations gave us clues to how much we still had to learn about the problem. We called in the research people, took a look at how the market had developed, how it was evolving, conducted focus groups, and talked to lots of consumers. We wanted to know: *What credit cards did they use? Which most often? For what purposes? What were the usual charging and payment behaviors? Why was the Green Card preferred?* We found out that consumers saw little advantage in the additional things the Gold Card delivered. The client had counted on those additional features to carry it; our research proved otherwise. Now we knew consumers had to be given reasons, other than the previously exploited features, why the card at its premium price provided additional prestige over and above its gold color.

> **Craig Middleton,** executive vice president
> and director, marketing and planning,
> McCann-Erickson Worldwide, New York City

Never underestimate the value of questions or the reward of research. Together they track the way to the true problem and establish where attention should fall. Together they reveal the appropriate audience to target for any given communication and the factors to which that audience would most likely respond.

Sometimes, the business of running a going concern so consumes clients that they have to be reminded of their publics and the important part they play in the health of their company. This public relations executive says management needs to be reminded time and again about it.

Somebody comes in. They've got a problem. They can't clearly identify it, so you have to spend some time and ask questions. They might say, "I need to send out a press release and that will solve my problem." You have to say, "Yes, you have to put out a release, but you have to recognize that one press release doesn't necessarily do the job. We have to first define the audience, what they need to know." And you have to say this to them [the client] over and over.

Jim Little, president,
First Communications Group, Inc.,
Findlay, Ohio

Sometimes, a simple and direct question often exposes how much clients might know about their market. The direct approach worked for this creative director. Once the client's perspective of his audience was known, the advertiser and his research staff knew where they had to place their research efforts.

Typically, we'll simply ask the client: *What do you see your marketplace as being?* We may discover, depending on the project and the marketplace circumstance, that they do or don't have a current or clear picture of who their target audience really is. In one case [a chain of amusement parks], we discovered that their approach was strictly directed to teens and that they weren't getting enough repeat business even with this population. They had overlooked a promising segment of the marketplace, the family. We conducted field observations noting which age groups were and were not coming to the parks, why they came, how often, what they liked, what they found lacking, and so on. This and other research corrected the client's view of their market and served to reposition their advertising approach.

Chuck Kent, creative director,
BBD&O Worldwide, Chicago

Remember, you're writing for a public, not for an audience of one—yourself. You may stumble on a great idea or have something important to say, but unless it serves the larger purpose, your particular public, there is little chance anyone will pay attention, including decision makers. Magazine publishers understand that principle well. Specialty magazines, particularly, keep a close tab on fluctuations in public preference. They know that advertisers take the temperature of the market as a matter of course and will not buy space in their publication if it fails to reflect the current mood of the marketplace.[13]

Consumer needs and moods change all the time, so the vigil should never let up, market researcher Karen Ritchie, McCann-Erickson Worldwide, told publishers and editors at a recent conference. The baby boomers are no longer twenty-something, she reminded them. Meet the new twentysome-things, she said, Generation X, whose values, attitudes, and outlooks differ sharply from their predecessors.[14]

Keep in mind that research includes still another activity—knowing your decision makers, understanding what makes them tick. In public relations and advertising, decision makers include your direct supervisor, a department head, an account executive, and through any one of these managers or through personal contact, the client. You need to find out who the decision makers are, what they expect, what their preferences and prejudices are, what it takes to "sell" them. It may be difficult, but, like learning about the problem, product, and audience, it can be done. You might even have to re-educate decision makers about their own industry, which was the situation in this case (see Chapter 3).

> Their resistance to change was very, very strong, and that was the interesting part of this program, that is, how we taught them [the client] the importance of various people to them, so they could see that each of those publics had an impact on their business in a very direct way.
>
> **Gwin Johnston,** CEO,
> Johnston Wells, Denver, Colorado

Getting to know the client's idiosyncrasies is a matter of professionalism, a maturing process, according to one public relations executive. He advises novices to observe and read as much as possible about the client beforehand and not to be timid about asking questions.

You soon learn to raise questions with skill. When we make contact, we don't initiate the questions right away. We just start the conversation going, then say: *By the way what does Joe think about these areas we've been talking about? How does he function in these areas?* You almost have to be an investigative reporter. Like the press, we ask the logical questions, the ones that fit the context, and not always, but usually, people will start volunteering information and pretty soon a pattern develops. The more you know about a prospect when you go to meet him, the better off you're going to be.

Joe S. Epley, chairman and CEO,
Epley Associates, Inc., Charlotte, North Carolina

The questions, of course, vary from case to case, but the approach to them is similar across all divisions of mass media. This advertising executive believes that questions work to the advantange of both client and agency.

Inquiries should tell the client we care, then they help us to know what their priorities are, how they think about the business. A little bit of small talk concerning them, their families, over a casual lunch is just a polite way of leading up to more direct questions.

Veronica Buxton, senior vice president
and group management supervisor,
Foote, Cone & Belding, San Francisco

She also said that they try not to know the client so well that the agency might be tempted to substitute something that should be sold for something that would, instead, please the client. The service objective—resolution of the problem—should never disappear from sight.

You may not be able to psych out all clients. Some reveal few personal clues. When that happens, this advertising pro says, do the next best thing:

Talk to other people who have had a business relationship with the client. In fact it's helpful to talk to those people even before meeting with the client. Then you can compare those comments against your own experience with the client. Things begin to fall together, and even the most mysterious figures begin to take on a personality.

Charles Crispin, president,
Crispin & Porter, Coral Gables, Florida

The discussion in this chapter centered around several key functions before a proposal can be written: namely, developing a body of knowledge concerning the problem, learning about the product, the audiences involved, and the decision makers. What one must do with that body of knowledge, how it contributes to the discovery of ideas for an implementation plan, figures large in still another set of key functions. That's what the next chapter is all about.

NOTES

1. M. Polanyi, *Personal Knowledge: Towards a Post-Critical Philosophy* (London: Routledge & Kegan Paul, 1958).
2. A. Einstein and L. Infeld, *The Evolution of Physics* (New York: Simon & Schuster, 1938).
3. J. L. Adams, *Conceptual Blockbusting* (San Francisco: Freeman, 1974); H. Larrabee, *Reliable Knowledge: Scientific Methods in the Social Studies* (Boston: Houghton Mifflin, 1964), R. Lefferts, *Getting a Grant in the 1990s* (New York: Prentice Hall, 1990); and R. D. Stewart and A. L. Stewart, *Proposal Preparation* (New York: John Wiley, 1984).
4. R. F. Rich, "Knowledge Synthesis and Problem Solving,") in S. Ward and L. J. Reed, eds., *Knowledge Structure and Use* (Philadelphia: Temple University Press, 1983), 287-312.
5. For example, see S. D. Brookfield, *Developing Critical Thinkers* (San Francisco: Jossey-Bass, 1987); J. S. Bruner, "On Perceptual Readiness," in J. C. Harper, C. C. Anderson, C. M. Christensen, and S. M. Hunka, eds., *The Cognitive Processes* (Englewood Cliffs, NJ: Prentice Hall, 1964); R. Schank, *The Creative Attitude* (New York: Macmillan, 1988); and J. D. Sinnott, "Model for Solution of Ill-Structured Problems," in J. D. Sinnott, ed., *Everyday Problem Solving* (New York: Praeger, 1989), 72-99.
6. See J. Woo, "Lawyers Often at Odds with PR Firms," *Wall Street Journal,* 22 July 1992, B5.
7. D. Leeds, "Uncovering Hidden Sales Objections," *National Underwriter* 95, no. 52 (1992): 9-11. Here Leeds is referring to a prospect's resistance to purchasing an insurance policy, but the psychology of resistance is not much different in the business of mass media or, in fact, in any human encounter involving a problem.
8. J. W. Getzels and M. Csikszentmihalyi, *The Creative Vision: A Longitudinal Study of Problem Finding in Art* (New York: John Wiley, 1976). The authors conducted one of the

few longitudinal studies on finding the problem, but their work applies mainly to how art students go about doing it. See also Polanyi, *Personal Knowledge;* and Larrabee, *Reliable Knowledge.*

9. J. L. Adams, *The Care and Feeding of Ideas* (Reading, MA: Addison-Wesley, 1986).

10. For leads on the techniques of research in the mass media, see E. K. Parsigian, *Mass Media Writing* (Hillsdale, NJ: Lawrence Erlbaum, 1992).

11. N. Miyake and D. Norman, "To Ask a Question, One Must Know Enough to Know What Is Not Known," *Journal of Verbal Learning and Verbal Behavior* 18 (1979): 357-64.

12. J. H. Behling, *Guidelines for Preparing the Research Proposal* (Lanham, MD: University Press of America, 1984), 39.

13. See M. Boisclair, "Publisher's Survey," *Magazine Week,* 2 November 1992, 24-8.

14. S. Donaton, "The Media Wakes Up to Generation X," *Advertising Age,* 1 February 1993, 16. Although Generation X gives advertisers a new consumer target, the baby boomers are not forgotten because advertisers are also turning their attention to other "hot" targets—for example, DINKS (dual income, no kids), Empty Nesters (seniors, no children at home), and Techno-Savvies (computer buffs, 48% of whom use their computers every day).

5

Pre-Proposal Activity II
Key Cognitive Functions

Insights will sweep through the corners of your mind at certain moments during the first stages of research. However, uncertainty will linger until other activities take place such as evaluation, organization, and analysis of collected data. Once these tasks are completed, the vision begins to clear, the real problem comes into view, and ideas on how to communicate the message and act on the problem suddenly begin to take shape.

Some call the discovery experience "spontaneous ideation," "a sixth sense," "intuition," or "instinct." Still others say the experience is a manifestation of one's "talent" or "creative ability." It's true, the "Aha!" moment seems to occur quite suddenly, but scholars and creatives will tell you it happens only after one has experienced the tedious work of research and lived long hours with volumes of collected data through weeks, months, or even years.[1] It may sound like drudgery, but it isn't. The search absorbs and seduces the explorer to carry on because the prospect of discovery increases with every advancing step.

At this point, you're ready to review the collected research, but that doesn't mean the research ends. On the contrary, the effort may continue even as you begin writing the proposal. There's always a need to cover an overlooked point, recheck a piece of data, or include a recently proven fact. However, the major part of the investigation must stop somewhere. That usually occurs when those involved feel they have a sufficient grasp of the facts concerning the problem and its peripheral factors to begin the discovery process.

Properly executed, the process will unveil more than the real problem, its peripheral factors, and information about the audience. It will also shape a data-driven conclusion statement about the problem, which, in turn, will suggest a theme focus or idea for the solution strategy.

Although philosophers, behavioral and cognitive scientists, and media practitioners agree on the merit of evaluating, organizing, and analyzing a mass of unrelated data,[2] only a few identify the means by which it's done in a particular context.[3] All warn against incurring bias in the performance of these procedures, but few suggest techniques to avoid such risks.[4]

MANAGING THE COLLECTED DATA

Science and market researchers evaluate, organize, and analyze data as a matter of accepted practice. They rely on standard methods to manage and interpret the results of scientifically conducted experiments, polls, surveys, market studies, field observations, and the like.

The research conducted by mass media writers is less formal. Nevertheless, they also evaluate, organize, and analyze data they collect, some of which may include results obtained from studies conducted under controlled research methods. Moreover, media pros follow a mode of research and report similar to the one practiced by science researchers, a mode long noticed by several researchers and finally organized into a procedural guide for media assignments exclusive of proposal projects.[5] Its presence identifies the disciplined mode of process and thought that exists in mass media professionalism. It also goes a long way in terms of avoiding bias and error in both media assignments and special projects such as media proposals. More about bias later, but first let's examine how one can improve accuracy through careful management of the data. That process begins with a review of the body of knowledge, continues with an evaluation, organization, and analysis of the data, and ends with an evidence-driven conclusion about the problem.

Evaluation

In this context, evaluation begins with a careful reading followed by frequent reviews of the researched material that you and others have collected. Self-inquiry directs the review and evaluation process. Refer to the self-inquiries in Chapter 2 to remind yourself about the "starter" questions to raise at this point.

Your data might include information from books, articles, product reports, market research results, audience profile studies, annual corporate reports, sales or production records, government documents, interviews, scientifically conducted studies—anything that informs the problem at hand. Careful reading and frequent reviews are necessary for several reasons. You need to be familiar enough with the mass of data to identify relevant from irrelevant information, substantiated from unsubstantiated information. In short, you "clean" the data, that is, separate the wheat from the chaff.

This cleaning process helps organize the data into a useful reference source for accurate analysis. As importantly, your decision makers will expect you to provide them with information about the problem that stands up to challenge, presents all sides of the issue, and includes peripheral factors that impact on the situation. They'll also expect you to come up with an accurate assessment of the situation and recommendations on how to deal with it. All that depends on how carefully and fairly you review, evaluate, organize, and analyze your data.

The key is to familiarize yourself with the data so well that you'll notice, question, and filter out unsubstantiated statements, false assumptions, unproven claims, and unstated premises. You need to watch for indications of bias, innuendo, and motive; also, arguments unrelated to the issue, underlying influences on the problem, or someone's conclusion that fails to match the stated issue or the facts or figures on record.

Rely on *relevant* data, that is, corroborated information related to more than one view of the issues surrounding the problem. Relevant data also inform, are interesting, unique, new, and stand out from all the rest. In addition, look for and question the use of undefined abstractions and jargon, omissions of necessary background and other facts or figures, and one-sided presentations.

If you're examining tables and charts, check for possible mistakes such as missing and erroneous entries or totals. One way to do this is to match the given information, including numbers, against information in other documents and records on the same issue. If these fail to agree, find out from the source of the documents why there's a difference.

It may seem as if more material would be eliminated than saved. That doesn't happen too often. In fact, the usual case is that one collects more information than one can use. But if exemptions do thin down the data, continue the research until all necessary gaps have been filled. Some questions always remain unanswered, which could mean you might have to conduct your own research study to get the answers—for example, a poll to learn if an organization truly carried out declared policies for its membership.

The goal here is to establish a reliable knowledge base. Remember, someone is going to examine your proposal argument in the same questioning manner as you examined information given to you.

The Organizational Map

Once you've cleaned the data, review them again and again. Internalize this body of substantiated knowledge until it becomes accessible to instant recall for assembling in whatever type of organization seems appropriate to the task. Since no standard method of organizing data exists for those in the mass media, the organizational configuration becomes a matter of choice. The nature of that configuration depends a great deal on the volume of data in hand and, particularly, the problem itself. Let the data suggest the mode of approach.

There are a few organizing styles that appear more often than others. For example, arranging information under groups related to topics, persons, places, events, or time. The information grouped under a category head may be recorded on file cards or kept in 3-ring binders or file folders.

For complex projects, pros build charts, tables, or grids, give each column or section a name, and then post appropriate elements of information into each category unit. This breaks down the data into units in a way that accounts for all the verified and relevant material and, at the same time, provides an organizational map, one that gives a panoramic view of the whole in order to analyze it.[6]

Some pros pin a series of information sheets to wall areas—another way of capturing a panoramic view of the whole. Others draw various types of configurations—for example, diagrams—and then plug in the details. Still others enter data into the computer and, if their program provides it, use the split-screen mode, placing text on one side of the screen and directions for use or development on the opposite side.

On less complex projects, some of the more practiced pros organize data in their heads, but that's dangerous for novices, occasionally even for pros. Use your own organizing method or one of the methods suggested here if it suits your particular set of data and seems like a system you could manage.

Whatever the organization, assuming you've included only verified and relevant material, your organization should provide you with an accurate view of the whole, allow access to any single part of the whole, and permit frequent and easy review so that all the details become an integral part of your thought processes. In short, organizing data simply means breaking down the whole into its various parts for the purpose of analysis and making determinations based on evidence that stands up to question.

Analysis

In this context, analysis means to examine the elements that make up each part of the whole and also to compare and contrast all the parts against one another to see how they do or do not interact. Look for similarities and differences, anomalies and discrepancies, agreements and disagreements, gaps and omissions, conflicts and contradictions. Look for links that illustrate relationships, correlations, patterns, or trends.

A sharp eye for any of these conditions will tell you where the weight of the evidence falls and why. The volume of elements in a single category may stand out more than others, or one category of facts may carry more power than other parts, or perhaps one item in a single category stands out from others in that category, or several related items in several categories join as a ground for evidence to the real problem.

The analysis function helps you find out what you need to know in order to draw an evidence-based judgment about the real problem, to form a substantive problem statement about the researched whole, and to render an informed decision about the most effective means of reaching your particular audience.

THE REWARDS OF SELF-INQUIRY

Whenever you face uncertainty in the performance of any of these functions, rely on self-inquiry. Framing unknowns into questions propels you into thought processes that do several things for you: They force focus on the issue, direct notice of things you should be noticing, and open doors to ways of obtaining answers. Moreover, transferring cloudy issues into self-inquiries acts as a challenge to given information and fosters sound judgment. This also acts as a stimulant in noticing hidden links, patterns, and trends, whatever is missing, or what is new, unique, or stands out from all the rest.

Above all, questioning leads to recognition of an order in the chaos of parts and triggers insight into the unity existing in a mass of disconnected elements. At the same time, the answer to the puzzle takes shape and articulation of a conclusion statement becomes possible. What's more, that statement not only stands up to challenge, it becomes the idea source for a creative communication strategy. The point is, you don't have to relinquish your creative abilities to chance decisions. That means that when implementation ideas start rising to the surface, you'll have the evidence at hand to defend their merit.

Let's assume your research is solid but that you still don't see data weaknesses and strengths even after framing probing questions. It's a good indication that you and the body of knowledge are still strangers or that your organization needs adjustment. You need to get better acquainted with the collected data. Review your organized material again, check where you may have gone wrong (try the self-inquiries listed here in the section "Avoiding Bias"). Make the appropriate adjustments. Then ingest the material, storing it in your mental retrieval bank so that you think about it spontaneously while jogging, running errands, driving to work, even while dozing off to sleep. Only after you've mastered every detail will those provocative questions work for you.

INSIGHT: PART PREPARATION, PART MYSTERY

Once investment in the body of knowledge, the evaluation, organization, and analysis has been made, the "Aha!" moment seems to come on suddenly and determinations seem to shape themselves almost effortlessly into statements about the problem and a supportable judgment about dealing with it. The fact is, all this has been fermenting in your mind from the point of problem consideration to the analysis phase. The moment of insight is simply the sum product of all your preparatory activity. The order in the chaos, the unity the evidence itself reveals, may seem to fall into place by itself, but it's really a synthesis of all the data-driven details you've turned around in your mind constantly without even realizing it.

Depending on the complexity of your problem, the conclusion statement may run for just a few sentences or develop into a substantial paragraph or more. Its content may include one, a few, or all of the following: a brief reference to the perceived problem, identification of the true problem (or a confirmation or modification of the perceived problem), a summary of the research uncovered, results of the analyzed data indicating reasons for correcting original perception of the problem, and a concise explanation of how the problem will be handled or corrected. It may also name and describe the audience(s) of interest.

The point is to be complete enough to give decision makers a fair picture of the whole, clear enough to avoid misunderstanding, yet precise, concise, and direct in order to give them a quick and easy read. The synthesized statement about the problem often acts as the fountain source of ideas for journalists and agency creatives who must translate hard facts into words and images that grab public attention. You'll see the outcome of synthesis and translation in the case studies below.

F. C. Bartlett calls moving from analysis to end point the "leap" from given evidence to evidence unmasked, and he characterizes analysis as the realization that objective evidence has properties of its own not immediately apparent in its specific parts.[7] Brewster Ghiselin sees the moment of discovery as a reorganization of the preparation and management that has gone on before "without which there can be no significant creative activity."[8]

These are inner workings of the mind that escape precise explanation. However, Bartlett and Ghiselin make one thing about the mystery quite clear. The "leap" across the dark abyss into the world of "significant creative activity" cannot be achieved without first accomplishing significant preparatory activities like the ones thus far described.

Again, much of that preparation and search for synthesis is stimulated by questions, some noted on paper and others expressed outwardly or inwardly. Creatives, including media pros, demonstrate the questioning attitude in all areas of their work, including proposal writing. It's all done so unconsciously that many practitioners are unaware of the internal dialogue or preparatory habits they carry out. Nevertheless, all these activities are easily detected in their descriptions of how they perform their work prior to writing a proposal.

As for how preparation serves composition of the proposal itself, very little relevant information found during the preparation pro-cess is wasted. In fact, much of the substantiated research data may be used in the written proposal (see "Development of the Proposal," Chapter 6), and portions of it may be visualized for oral presentation before decision makers. Visuals may include such devices as videotapes, slides, overhead projections, flip charts, storyboards, and other like techniques (described in Chapter 10).

AVOIDING BIAS

Studies show that personal bias always stands unnoticed as the ever-present enemy. Unless checked, one has the tendency to ignore certain items of information and retain only those that confirm a personal conviction or a favored hypothesis. That kind of researcher will miss seeing the real problem, attend to the wrong audience, and will most certainly set up an implementation strategy that invites rejection.

Scholars in problem solving and critical thinking have found that questioning one's own motives defends against committing biased judgments.[9] Self-inquiry, they note, is the mark of a creative problem solver. If the insistence on self-inquiry sounds like a repetitive refrain, even when applied to curbing personal prejudices, it's intentional.

Just keep in mind that self-inquiry stimulates the thought processes so that the functions required in proposal preparation can be accomplished as accurately and thoroughly as possible. Roger Schank refers to self-inquiries as "remindings" that give one something to think about, and Daniel Reisberg sees them as "inner speech."[10] Still others interested in creative thought simply call the questioning attitude the habit of "thinking out loud" or carrying on an "internal dialogue." No matter what the label, the sense of its thought-provoking force and reason for being remains the same.

To avoid the tendency to bias, maintain a keen awareness of your own biases, values, and inclination to hold to a position when the evidence proves otherwise. Keep an open mind when reviewing collected data, selecting relevant items for your organizational map, and looking for weaknesses and strengths in the data during analysis. Prejudicial judgment will, without a doubt, thrust you headlong into wrong conclusions, weak ideas, and strategy presentations that set you up for challenge, even rejection.

To keep your impulses in check, ask yourself these critical-thinking questions:

- *I must look honestly at myself. What are my interests, values, beliefs, prejudices, and assumptions?*
- *Have any of these interfered with a fair selection of reference sources?*
- *Have any of these clouded my consideration or judgment about the evidence?*
- *Have any of these interfered with a fair selection of data items for my organizational map or my analysis of them?*
- *Have any of these led to oversight or elimination of data I should have included?*
- *What data must be reinstated to account for omissions and to prevent false analysis and misconceived conclusions?*

If the key research and cognitive functions you've read about thus far seem like a lot of hard work for a media proposal, you're right, they are. But it's necessary preparation that delivers its own reward. Although unheralded as applied research and mind-searching headwork and usually mistaken as "talent," it's the kind of activity that goes on in the mass media. Those who respect its value are the ones who are noticed by their supervisors as problem solvers and creatives, people that employers like having around.

TESTING THE SOLUTION IDEA

Testing the implementation plan is not general practice among journalists, although they might discuss the analyzed outcome and implementation idea with colleagues, editors, or others. To inform is the journalist's purpose.

The public relations goal is also mainly to inform, but it usually includes a sales factor—selling a company's new position (image), restoring a company's reputation following a crisis situation, announcing product improvement or company development, and the like. As in journalism, their implementation ideas are cleared through levels of in-house personnel, sometimes to outsiders familiar with the problem. But then they may be tested on a representative group of the target audience.

The ultimate goal in advertising is to sell a product, sometimes the company's new image, or to re-educate sales personnel, support a community project, or just to get a read on human behavior, attitudes, or opinions. As in public relations, ad agencies often test the impact of their creative ideas on select public groups before proposing them to the client and before investing the time and dollars necessary to carry out their creative propositions.

If, for example, a campaign idea randomly tested on a representative group of people motivates only a few, chances are it won't work on the rest of that population. So it's back to the drawing board. Conversely, positive feedback from a knowledgeable group concerning a solution strategy means the plan becomes part of the proposal content. In journalism, a test with colleagues may elicit a better presentation idea than the one you had in mind.

HOW THE PROS DO IT

Print and Broadcast Journalism

The investigative reporter whose comments appear below had written dozens of proposals for enterprise stories, but for this particular story she kept her idea under her hat, conducting the research as time permitted from other assignments (see case introduction, Chapter 4). It wasn't until she was well into her research process and had something to report that she spoke to her immediate editor about the project. Formal overtures to senior editors came only after the data proved powerful enough to convince decision makers that the project was worthy of publication. Here's how she describes her particular system of organization, analysis, and synthesis:

> After you've been working on something for two or three months, you just have volumes of notes and data. So I do have a system where I go through each. . . . It's kind of hard to explain . . . but I start out with blank sheets of paper, a legal pad, on which I place broad titles or categories at the top in order to begin to try to structure the data. One category might be "Scope" where you're laying out the scope of the problem. Another category might be "History" where you're talking about the history of the problem. . . . All these categories, by the way, later help you structure your story when you come to writing it. Another might be "Future," another might be "Reasons" for the problem, another might be "Countermoves," that is: *Who's trying to work against your efforts and why?*
>
> Then I begin to go over my notes, and I systematically begin to number or alphabetize or in some way index my notes so that each statement, each piece of information is numbered and then placed under one of these categories. It's very time-consuming, maybe several days, and in some ways boring. It's a process editors don't necessarily understand or appreciate, but when you're ready to put all this into English you have sectioned data for a proposal and an outline for a story, and you also have the story in your head. Basically, you've refamiliarized yourself with the data to such a great extent that it allows you to throw away your notes because with these five or six pages that you have you see your proposal and your whole story and know where to find any detail.
>
> Once I've got everything converted from notes to this outline, I then take a red pen or whatever and I begin to look at what the patterns are, what the related materials are within each of these categories. That's where a lot of the thinking process occurs and I kind of internalize the whole thing and consider what the message is going to be. You need to have some idea or statement in mind from the start. I don't always have one, but I do have to be completely open to the fact that

it will be modified or changed, and that happened in this case. You have to have some focus initially, otherwise you'd be thrashing around collecting irrelevant data endlessly.

To understand what the message is you have to review your notes and to do it more than once. Everything I have from my notes goes on those sheets. I ask: *Where's the strongest material? What's really the problem statement? The most interesting quotes? What material repeats itself? What's not as important as other material?* So just from the writing point of view I'm trying to eliminate a lot of names and so forth. I try to figure out: *What needs to be said? Who says it most clearly?*

Originally, I had proposed something along these lines: "Twenty years after the advent of rape crises centers and sexual assault awareness, rape victims continue to say they're treated badly by law enforcement." After looking at the collected data, the statement was more like "Nearly 1 in 4 women who reported rape or attempted rape to the Oakland [CA] police department were told that they were lying, sometimes before the case was investigated, and sometimes the reports were never investigated." No relationship at all to the original statement, but that's what the data said was the message and that's what you have to use no matter what you thought originally.

Candy Cooper, investigative reporter,
San Francisco Examiner

Complex projects usually require an organizational system that maps the data and makes it available to summary review, a device not unlike Cooper's system. As indicated earlier, less complex projects are organized in various ways—entered into file folders, tabbed loose-leaf binders, computers. However it's done, there's always some kind of organization that provides an actual or mental map so the information in it can be analyzed in isolation or in group discussions. Not every reporter uses Cooper's particular organizational system, useful as it is, but some kind of data management and analysis always takes place. Whatever the approach, total immersion in all the data collected is an absolute requisite, as Cooper indicates. Without familiarity with the material, neither your independent analysis nor your contribution in a group discussion will count for anything.

Group analysis (also called "brainstorming") was the approach in the next case. This special projects editor had been
reporting stories of child killings in Detroit's schools and neighborhood streets for some years. Steeped in the details of Detroit's
reported child killings, she had also kept clippings on similar
reported incidents in other major U.S. cities. So the background
of this modern-day problem was available to her from both
memory and filed records.

When the number of child killings in and around Detroit
increased alarmingly within a six-week period, she and her managing editor, Bob McGruder, felt that the problem had to be
redefined not just as individual tragedies but as a collective one.
Meanwhile, several conversations and meetings with McGruder
and her six-member team were held. One of those discussions
took place after all team members had studied the data. The
collection included news clips on local incidents and those in
other metropolitan areas, results of calls to other major newspapers to learn about their current coverage of child murders, stats
on child deaths in major U.S. cities obtained from the FBI's
Uniform Crime Reports, and, after the initial proposal was approved, interviews with teachers, parents, child psychologists,
and school counselors.

> From the beginning, Bob was very interested in trying to find
> a way to make the children's voices heard in this and he
> ascertained this after looking at my material. I think it was at
> the first meeting after our initial proposal was approved,
> somebody said, "Well, we know how to define the children
> who were killed as the victims because we've done individual
> stories on them. *But are they the only victims?* Look at the
> impact here on the living [referring to news clips and other
> collected data]. The real victims are the children who have
> witnessed the killings and are affected by them. These are
> children caught in the cross fire [the conclusion statement
> which became the story theme and basis for the series title].
> That's what needs to be examined now." We later did not
> only a local but a regional and national story using this
> approach.
>
> **Jane Daugherty,** projects associate editor,
> *Detroit Free Press*

The effort by Daugherty and her team resulted in a special report under the theme title dictated by the data, "Children in the Cross Fire," published over several days in May 1992. The stories covered ten full pages of copy with graphics. When word got out about the team's comprehensive coverage, intra- and interstate requests for copies of the story led to reprints of the series in the form of a special supplement. The team had not only quantified child murders locally, regionally, and nationally, they also had explored the psychological impact on the surviving children and how parents, teachers, psychologists and counselors were helping them cope with their anxieties.

Data organization and analysis are not much different for those in broadcasting. This host and executive producer of a daily hour-long interview program for Connecticut Public Radio (see Chapter 3), says that media people are constantly organizing data in their minds, mulling over what they've observed and learned.

> We absorb and store everything. I spend tremendous amounts of time researching, reading, and studying for shows. Our show is a blend of highly planned and structured programs and that reinforces the spontaneity so crucial in our work. Everything we do in life is about the work, whether I'm eating a meal, seeing a movie, or reading a comic book or encyclopedia, it all feeds into the mind's computer, and I think all of it somehow nourishes that creative voice that tells us what's important and interesting, and gives us our ideas. I come out of a print news background and the same standards are in effect in radio and in TV because I do both.
>
> **Faith Middleton,** manager and executive producer, WPKT, National Public Radio, New Haven, Connecticut

You can hear echoes of Middleton's sentiments in this Detroit TV reporter's comments. She had covered many of the city's fires for her local station, collected volumes of data, and observed firemen at their jobs for some time. She proposed doing a broadcast on one of the city's firehouses, a program demonstrating more than just the heroism of firefighters. She wanted to convey what she had observed over the years—firefighters' passionate sense of responsibility to their jobs. She characterized them as "neighborhood warriors" who manifested a spirit of family, community loyalty, and devotion to their jobs.

Firefighters had different reasons why they risked their lives almost every day for total strangers or tolerated the boredom of inactive days, false alarms, and calls to put out dumpster fires or grease fires in kitchens. Earning a living held the lowest priority on their list of reasons. Here's how this award-winning broadcaster manages and makes decisions about her data:

> You do a lot of research that never gets on the air, data like local and national stats [on fire reports], actually enough to write a book on the *War and Peace* of fire fighting, but you need all of it as a basis of knowledge.
>
> I have a system of file folders marked with the types of information in them. I review these a lot, highlighting comments, sound bites, appropriate video. I look for what's truthful [substantiated data], that's first and foremost, then what's relevant, and third, what has emotion, impact, something the viewer will remember. It turned out that this was the busiest firehouse not only in this city but one of the busiest in the nation. That's what the data showed. So along with the devotion, attitude, and heroism of these firefighters that became one of the themes in my story.
>
> **Ann Thompson,** reporter,
> WDIV-TV, Detroit, Michigan

Like print and broadcast journalists, creatives in public relations and advertising are just as savvy about collecting and managing data and letting results direct the solution strategy.

Public Relations and Advertising

The crisis situation brought to Denver-based JohnstonWells by a blue jeans manufacturer required extensive research into the company itself and involved more audiences than the company had realized: the factory operations group, the employees, distributors, retailers, sales force, and disgruntled customers (see Chapters 3 and 4).

Research information collected about the company's history, policies, and needs along with data derived from field investigations, interviews, and other research all had to be managed somehow so that the real problem and methods of solution became evident. After introducing initial research results to the client and getting their approval to move ahead, the agency began closing in on a creative strategy to resolve the problem.

> We synthesized all our research, particularly the interviews, then put together a grid. The grid showed the key areas where we really needed to do some work. For example, we had categories like "Current State," "Future State," "The Gap Closing" . . . that is, where we wanted to be in a particular area and what we had to do to close the gap between the current situation and a future state [the "objectives"]. This is a company undergoing tremendous transition [from mainly a company-preferred position of anonymity to a publicly visible manufacturer of a popular product] and it needs to understand what's happening in order to respond to its organizational needs.
>
> **Gwin Johnston,** CEO,
> JohnstonWells, Denver, Colorado

Johnston's team had multiple problems to deal with, one of which was boardroom fear that if the company became too visible and too successful a non-union shop would then seek unionization. These peripheral problems were handled as they became apparent during data accumulation and provided some solutions to the problem of unhappy distributors, retailers, customers, and employees.

Dealing with multiple problems is not uncommon in public relations. Kelsey-Hayes, one of this agency's clients, had long been perceived as just a supplier of steel wheels for vehicles. In recent years, this automotive parts manufacturer had invented and developed many other nonautomotive products and wanted the global market to know about it. To do that, the agency needed to get rid of an outdated image and also establish believability that this automotive parts company was also a trusted high-tech manufacturer. At the same time, the agency had to deal with an impending merger, the painful task of employee layoffs, and a movement toward unionizing. Here's how this public relations executive and his team researched and managed the mass of data collected to resolve not one but several client problems.

> We start every project or client relationship with research. It [the research] could be very significant, as it was with the Kelsey-Hayes project. We conduct focus groups, qualitative research to identify the problem, and surveys or simply sit with the CEO to determine what the situation is. In this case, we also did a media audit; that is, calling automotive news and trade editors to determine their perception about Kelsey-Hayes because they're close to the industry and are an important pipeline to customers.
>
> To forge a program, we look at the collected data and examine all of it. For Kelsey-Hayes, it was more than usual. We put up flow charts, lots of them. I will draw a horizontal line and above the line I'll put everything that's unique, for example, about our client and the company's products. Everything that's the same [in comparison to similar manufacturers and similar products] goes below the line. Then I'll conduct a creative session where we evaluate all the data [group analysis]. We want to get a handle on what we're working with, which problems need priority attention. We look at all the unique factors, compare them with sameness items below the line, sift through everything. It's a review that not only identifies the main problems and solutions for them, it also bubbles up ideas for tactical activities. It all comes together in the analysis. The light goes on and you say, "Okay. This is it!" The program is easy to write once the analysis is done.
>
> **Michael O. Niederquell,** executive vice president, Anthony M. Franco, Inc., Detroit, Michigan[11]

The size and organizational makeup of agencies may vary, but it's the disciplined practices of creative members that "bubbles up" the surge of ideas, as Niederquell points out. If you find yourself in a large agency, you will probably have the advantage of in-house research and marketing experts. But make no mistake, you play a vital role in the process of research and data management.

You and other members of the research and marketing team share information collected about the problem. Each member usually records the information either in a free-form report, fills out a standard agency form, or makes it known at discussion sessions. Several of these sessions take place until agreement is reached on what the data say.

BBD&O's project was a competitive pitch for the Six Flags account, a chain of six theme parks located in strategic areas from coast to coast (see case introduction, Chapter 4). The client wanted a consistent advertising campaign that all their parks could use and that would maximize the appeal of the parks and increase attendance. The comments of this advertising executive illustrate how a campaign catch-phrase rises naturally from the results of thorough research and disciplined data management.

> BBD&O is very big on consumer research, particularly for developing strategies, to have a good foundation. We did focus groups, field observations, quantitative research in terms of what target groups were looking for. We questioned the client and listened.
>
> One of the things we learned from our research was that they weren't getting repeat business and were appealing to a limited audience, strictly teenagers, while overlooking a viable audience, the family. And their past advertising [an important clue] never focused on the "end feeling" after experiencing the rides. Data from focus group surveys and our field observations were brought to the table and discussed. One thing was strikingly clear: Park visitors, teenagers and families, held a vivid memory of the excitement they had experienced at the parks. So that was something we focused on. In fact, it became one of the advertising themes we proposed in our creative strategy plan: "Have the time after time of your life."
>
> **Chuck Kent,** creative director,
> BBD&O Worldwide, Chicago

In smaller agencies, labor is less divided and procedures less formal. Those involved in the problem-solving process may have a much larger share in the agency's research and data management functions. In small agencies, like this next one, personnel have easier access to their superiors and more opportunities to carry on a one-on-one dialogue about the problem and the data.

In this case, the agency had been invited to plan an advertising campaign for a resort complex located in Ocho Rios, Jamaica (see Chapters 3 and 4). Although the client was new to the agency, the product and the business of promoting resort areas was well known to the agency's president. Nevertheless, it took several meetings with the client, numerous questions, and extensive research into public perceptions and the attitudes of travel agents toward the product as well as study of past media use, current market conditions, and the effectiveness of the resort's own sales representatives.

The president and his team discovered that the client's position as an all-inclusive resort had been all wrong for them; also, that they were overadvertised in the popular market and underadvertised in the affluent market that was better suited for the ambiance of this particular resort. The weak occupancy rate, the agency team found, was really due to these conditions plus a sales force that had to be re-educated about its product. Here's how they managed the data to arrive at these conclusions:

> We set up some categories. The primary ones were "Situation," "Problem," "Objective," "Strategy," "Execution." In "Situation," we covered the competitive analysis including subcategories such as product, image, economic environment. In "Problem," we covered research issues. In other words, the identification that we had, deficient trade awareness, deficient consumer awareness, and so on. "Problem" could also be labeled "Opportunity." It all depends. That is, we might say "Based on this problem we have an opportunity to change awareness in this, this, and in this way" and then explain how we'd do that. We ask: *What is the position we want to arrive at? Yes, we're priced all-inclusive, but what's more important? To be known as an all-inclusive, or to be known as one of the best resort complexes of the Caribbean? We have a beach, but it's*

truly not defendable. What kind of resort has 90 swimming pools? We have that. Now that's defendable. In fact, that question became the catch-phrase in our initial ad.

Charles Crispin, president,
Crispin & Porter, Miami, Florida

The Crispin team completed no forms or elaborate research reports. Rather, at first they worked solely at the dialogue level with each other and the client. The written proposal for the client containing the basis for their conclusions came later.

Sometimes, research and data management functions are done without physically categorizing the data or drawing up elaborate charts, grids, and the like. That was the case in the next example (see case introduction, Chapter 3). This pro says he does much of his work mentally but admits that he spends a great deal of time reviewing and studying the collected data. Also notice that an internal dialogue drives and controls his mental management of data organization and analysis:

When I look at what we have, I want to know: *Where is the product in the market today? Is it a growing or declining share? Is the product being supported with dollars at a rate above or below previous standards? Where is the competition today? What's relevant to sell to this particular audience under the existing conditions?* You can determine what's relevant by asking all the questions I've just named. The questions are never the same. It depends on the problem, but these are fairly basic ones.

Philip Smith, creative director,
NKH&W, Kansas City, Missouri

Whether data are organized formally, informally, or mentally, it's clear that deep involvement with the collected information is an absolute necessity. Without that involve- ment, a clear understanding of the problem remains a remote possibility. Moreover, appropriate questions for either organization or analysis simply would not occur. When involvement, understanding, and critical examination fall short, the "Aha!" moment of discovery remains a stranger to personal experience. The good news is that when all pre-proposal activities are faithfully performed success is more often the case. Then, as these and other pros in this text indicate, it's an easy stride into the next phase—writing the proposal. Chapters 6 and 7 help you understand how to execute that task.

NOTES

1. For example, see F. C. Bartlett, *Thinking: An Experimental and Social Study* (London: Allen & Unwin, 1958); J. S. Bruner, "On Perceptual Readiness," in J. C. Harper, C. C. Anderson, C. M. Christensen, and S. M. Hunka, eds., *The Cognitive Processes* (Englewood Cliffs, NJ: Prentice Hall, 1964), 225-57; and J. M. Ziman, *Reliable Knowledge* (New York: Cambridge University Press, 1978).

2. J. S. Bruner, *A Study of Thinking* (New York: John Wiley, 1986); L. B. Greenfield, "Teaching Thinking Through Problem Solving," in J. E. Stice, ed., *Developing Critical Thinking and Problem Solving Abilities* (San Francisco: Jossey-Bass, 1987), 5-22; H. A. Larrabee, *Reliable Knowledge* (Boston: Houghton Mifflin, 1964); and R. E. Rich, "Knowledge Synthesis and Problem Solving," in S. Ward and L. J. Reed, eds., *Knowledge Structure and Use* (Philadelphia: Temple University Press, 1983).

3. For example, see C. E. Moustakas, *Heuristic Research* (Newbury Park, CA: Sage, 1990); and E. K. Parsigian, *Mass Media Writing* (Hillsdale, NJ: Lawrence Erlbaum, 1992).

4. For bias-avoidance techniques in media work, see Parsigian, *Mass Media Writing.*

5. For example, see L. Bogart, "Social Sciences in the Mass Media," in F. T. C. Yu, ed., *Behavioral Sciences and the Mass Media* (New York: Russell Sage, 1968), 153-74; and J. Tankard, "Reporting and the Scientific Method," in M. E. Combs, D. L. Shaw, and D. Grey, eds., *Handbook of Reporting Methods* (Boston: Houghton Mifflin, 1976), 42-80. For the procedural guide to media assignments other than proposal projects, see Parsigian, *Mass Media Writing.*

6. For additional ideas on setting up an organizational map, see Parsigian, *Mass Media Writing.*

7. Bartlett, *Thinking.*

8. B. Ghiselin, *The Creative Process* (New York: Mentor, 1963, 7th printing), 28.

9. S. D. Brookfield, *Developing Critical Thinker* (San Francisco: Jossey-Bass, 1987); H. G. Gough, "Imagination—Undeveloped Resource," in S. J. Parnes and H. G. Harding, eds., *A Source Book for Creative Thinking* (New York: Scribner's, 1962), 217-26; and R. Schank, *The Creative Attitude* (New York: Macmillan, 1988).

10. Schank, *The Creative Attitude,* 98; and D. Reisberg, *Auditory Imagery* (Hillsdale, NJ: Lawrence Erlbaum, 1992), 73.

11. Mr. Niederquell is now president and CEO of his own company, Quell Communications Group, Inc., located in Troy, Michigan.

6

Writing the Media Proposal I

Key Components

K ey components are those units of information that identify the problem, explain how you intend to deal with it, and clarify details related to those two principal matters. Selecting the title for each component usually is left to the proposal writer or to members of the project team. However, that choice is directed by the basic message contained in the unit of information. So the labels attached to the components listed below are simply representative of the types of components and unit content that petitioners frequently include in media proposals.

The absence of a standard format may be disconcerting to the novice, but working from a prototype is uncharacteristic in the composition of media proposals. What is characteristic is the disciplined preparatory process that proposals demand, which then renders the freedom of creative choice at the point of composition. That doesn't mean your creative choices will be arbitrary or so flimsy they'll collapse under challenge. Rather, those choices will be based on a substantiated body of knowledge on which you can rely for composition ideas and content.

Earlier, you learned that the researched data would either confirm the perceived problem or reveal its true nature, produce a conclusion statement about the problem, generate ideas for developing a solution strategy, and suggest a theme focus for a mass-distributed public message. That same body of knowledge will again tell you what components your proposal requires and indicate, as well, the content and title for each unit of information. But even as these clues open up before you, never lose sight of the ultimate purpose: The media proposal must convince someone that you have solid reasons for proposing a strategy designed to respond to a particular problem and, at the same time, fulfills the decision maker's needs and purpose.

Like any other creative enterprise, the composition of a media proposal and its specific units of content depends on your grasp of the body of knowledge; meaning of course, that unless you've gone through the preparation process to identify the true problem you cannot know how to respond to it or determine what units of information will construct a convincing presentation. Knowing all the details surrounding the problem and the evidence supporting those details is an absolute before important units can be determined and named.

If this sounds like you'll need another review of the data, you're right. The exercise of review and evaluation you performed to reach a conclusion about the problem will help. But another review facilitates the process of composition, a different kind of cognitive and organizing activity. Be reminded, you're now working from an evidence-based conclusion, a codified and analyzed body of knowledge. That doesn't mean thinking ends— not by a long shot. That dimension of reasoned thought continues to the end. It does mean you now have a reliable base of information to work from.

Because you do have a solid body of knowledge, you'll most likely use a good portion of the whole or very definitely its most important points of information (more about that in Chapter 7). Your aim at this point is to identify significant sections of information that must be included, to name them and understand how they should be ordered into a format design. After reviewing the data and identifying units of information, make a list of these units and then draft an outline prioritizing units in an order of importance that promises a logical flow of information, speaks to the purpose of the project, and allows decision makers an easy read.

The order in which you list those components depends on which units of information contribute to building a persuasive argument; also, how one unit of information follows naturally from the last and effects the same end. Always keep in mind the priority of problem, solution, and the details related to each because these are the units that tell decision makers whether their needs/purpose will be met. This holds true whether the proposal is presented in written or oral form or as a leave-behind document following a personal or team presentation. The list below will give you an idea of a common order, but again keep the purpose of the project in mind and all the data that apply to each of its various units of information.

In short, the creative process of composing a proposal is as fluid as the preparatory process. It takes as much, perhaps even more, sensitivity to all possible needs that may radiate from the problem and its solution and raises an even greater urgency for critical/creative thinking.

Believe it or not, order does exist in all this chaos. Part of that order is knowing your problem and the research so well that every detail lies captive to your reach. Another part is self-inquiry, asking yourself questions about what components should be included and how they should be ordered (see a later section here on "Order of Presentation"). You'll find yourself constantly thinking about components, their order, titles, and content. Helmholtz identifies this type of absorption as "thinking at the sub-conscious level," a typical characteristic of the creative mind (see Chapter 2).

Scott Lewis, a reporter for WJBK-TV2 in Detroit, says that when he's engrossed in a complex project he's "like a zombie. My wife may be talking to me, but I'm not hearing her because

I'm churning everything in my mind over and over again, visualizing the order of presentation, always asking myself questions about it and what I need to say about what."

A CREATIVE OPPORTUNITY

Don't be put off by the structural fluidity of media proposals. In fact, it's precisely that feature that finally turns a disciplined preparatory process into a creative opportunity. Use your experience with the researched and analyzed material to make informed decisions about identifying and naming units of information, designing a format order, and deciding what to put in each unit and how to say it.

There's no mystery about identifying units of information. Just think of components as sections of information in a file drawer, each with its own label and placed there for selection as the situation demands. Feel a need to review the data once more? Go ahead—and don't be embarrassed about it. Some parts in the body of knowledge are more complex than others and require more reviews. The data will speak to you in time.

Listed below are the types of section components that appear in media proposals fairly consistently. Get to know them. Understanding their purpose and what ordinarily goes into them will help you recognize component units for your proposal and appropriate names and content for them. Temporarily, use the labels listed and mark whatever data in your body of knowledge apply, using an abbreviation or initials of the given label.

The model shown below is not written in stone. In the interest of brevity, proposal writers sometimes combine several units of information into a single component. For example, the second and third sections listed below may become part of the first either in a single paragraph or in several paragraphs. How you handle this depends on the complexity of each of those sections and how much detail in a component can be tolerated by your particular decision maker. If a series of brief sentences takes care of all three, then combine them; if not, allow a separate section for each. If you happen to know how decision makers, those inside and/or outside your media house, like to see components organized and named, let that be your guide.

In fact, some decision makers prefer to listen to a proposition rather than read about it (see Chapter 9 for pointers on oral presentations). If you know that's the case, defer to their preference but organize your proposal on paper anyway and in a manner that's complete yet concise and facilitates understanding. In any case, be sure to prepare a written leave-behind report that covers and details your oral presentation. It gives decision makers a document to hold in their hands and review and study at will.

KEY COMPONENTS, CONTENT, AND VARIATIONS

The following components represent some of the sections most frequently included in media proposals. The labels attached to them are ones commonly used, but you may see them named otherwise.[1] If you use the labels given below, that's fine; if you choose ones of your own making, that's fine too. Just make sure that each component title relates to its content or some key feature or features in it. If your media house has an established set of component names, then follow the house style. As you review the following section heads, notice particularly the basic content that each requires.

The Problem

☐ Provide a clear statement of the perceived problem and whether research confirmed, modified, or disconfirmed it. If modified, restate the problem and justify the modification with evidence for doing so. If disconfirmed, provide a clear statement of the true problem. Give reasons for the change and evidence that substantiates existence of the real problem. If the evidence runs long, place it in a separate section or on a following page(s) under its own title, such as "The Facts" or "What We Learned." If you have evidence concerning why the perceived problem remained hidden from view, give it.

Rationale

☐ Include a statement justifying attention to the matter at this time.

☐ Show evidence in support of the statement.

Objectives/Goals

☐ Explain the purpose of the proposal. Describe what you hope to achieve over the short term, over the long term.

☐ Give reasons or evidence justifying the stated objectives and/or goals. The terms *objectives/goals* carry meanings in journalism that differ from those in public relations and advertising. In journalism, the terms are used interchangeably, but a short-term objective might be to alert public attention to the practice of releasing convicted criminals before they haved served their minimum sentence. The long-term goal might be to monitor public response to reports of this practice in the interest of polling citizen concern about public safety.

   In public relations and advertising, both terms are used by petitioners to indicate understanding of what the client expects to receive. However, the term *goal* carries a more general long-term reach to it. The end point to be achieved might be to restore consumer confidence in a client's product—for example, a motor vehicle that proved to be unsafe in collision situations, resulting in severe injury and even death. The short-term objective might be to recall current vehicles and correct the problem to prevent further injury and loss of life. The objective is more specific and lends itself more easily to the devices of audit and measurement.[2] Goals usually are too abstract for measurement. To assure your understanding of the terms as they're used in your media house, ask.

Audience

☐ Describe the audience affected by or interested in the problem. Journalists often give a brief reference to the audience in the rationale or in a unit of its own, especially when describing the results of a polled group around which a story will develop. But in public relations and advertising, petitioners go to great lengths to characterize their audience(s); for example, the description might include the numbers in a certain population of interest such as working mothers or teenagers. Then the population of interest may be broken down into subgroups according to their numbers in various age groups and may include their sex, education, occupation, affiliations,[3] needs, habits, preferences, complaints, and their relationship to the problem,[4] or petitioners may concentrate on those characteristics for more than one population of interest.

☐ In layman's language, explain the methods used to obtain the profile and any other evidence verifying statements made about the audience.

The Operational Plan

☐ Outline the implementation plan or strategy designed to respond to the problem.

☐ Include a statement of confidence that the recommended plan will meet the intended purpose of the proposal.

☐ Provide evidence in support of that belief. In journalism, it might be the results of a survey or poll. In public relations and advertising, the results of a survey or poll would serve the same purpose as would the results of a laboratory experiment or field test. Also, if a similar strategy resolved a problem not unlike the current one, that could serve as a support statement.

These are just the bare bones of a proposal. Depending on the scope, breadth, and depth of the project and the expectations of your supervisor and/or client, the proposal might exclude or combine some of these components or include several more beyond those already given.

Some Extras

Inclusions are less certain in journalism than they are in public relations and advertising. In fact, of the following possibilities, only the units "abstract" (or "overview"), "time line," "services," "budget," and "confidence statement" are usually included in a journalistic proposal, but all are common fare in public relations and advertising proposals.

Table of Contents

List all major units and subunits and their page numbers.

Abstract

Also called "executive summary" or "overview." Briefly describe the problem, intended audience, why the problem deserves attention at this time, the purpose or objectives and/or goals of the task at hand, the strategy, and a general introduction to how the petitioner plans on realizing the recommended strategy. Elaboration of these items and other components will then fall under their own special headings in following pages and, in public relations and advertising particularly, cover such information as:

1. *What special programs and recommendations are planned and why.*[5] These may be training programs for sales and other personnel or for executives who must know how to respond to the press, union leaders, politicians, and activists. Other programs may offer tips for executives' public appearances, a written speech and delivery style for same, or suggestions for community outreach activities. Recommendations may also include methods of increasing product output to allow overworked employees more free time, creation of a new logo for a company seeking a new image, and/or a campaign theme for a new product.
2. *Which mass media channels will carry what messages and why these channels were selected to support a program.* Stats for this part of the

argument are customarily provided by the agency's marketing division.

Time Line

Outline what you intend to do and when for the editor, producer, or client and when you expect to complete the job.

Services

Describe the types of services and/or equipment required and explain why you'll need them.

Audit Plan

If you're going to "track," that is, assess the success of your recommended plan, explain what and how you're going to do it and what specifically you want to learn from the exercise.

Visuals

These rarely, but can, appear in a journalism proposal—for example, a pie chart indicating the percentage of public funds used for supervisor travel expenses as opposed to the percentage spent on the mandated purpose of a city department. In public relations, visuals are a customary part of a proposal—for example, a table indicating percentages of production rates at various plants over a period of six months, a chart showing numbers of certain subgroups in a population of interest, or a map of a region singled out for a community outreach program. In advertising, such visuals may also appear in the proposal. Additional ones may include a sample of recommended public communications—for example, the layout of a brochure, a sales guide, a sample magazine ad, or a storyboard showing a series of sketches indicating what will be seen and said in a television commercial.

Sometimes, the proposal may simply list the public communication possibilities available within budget limitations. If samples of planned communications are produced, these may be tested for effectiveness with focus groups or some other type of field trial before presentation to the client. A favorable outcome adds strength to the argument that your recommended messages are based on fact, not supposition. Or your proposal may give just a statement of the results and why your agency feels the recommended communications will do the job. Still another alternative is to provide an example(s) of how the recommended communication strategy worked successfully in similar cases for other clients (if you name the client, be sure to obtain the client's permission beforehand).

If results of a pretested communication prove disappointing, modifications are made before any examples are shown to the client. If the client had seen these before testing, your proposal might also give an explanation as to why modifications were made and why the agency now feels the modifications will produce expected results.

Budget

Detail the cost of all named services and needed equipment. Journalists will include a cost estimate of those items along with travel costs and whatever out-of-pocket expenses may be incurred. Public relations and advertising agencies tabulate the hourly time cost devoted to a project by staff members and whatever other costs may be incurred by the agency or members of its staff.

Confidence Statement

Conclude by elaborating your or your media house's qualifications to do the work. Journalists might point out other successful enterprise projects they've done. If this is a first, name the major assignments you've done that impressed editors and/ or generated good public response. Public relations and advertising agencies usually include the resources they own to handle the job and the names, titles, and experience of all personnel assigned to the project, perhaps singling out certain persons who have successfully completed other projects similar to the current one. Another section of the proposal may list the clients in industries similar to the one in which the prospective client is involved.

Inclusion of any of these elaborations depends on the scope of the project, the petitioner's knowledge of what a particular decision maker expects to see in any given proposal, the decision maker's knowledge of or experience with the petitioner's expertise and resources, and what the decision maker is willing to underwrite.

ORDER OF COMPONENTS

Whether you put it all down on paper at once or just parts of it in serial form, the format order of components in any presentation, written or oral, is dictated by the process of logical development. To appreciate the logic of proposal presentation, put yourself in decision makers' shoes. Ask yourself: *If I were the decision maker, what would I expect to see first, next, after that?* A pragmatic way to begin is with the problem itself and the objectives/goals involved. The rest will fall naturally into place.

Suppose you were the decision maker. You'd want to know:

- *Does the petitioner understand the perceived problem?*
- *What's the real problem here?*
- *What reasons does the petitioner give on why this problem is the true problem or is so important?*
- *What evidence supports those reasons? Is the evidence reliable, verifiable? How so?*
- *What solution strategy is recommended? Is it the right strategy? Will it work?*
- *What evidence does the petitioner give to support a claim/belief that it will work? Is the evidence reliable, verifiable? How so?* The petitioner's argument here is important because it tells you if the petitioner's purpose coincides with yours and to what extent the petitioner is committed to the task of resolving the declared problem or need.

You'd want to make sure the petitioner understands the needs of the primary audience and how the problem relates to that audience: *Who's interested and concerned? Why? What is it that we want the audience to think, feel, understand, or do? Who will react favorably, unfavorably, and why?*

You'd also want to know how the petitioner intends to implement the project, how long it will take to do what, what exactly the implementation will entail in terms of required resources and their cost, perhaps why the petitioner has chosen this particular strategy over all other possible strategies and what concrete evidence is given for that choice.

In the instance of public relations and advertising proposals, you as the decision maker would want to see if the petitioner knows how and where to place the public message for greatest return. You'd want to make sure that the cost of implementation is going to be worth your $$$ investment. The "pay back" aspect of the recommended program is of vital concern to you. In fact, you might want answers to the following: *How long before I can see some results from the recommended program?* (or) *How long will it take before sales from advertising begin to pay the advertising costs and show a fair return on my investment?* According to one account group supervisor, if "pay back" time runs under a year, that's "very good."

You'd also want to know if the agency you've selected is qualified to get the results you expect, if the agency intends to conduct an audit of its implementation strategy. After all, you wouldn't want to throw good money after bad. You might also expect to see any additional information your particular problem demands and, most important, that facilitates your quick and easy review of the proposal.

Throughout this role-playing exercise, however, keep in mind all the clues you've picked up about your decision makers—their ways of thinking, what they expect, their limitations and concerns, and the like—because those clues will have some bearing on how decision makers play out their role as judges. Of course, client expectations are often unrealistic or off the mark. In your ordered presentation and without embarrassing decision makers, let your research evidence show you're right on the money and where they must now focus their attention for best results from their investment.

Just remember, any order inferred here could be drastically altered by other developments or factors introduced along the way. If that happens, depend on the principle of logical presentation and, again, place yourself in decision makers' shoes. You need to be open to modification and change. That's the nature of the media business. It may seem chaotic and uncertain to some, but remember you have a disciplined process to guide you and the ability to think critically as well as creatively in the face of adjustment. Together they help you maintain some semblance of order and do a professional job.

TESTING THE FORMAT DESIGN

Test your design by visualizing first the whole of it, then unit by unit, page by page. Meanwhile, ask yourself these questions:

- *Does the design flow logically from one component to another?*
- *Is the arrangement such that each new component responds to a need left unanswered by the previous component?*
- *Is the format presented in an easy-to-read, easy-to-follow manner?*
- *Does it have a discernible pattern, an identifiable beginning, middle, and end?*
- *Do component titles fit the content? Are they self-explanatory? Do they describe the content appropriately?*
- *Are charts, tables, and/or stats placed relative to the component they intend to support?*
- *Have I included all the information I would expect to see if I were the decision maker? If not, what's missing?*

Another way to visualize your format is to use a separate piece of paper for each component. Plug in items you plan to use and then give each a title. Shuffle the pages around until you find a logical place for each component. You can do the same thing using large file cards for each component. On each card, put down one or two lines describing the gist of each component's main points. Title the components. Then spread out the cards and look at the whole to see if each component follows appropriately from the one preceding it, if main points of information on each card follow appropriately from those preceding them, if the title is appropriate, and so on. Then check the whole for a logical flow of information. *Do the units connect like links in a chain, or does the flow collapse at any point?* If the latter, rearrange the cards until you have a linked chain that reads like a narrative.

Writing a proposal takes a great deal of persistent effort and solid judgment. Both grow out of experience with disciplined process, a verifiable knowledge base, and critical/creative inquiry, including inquiry into your own motives and judgments. Aside from those activities, fortify your good judgment by keeping your antennae on alert during meetings, attending to details as well as to the larger picture, and responding quickly to editor/ producer direction or account executive/client requests.

ABOUT COSTS AND BUDGETS

Keep in mind that the cost of any project is important to all concerned. Public relations and advertising agencies are particularly cautious these days. If you sense or learn that the client is inclined to keep a tight purse, ask yourself: *If the client is reluctant to go the whole nine yards necessary, how far will the client go? Is that distance worth the agency's investment of resources, personnel, time, and effort?* If not, the agency, although anxious to do business, may turn down the opportunity and even suggest the name of another agency, perhaps a smaller one, to do the job.

If the agency wants to handle the project, it may suggest a strategy that costs the client less money and avoids a drain on agency resources—not a minor issue. For example, the ad agency Margeotes Fertitta & Weiss "fired" a client, refusing to do any more ads for the client's product, Remy Martin (cognac), a small but prestigious account. The agency simply decided the payoff was not worth the trouble and notified the client that it would not renew its contract. Usually, advertising reporter Kevin Goldman notes, it's the other way around.[6]

Still other "firing" incidents were pink slips issued to the Chi Chi restaurant chain by their ad agency D'Arcy Masius Benton & Bowles, to the Domino's Pizza regional group by Bayer-Bass-

Vanderwarker, to the Ponderosa Steakhouse chain by N. W. Ayer, and to the Howard Johnson's motel and restaurant chain by Interpublic Group-Lintas.[7]

The protracted recession of the early 1990s forced clients to tighten their belts. Agencies had to do the same. No surprise here —it's just smart business. The reward for financial and creative investment must be substantial enough to sustain the reputation and life of any media house, the well-being of which its members depend upon for their weekly paycheck. That truth applies to print and broadcast houses as well.

It makes no sense to set down a typical budget here. No such model exists because no two implementation plans are similar enough. Each strategy calls for various types of services and equipment, different needs and requirements.

Print and broadcast journalists tell their decision makers what they'll need to do the job. An in-house person practiced in developing a project budget then decides if it can be done as planned or if adjustments must be made. Public relations and advertising agencies also have in-house specialists who make those decisions, but the petitioner still has to tell them what and who they'll need and for how long.

ABOUT LENGTH

The amorphous nature of media proposals significantly limits what can be said about how long or how detailed the media proposal ought to be. The variety of those boundaries marks one of the principal differences between journalistic proposals and public relations and advertising proposals. Moreover, content length and breadth differ between "internal" and "external" proposals.

Journalistic proposals are mainly of the internal variety; that is, they're reviewed by supervisors, editors, or producers in-house and the review process ends there. Internal documents related to proposal preparation at public relations and advertising agencies pass through the same internal review, but here department supervisors and account executives are the judges. However, the process doesn't end with them. An external, formal document is then prepared for the client who is the ultimate judge.

Internal Proposals

Print and broadcast proposals issued by a petitioner might run no more than a page or two, but for a complex project or one executed in phases, sometimes five or more pages are required. The object is to be brief, yet thorough and informative. To achieve that end, petitioners put information in short paragraphs or list main points prefaced with a bullet or similar symbol and a few brief sentences of explanation under any point that needs it. Decision makers in print and broadcast houses have little time to wade through pages of reading material. In fact, and unless otherwise required, they prefer to see it all on no more than three pages. Then they'll call the petitioner in to answer questions, or they'll return the initial proposal with comments and questions written in the margins. Internal proposals in public relations and advertising usually run longer than three pages, but again the aim is to make it simple, concise, and easy to read, yet thorough and informative.

Informal Beginnings

Very often, many of the components listed above appear in serial form as office correspondence. For example, journalists may verbally introduce a story idea to their editor, state the problem, and provide a rationale for it. If the editor is interested, the next step is a written report repeating the essence of the verbal introduction, the data thus far accumulated, and the names and IDs of interviewees available for contact. Several progress reports with additional components may then follow the first document—if travel will be involved, for what purpose, the cost of same, how long you'll be away, and so on.

Public relations and advertising personnel operate under similar informal beginnings if the house is small or even medium-size. In large agencies, however, staff members in several specialized areas (research, marketing, media, creative) write out formal memoranda as preparation progresses, or they fill out forms specifically designed for internal review. Much of the accumulated information ends up on the account executive's or group supervisor's desk.[8] The material is then reviewed, discussed, and considered by the proposal team for inclusion in the document as component content. The document may be refined several times before the head of the account team reviews it again and before it's presented to the client.

In many cases, and before all this begins, all the client may see is a two-page business letter outlining the agency's findings, a projected budget, and a statement that the agency is prepared to deal with the problem if the client so chooses. If the client is so inclined and the budget's suitable, the client will ask for more details. Phone calls, face-to-face conferences, and additional research will then precede composition of the final document.

Anticipate the Decision Maker

Whether you're a journalist or a public relations or advertising writer, be prepared to respond to any aspect of any one of the basic components listed above. That also applies to any other aspect related to your particular project. Perhaps you overlooked something in your initial development or misjudged decision makers' needs or personality quirks and left out something important to them. Just be prepared to give a ready answer.

For example, if it doesn't appear in the proposal, a journalist might be asked: *How much time will you need? How many members of the staff will it take? What equipment will you need? When can you get it ready for publication/air time?* These issues are important to editors and producers because they need to know the resources they're left to work with in order to run the daily operation.

The journalist also might be asked: *Why is this a timely issue?* (an absolute in winning approval). *What assurance do you have that these facts are true? Who exactly do you have lined up for interviews on issues A, B, and C? Are they willing to go on record? What do you know about them? Have you verified their statements? How? Do you see this as a one-shot deal, an occasional story, or a series?*

The latter question is usually a board decision, but there's no reason why you can't make a suggestion as to how you think the creative presentation should run. You could include brief answers to these anticipated questions in your proposal; otherwise, stand ready with a response, and when challenged on any point, be sure you have data to back it up.

Also, be prepared to make changes in your original plan. As the work progresses, new information and editorial demands will necessarily introduce adjustments and modifications. Your editor or producer knows that, and you should expect it, even delays. In fact, you may be asked to temporarily drop your project to take care of an urgent assignment.

Sometimes, an enterprise project can be finalized within a reasonable length of time. But if the project is a major one, it may take months, perhaps more than a year, and that is why staffing for the project could become a problem. In any case, anticipate the length of preparation and production and give yourself plenty of leeway. You might have to deal with unexpected hold-ups or events. Another precaution: Whether you present your proposal orally or in written form or in both delivery modes, anticipate and be prepared to answer questions you believe decision makers will raise—and they always do.

The Best Defense

In public relations and advertising, questions from the supervisor, account executive, or client are far more difficult to anticipate, but it can be done even with problems never before encountered. As in journalism, the best defense is curiosity. Before the confrontation, immerse yourself in all the facts plus any factors that radiate beyond them. Whatever question this exercise generates in you will probably be a question you can anticipate from either the account executive or the client. Be prepared to respond. Discuss the problem with your colleagues or group supervisor. That always helps. If it doesn't, it may be that the client hasn't provided full disclosure. Ask the one in charge to raise the issue with the client.

Of course, it's easy to overlook something. If you're asked about it, don't say "I'll try to find out"—that's wimpish—and don't say "I'll try to get back to you tomorrow" but, instead, say "I don't know, but I'll have an answer for you by such-and-such time tomorrow." Then get on it and follow through on your promise. The display of self-confidence and reliability is a sure way to win both supervisor and client confidence.

If you know your problem situation thoroughly and the details concerning its solution, chances are you'll have ready answers for most questions that are raised by internal judges. As for the ultimate judge, the client, that decision maker mainly wants reassurance about issues like these: *How do you know this is the problem? What's your basis of confidence that your approach is the answer? Have you done this for anybody else before? Who? Did it work then? How well? Why is it right now? How long will it take to get out the message? How much will all this cost?* If you've followed the preparatory process recommended, you should have ready answers to these and any other questions.

External Proposals

All media proposals pass through an internal review, after which, if approved, they evolve into external proposals, the format design of which becomes much more complex, with each proposal taking on added volume and a format order exclusively its own. Also, because the research effort may be more extensive and quite costly, a more detailed coverage of research results is usually required. Or if implementation may call for various types of media use or personal contact, more descriptive explanations must be given regarding what channels will be used for what, where, when, why, and how.

So aside from the basic components that often appear in internal proposals, additional ones may come into play, thus increasing the volume. It's possible to write a five-page public relations or advertising proposal, but some can run up to 50 or more pages. These are then spiral-bound or looseleaf-bound and tabbed into labeled sections. These high-volume external proposals also are known by other names—action plan, program, planning book, and the like.

SOLICITED AND UNSOLICTED PROPOSALS

These are terms more often heard in public relations and advertising circles than in print and broadcast journalism. Nevertheless, the intended meaning of these terms applies across the board. In journalism, a "solicited" proposal is akin to an assignment from a special projects editor to members of a special projects team, usually in the form of an extended office memo. An "unsolicited" proposal is more like a story idea that a journalist proposes or a project that a special projects team member initiates.

However, in public relations and advertising, the meaning of these terms is far more specific and familiar. In those environments, the difference between a solicited and an unsolicited proposal is the difference between an agency seeking a client's business (solicited) and a client sending an RFP to an agency (unsolicited). Although an agency may receive an RFP from a client "of record" (the client numbers among the agency's list of accounts currently on record), the client is free to send the same RFP to other agencies. The agency of record, of course, is also expected to follow the fortunes of its various clients and to bring any potential problems to the attention of those clients. That responsibility might be seen as a bid for business, but such activity is more in line with providing the service the client expects from its agency of record.

OTHER DIFFERENCES

Proposals prepared for media houses differ from proposals written for funded media projects. For funded media projects (see Chapter 3), you rarely have the opportunity for personal contact or the advantage of clarifying issues with the funder, and you'll only be writing one proposal. In private industry, however, and as suggested earlier, personal contact is necessary and frequent, clarifications ongoing, and more than one internal document may be necessary before the final one is composed.

Also, as pointed out earlier, in print and broadcast journalism, your first proposition may be a brief mention to the editor during a chance meeting in the hall, during a coffee break, or in the office. The editor or producer may say "Okay, that sounds good. Show me what you've got so far." You come back with an initial proposal, which then goes into a decision process by other directors. They may come back with some questions and directions, or they may say "You've got a good idea here, but we think you need to take another approach" or "You need to avoid this and include so-and-so." You look into it, and if their recommendations are justified, show them what you found out. If they're not justified, say so or write a memo explaining why and noting the evidence in support of your explanation.

In public relations and advertising, the initial contact may simply be a luncheon meeting, phone call, or letter from a prospective client giving their version of the problem (sometimes called a *statement of work*, or SOW). If, however, the client is an established account, the agency may bring the client's attention to a problem during a business or luncheon meeting called for that or any other purpose.

However the process begins in either journalism or public relations and advertising, frequent meetings will follow in an effort to arrive at a mutual understanding of the problem, the extent of decision makers' willingness to invest in the solution process, and any other matter that may be of concern to them or the media house.

It bears mention again—your cause may be lost unless you're *prepared* to answer questions at in-house meetings you attend to discuss your progress. If you don't happen to have a ready reply, use the response given earlier in this chapter: "I don't know, but I'll have an answer for you by such-and-such time tomorrow." Furthermore, hand in periodic reports of your progress, even though no one has asked for them. It reassures decision makers that you're on top of things. The information exchange is simply part of the process as research continues and information emerges to give everyone the confidence that your final proposal merits support and that a creative piece worthy of public communication will result.

THE ULTIMATE PURPOSE

The high stakes involved in sustaining the life of a media house also depend on how effectively you argue and present a proposal's various components not only to win approval from decision makers but to present a strategy that will win an audience for your media house, secure, and/or sustain a client. That's the ultimate aim.

Follow the problem-solving process, raise critical self-inquiries (those provided in this book and those you're impelled to ask about your specific project), take notice of decision makers' mind-sets, personality quirks, and needs, and thoroughly internalize your evidential base of knowlege. The design of a media proposal will then take on its own imperative form and persuasive merit, as well as justification for its cost.

HOW THE PROS DO IT

Although well prepared to compose a proposal, pros continue to do a great deal of thinking before attempting to put all its many parts together into a whole piece. For example, notice how all their judgments, including the solution strategy, content, and shape of the proposal, flow from identification of the true problem and the data collected concerning it. Notice, too, how often and in what instances pros rely on critical and creative self-inquiry to help them make their decisions. No predetermined format designs here. The petitioner follows the direction of a specific problem and what the data show are its particular needs for solution and communication to its public(s).

Print and Broadcast Journalism

This investigative reporter proposed a feature series that would draw attention to community constructions that developers had been building on toxic land, namely, a downtown Detroit river-front project called Harbortown, which consisted of a shopping mall, condominiums, and apartment buildings.

The journalist's proposal ran about three pages and was titled "The Harbortown Project." He introduced the problem of construction on contaminated land along with findings drawn from extensive research on how the project slipped through the cracks at both state and city levels. His research not only covered this project but others planned for construction on toxic land. He also included the questions he sought to answer: *Was the Harbortown area cleaned up before the project was built? If so, what level of cleanup? How dangerous are the toxics at Harbortown and other areas?*

As for order, the reporter knew his editors preferred to see a clear description of the problem up front, then evidence for it, followed by the questions the petitioner intended to answer, and an outline of planned stories and what they would contain from what sources.

> For the Harbortown project, I outlined a three-day series [implementation strategy], and the editors talked about it and decided it would have a stand-alone section so that all the stories could be combined in one place. It varied the contour, the shape of the series, but not the number of stories. At the end of the process, I discovered some additional information that led to a few more stories than we planned on. So I cut back on another story that I thought would be bigger than it was.
>
> Generally, editors expect to see a brief, cogent overview of the story, also some details; that is, what we know, relevant facts and information, sources used so far and planned, reliability of these, what we expect to find, how we might frame what we find for the reader, and the story's relevance to readers [audience interest]. I also include the amount of

space I believe it'll take, but I don't know that everyone does this. Many reporters just prepare a list of stories they think they need to do in order to shed the greatest light on the subject and suggest how and when they should appear so readers can take it all in gradually.

> **John Wark,** investigative reporter,
> *The Detroit News*

Wark's proposed series developed into a front-page story plus two inside pages in a Sunday edition during August 1991. Additional stories in the series followed the next day in an eight-page inside section. He titled the series "Poison on the River Front," an apt description of what his analyzed data revealed.

Mike McGraw (see case introduction, Chapter 4) handles his proposals in much the same way:

> After hearing the problem [statement], editors here, first and foremost, want to see your evidence, some strong evidence that a significant investment in time and money is going to turn up something and whether it's going to be worth it. I always include the time I think it'll take, the personnel required, and the time they'll need. But about presentation and space required, my attitude most often is going to be that I really don't care that much. My primary goal is to get the information out there. But I will, at times, suggest ideas for presentation for no other reason than just sheer experience with the information. You'll find on many huge projects that is almost as much a reporter function as it is an editor function. The most important thing is to identify the problem as it really is and then prove to your editors beyond a shadow of a doubt that it exists.
> And I never go into an interview without having researched the source or having tested my questions.
> Finding solutions to getting the story is the hardest part of the job. You have to have a state of mind for journalism, and a very large part of it is a questioning state of mind. Nothing goes right without it. I didn't believe this before as much as

I do now. I also think that we as project reporters have an obligation to suggest potential solutions when we put out a problem.

William M. (Mike) McGraw, projects
reporter and reporting coach, *Kansas City Star*

If you've won the respect and trust of your editors over the years, you may not have to produce a "hard sell" or even write a proposal. Robert Capers, a veteran reporter, had suggested an "occasional" story to his special projects editor (called "occasional" because the proposed story was neither sensitive nor controversial). Because editors trusted Capers' judgment and his work, his verbal suggestion proved sufficient. Yet, and despite his track record, he chose to provide evidence of his background knowledge of the problem idea. Capers' story focused on nursing home care and the timely subject of elderly patients' rights.

Much of what I had learned [about the problem] was accumulated over many years and stored in files. I knew a lot about it and also had been writing for some time about medical ethics, hospital policy, and patient autonomy. This was an occasion where we redefined nursing home patients and their care [the problem idea]. So I knew a lot about this in general, but less about it in specific terms [the growing awareness of patients' rights, particularly those in outstate as well as instate nursing homes]. The story was inherently of interest to a lot of people, and I knew it wouldn't take much for me to convince an editor that there's something here. In most cases, I don't have to sell the stories very hard. I just told him [his editor] that there are many nursing homes out there and many residents living in them with family members, all of whom would be interested, and that they would want to know what seemed to be a fundamental change in the way nursing homes were providing care to residents, that is, growing willingness of doctors to communicate, recognition of patients' rights to make life and death decisions for themselves, and that residents were no longer regarded as incompetents but as people who needed the kind of care given to children [the rationale].

Capers added that when he was special projects editor what he expected his reporters to give him was

> something on paper that was new, something I hadn't read about, something important, something that surprised me a little bit. I'd also look for something that affects a lot of people or something that showed a lot of money was being wasted. To generate enterprise ideas, I'd say [to his team]: *Look, here's what's happening here, there, also here. What do these things mean? What's going on in the area of resource recovery? Is there something new in cancer therapy that we haven't written about and ought to? What's all this stuff about arterioscopic surgery?* I'd talk to reporters about how long it was going to take. I wouldn't expect it on paper. I might ask about the amount of space it would take, whether it would be a one-shot deal or series. It would depend on how refined the idea was. If a suggested idea evolved into a three- or four-day series, yes, [I'd want] a written proposal, and we'd also talk about photo possibilities and graphics.

> **Robert S. Capers,** staff writer,
> *The Hartford Courant,* Hartford, Connecticut

Capers admits that not every proposal can be sold on foot and that he has written out proposals many times, principally, he said, to refine the enterprise idea for himself before presenting it to the editor. Capers was awarded the 1992 Pulitzer in the category of explanatory journalism for his series on the Hubble space telescope. He also won the Premier award from the National Aviation and Space Writers Association for his earlier series disclosing what went wrong in the construction of the telescope's mirror.

Like Capers, Candy Cooper (see case background, Chapters 4 and 5) believes a rationale should promise a good story; that is, it should

> explain why the public has to know about this, whether it has the impact of some kind of public-service value to it, whether it has the potential to change something, whether it's a

problem that's never been looked at before, or if this is a way it's never been looked at before. You have to give editors a really good answer to why they would want to do this story, give space and time to your topic. This is the point where the selling of your idea has to happen.

Candy Cooper, investigative reporter,
San Francisco Examiner

Victor Solis, an NBC producer based in Europe, says he usually sounds out his ideas with an editor before putting anything down on paper. Once the editor agrees, the major part of his research begins (primary research) and much of that effort, he explained, goes into the proposal. In fact, for the features he produced during the 1992 Olympic Games in Barcelona, he said he used 100% of his research (see case introduction, Chapter 3).

The proposal must show the facts, your background knowledge of your ideas. The research is what your proposal must be based on, very little on personal knowledge. When you're proposing, you become a salesman. If you want to get your stories aired, you have to sell them. So you start with basic journalistic facts: *Is this an interesting story? Is it a compelling story? Is it something that will move an audience one way or the other? Is it an important story? Is it a story that will make people think? Is this a story that will give good, useful television?* If I can answer yes and give good reasons for each answer, it's a go [rationale and evidence for same]. If the reasons don't stand up, it's not a go. And always, the human factor is always the main thing.

Aside from the recommended story and the research I've done for it, I'll usually give my editor the length of time I'll have to spend on the story, the anticipated cost, which is of some consideration to the editor. If you've worked with an in-house financial manager for a while, you get a feel for cost. I also include the logistics involved, things like travel involved, the shoots, also which of these will be interviews, which videotaped, the number of people who will be involved, the type of equipment needed, all of which are cost-related but secondary to the main theme which is: *What is this story about?* [the problem] *Why is it important?* [the rationale] *Why should it be aired?* [facts supporting the rationale that also include reference to audience interest] You have to answer each of those questions in quite a bit of detail not only in terms of content but in terms of visuals and sound as well.

You put down everything that goes into this story, all the five Ws and the how, the questions you'd want answered if you were a member of the audience. All these things help sell your story. You get down to other details like, well, you might say "I need a cameraman for three days and he's going to have to bring in a wide-angle lens to make sure we get a panoramic view of the harbor [of Barcelona]." Or if it's a drug bust, you'd say "I need the cameraman to bring in a special night scope or infra-red scope." During the war [Persian Gulf], I made a request for a night scope for night shooting and 8 mm cameras because they're smaller and more compact. No shot-for-shot details. That comes at pre-scripting time.

Victor D. Solis, producer,
NBC News, Europe

When Solis gets a turndown on a first proposal because the editor says "It's not cost-effective," he says he keeps on pitching his project as long as it's timely and a solid idea. He keeps probing with questions like "Well, how about next month or so?" Solis admits he's had plenty of rejections, but he says, "If the story's there, it'll override the resistance to cost."

Public Relations and Advertising

Proposal composition in public relations and advertising is more complex, but the units of information are similar. Hud Englehart, a Chicago public relations executive, led a team working on a proposal for United Airlines (see case introduction, Chapter 4). Here he describes what went into the agency's proposal and how a simple question during an early client briefing helped pave the way to solution strategies:

What a client wants to see in a proposal goes all over the lot. Sometimes, they don't know and you have to make the decisions, and that's what makes this business so fascinating.

I think most of all what a client really wants to see is a solution to his problem or the issue. If you miss that [the true problem], you might as well not give it [the solution].

We have RFPs come in here saying what they want are capabilities, and I just wince at that because anybody can show you a whole lot of nice words on paper and tell you about offices around the world and so forth. But none of that proves anything about your ability to solve problems. Often, we'll get on the phone and say "I know you want capabilities, but give us a problem so we can demonstrate our capability." Demonstration is the key word. You need to demonstrate your agency can solve the client's problem.

You'd be surprised to know how many people in business do not realize that our business is a problem-solving business. You still have lots of people who think the media is just a nice thing to have and they just want newspaper clips all over the place. They don't understand that at the end of what we do there is, hopefully, an action. If I ask the question *What do you want to have happen when I'm done communicating?* it puts a whole different spin on what we need to be thinking about and what we need to do to help the client.

We won the UA business because three things stood out in our proposal. First of all, we demonstrated our experience in the airline business; that is, we showed we understood who was flying, why they were flying, and that we understood the nature of the competition [knowledge of problem, product, audience, and marketplace]. I suspect a lot of that came because we were the agency of record, but we're also fairly good students of the airline business. Secondly, we had a creative solution to the problem [implementation strategy]. The communications with the idea of passenger service worked perfectly with their need to communicate more strongly with the workforce and about their role in the success of the airline. All that went into our presentation, and the creative strategies themselves evolved to a very large extent from all our research work. Finally, we were able to demonstrate with a fairly tight budget [description of costs for services rendered] that we could deliver on the promise with the number [of dollars] that we said we could.

Of course, the first quarter of the presentation was a rationale on why we were doing it the way we proposed, a dissertation, if you will, which led the client down the road of "here's the strategy, here's the way we're going to do it and why." Because we were the agency of record, we didn't have to get into what we'd do mediawise. In other cases, we might have to prove that a little. And the way we do that is generally with a case history approach. We'll say, "For this client we were asked to do this and this is how we got it to happen." The other way you demonstrate credibility is by what I call "name dropping" [a list of other clients served and/or kudos from other clients].

> **Hud Englehart,** executive managing director,
> Hill and Knowlton, Chicago

This particular proposal filled nearly 100 pages. It opened with the problem as Englehart's team found it to be, not as the client thought it was, and included the evidence that supported that discovery as well as the strategy to resolve the problem. Content also included the bios of people working on the project, charts plotting various research findings, a hard copy of the slide presentation, the narratives that went with them, and a variety of other print and creative materials recommended for public communication. Englehart said, "You have to put everything in your program book (the written proposal) that you're going to say verbally in the stand-up presentation."

In the following description of component use and presentation order, agency executive Michael Niederquell indicates the kind of format his public relations firm usually follows (see case introduction, Chapter 5). In fact, he says all their proposals begin with a

> clear identification of the problem [problem statement], what goals we're trying to achieve, our way of achieving the goals, and then we define our tactics to overcome any obstacles in order to realize our objectives [solution strategy]. That may include not only the overall objectives but also the marketing and image goals. Below that, we have communication goals, then supporting tactics [evidence for establishing viability of the solution strategy]. The communication goal may not be among the client's own goals, which may be

changing the image or increasing the bottom line [the profit margin]. We also include a budget and an audit plan. The audit could be a simple media evaluation that includes a quantitative dimension in order to measure the success of our media recommendations. The results of the audit, of course, are provided after the fact [once the strategy is put into motion].

Michael O. Niederquell, executive vice president,
Anthony M. Franco, Inc., Detroit, Michigan

There's no "cookie cutter" proposal, warns public relations executive Joe Epley. At his agency they rely on the questioning attitude to help them decide what to include in their proposals (see case introduction, Chapter 4). This approach, he explained, usually plays out into a presentation format of the proposal. In some cases, he pointed out, the presentation may be no more than one to three pages on agency stationery.

First we ask: *What is the client's situation?* Then: *What are their PR objectives? What can we do to achieve those objectives? How would we go about it?* We ask: *Who the client team would be in our relationship with the client? What factor in our experience qualifies us to do this job? What are our financial arrangements?* Then we always close by asking for the [client's] order, saying that we're ready to go to work as soon as the client signs the enclosed letter of agreement.

If the client agrees, more questions come up at meetings to make sure that both the agency and the client are operating on the same wavelength. At Epley's agency, it's also common practice to discuss the proposal with the client throughout the development process before submitting a final proposal. He has found that

it saves more grief than anything in the world. Talking things out with the client also tells us whether or not we're "column fodder" [some companies chart one agency against another in columns of merits and demerits before granting a go-ahead]. Some clients will already have a firm that they either want to give the business to or they're already working with,

and basically all they want to do is get a check on them to
make sure the PR firm is right for them. We absolutely try to
avoid that because you can spend an enormous amount of
time in proposal preparation and still not get the business.
If we learn we're "column fodder," we try to determine how
much the account is worth. If it's not worth our time, we may
decide not to do it. If it is, we might go through the motions.
Your one sure safeguard is constant questioning—of yourself
as well as the client—and most important of all, listen, listen,
listen. You've got to be able to read the client. It's not what
they say. It's what they don't say. The point is to get them
talking by raising questions and then to listen to what they
say [and] what they haven't said.

> **Joe S. Epley,** chairman and CEO,
> Epley Associates, Inc.,
> Charlotte, North Carolina

Don't be afraid to ask the client if other agencies have been
approached, Epley advises. If it's a government RFP, they're
obliged to tell you. Private enterprises sometimes tell you, sometimes they won't. If disclosure is not made, other sources of
information can be researched, but sometimes, Epley says, you
may never find out if you're "column fodder" and you just have
to decide whether to take on the client or not.

Decisions in advertising regarding proposal presentation
drive forward in much the same way, and they're always generated by the same fuel—critical and creative questioning. That was
the case for Craig Middleton (see case introduction, Chapter 4).
The proposal for American Express opened like most proposals:
a clarification of the problem as research revealed it and then an
explanation of why the identified problem would be the focus of
solution attention (the evidence). Middleton explained that all
other proposal content emerged from answers to questions and
issues raised during research.

For example, research data provided the basis for a statement
distinguishing the gold card from the green card, a description of how it was possible for two prestige cards to coexist

without one blotting out the prestige of the other and that was simply the qualifications one had to meet for either one or the other card. The 5% number became a very important figure because we found that only 5% of the population qualified for the gold card, a factor that put them in a very special group and gave us a clear definition of our target audience. It also told us that we could market the green card on one level of prestige and the gold card on still another level of prestige and do it without encroaching on one or the other's market value.

In addition, results from research gave us our creative strategy which we outlined in the proposal. Research provided the creative leap that led to our unique point about the gold card holder: Gold card holders are responsible money managers, special individuals, not just because they made money but because they are astute money managers who can be trusted as responsible creditors. It added a higher level of prestige to the gold card. The gold card promised special treatment wherever it was used by the card holder. That became the creative focus of our creative strategy.

I have to say at this point that our executive vice president and director of creative strategy development, Bruce Nelson, deserves all the credit. Bruce is a very creative guy, a writer. What makes him remarkable and this whole process remarkable is that he, a writer, was the one who drove the analytic process, and that is not very usual. From the start, Bruce took a look at the problem and said: *Is it possible that there are two levels of prestige on an essentially functional card?* Then he set out to either prove or disprove that possibility. All the studies, focus groups, and so on were measured against Bruce's hypothesis. Research results showed that, indeed, there was a reasonable reason for two levels of prestige, that the market could split comfortably, and that one card would not hurt the other. Bruce isolated the problem, identified the causes of the former failure, drove the whole process of consumer exploration, refined the definition of the product, and ultimately wrote the ads. Being a creative person, Bruce is loathe to accept the fact that pure functional distinctions [of the credit card] are sufficient to drive the success of a product. He looked at what had been done in the past and determined [that] motivation to use one card or another had to be something beyond its features. So his question was:

What was that? The research gave us the answers, and we put them in the proposal.

Craig Middleton, executive vice president
and director, marketing and planning,
McCann Erickson Worldwide, New York City

Along with the customary opening and creative focus the American Express proposal included a summary of the problem and related evidence, a detailed budget, time line, and comprehensive auditing plan. As in most instances across all divisions, proposal parts may develop either as a whole piece at once or in sequential form and then be pulled together for presentation as a whole. In the American Express case, introductory content represented one document in the sequence, the marketing plan another, and then a media plan. Separate departments usually develop each document in the sequence, and then they're brought together, refined, and readied for final client presentation. Taken together the proposal segments could very well be seen as a "program" or "planning book."

Sequential development by various departments in advertising agencies is not unusual, and the extent to which research and analysis is carried out for each sequence is extremely thorough. It has to be because all those portions together contain the solution to the problem. A case in point is the new-product proposal designed for Chrysler's new Jeep model, the Grand Cherokee, an account of record at Bozell Worldwide (see case introduction, Chapter 3).

At Bozell, the proposal is called the "planning book." Several Bozell divisions were involved in providing material for this planning book. Contributions came from the departments of research, marketing, media, strategic planning, the account executive's office, and the creative department. The reports summarized research findings that identified the client's true problem, the appropriate target audience and their needs and preferences, a marketing strategy, media plan, and creative approach. Together they added up to render the solution, the creative idea, and a plan to execute the implementation strategy. The high-lights of these reports were then considered, discussed, con-densed, refined, and finally written into the planning book. In the commentary below, notice the value the advertising execu-tive attributes to these internal reports.

Notice, too, how details such as the "national perspective," "regionality," "car-line personality," and the dealership factor become new dimensions in this proposal simply because they applied to this particular problem and its solution. As pointed out earlier, those hidden components come into view quickly when you place yourself in the client's shoes and ask yourself the kinds of questions suggested in this chapter.

> We live and die by those documents [the reports from all the departments mentioned above]. Everything is research- and consumer-driven. You learn it, update it, revisit it, internalize it, but you don't have to go through the process. It's the material the creative department works from to plan their campaign strategy, and they learn it in much the same way. All this may go to the client in separate presentations before we actually produce the visuals for the final presentation.
>
> For the planning book, we identify the key marketing problem, describe where the target market is, what our advertising intends to achieve [the objectives], we talk about that from a national perspective, and in this case we pointed out how our dealer advertising association would dovetail with that, how the two relate to one another, then a simple statement of our car-line position, something we call the "car-line personality," and on which vehicle in the line it'll be focused. It's referred to as the "focus vehicle" in the line of vehicles to be included in the campaign strategy. Then we take each one of these and put them in the executive sum-mary component in the beginning of the planning book.
>
> Other components include the research strategy, the me-dia plan, in which are included all the important points of infor-mation from reports made to the account group from the divisions I've already mentioned. We include a budget plan and regionality overview [areas across the country where mar-keting of the new product line would take place]. The planning book is actually the basis for our oral presentation, which is

a synthesized version, something that can be used in a visual presentation such as an overhead or slidefilm projection. It [the visual presentation] will say the same things as the planning book, but it's done in at-a-glance convenience.

Each one of the book's various parts may take a series of meetings where clients make their inputs and, perhaps, modifications. For example, we try not to have the strategy session turn into a budget meeting. Obviously, they go hand in hand, but at times you have to draw some distinctions between how you choose to position your cars and how you choose to execute the plan. The creative work, too, goes into a separate discussion session. Then the planning book is written in final form and left as a leave-behind at the final oral presentation where we usually demonstrate the creative executions. We don't formally test our creative executions. We're more interested in listening [to focus group participants]. We want to capture their experience of touch and feel [with the new vehicle] and get reactions, but we don't want somebody else to judge that this [creative] piece is better than that [creative] piece.

Thomas J. Deska, managing partner
Chrysler Corporation,
Bozell Worldwide, Inc., Southfield, Michigan

It's important to become familiar with the components of a media proposal, especially the ones relied on most frequently, because that knowledge helps you decide about other dimensions of the proposal. Moreover, knowing about them helps you build your format in a manner expected by your media house and helps you recognize the house vocabulary for certain components. Speak their language, know the concept to which the vocabulary applies, and test your perceptions and judgments about what is expected by asking yourself the questions you feel your editor, producer, supervisor, account executive, or client would raise concerning the problem at hand and its solution strategy. Let your critical/creative thinking processes work for you.

Media proposals need not—should not—pour into any prefabricated mold. Nor should you assume that you can just sit down and bang out a proposal because you believe in your idea, that the merit of your idea alone will win over decision makers. Not so. You need to realize that not a word can be written unless you've accumulated a solid knowledge base and asked yourself critical questions all along the way. That prelude releases the creative logic needed to format a proposal, to write appropriate content for each component while giving it a style that informs yet facilitates review by decision makers. More about that in Chapter 7.

NOTES

1. A shared vocabulary in the mass media is nonexistent. In fact, different houses within a single media division rarely use the same words for similar items or functions. The terms used in this book to identify proposal components represent those used by some in the industry but not all. For example, *problem statement* is used occasionally; other times, the term is *problem description, problem situation, strategic opportunity, situation analysis, introduction, background,* and the like. Other components, too, are identified differently from those listed herein. However, the label attached to each component given here reflects the subject content belonging to it. Let the subject matter of the component guide your understanding of labels you might see at your media house or in other contexts.

2. Public relations and advertising agencies "audit" or "measure" more than one outcome of a recommended program ("audit" refers to a check, an examination to assess the merit or outcome of something; "measurement" is more a quantitative determination of an outcome). Measurable elements of the program might be the marketing plan—for example, the value return from using certain channels of delivery of a message—and the communication strategy, where the latter typically sets out to change minds or behavior about something in its attempt to predispose the audience to a given service, image, product, or idea.

3. Often referred to as a "demographic" profile.

4. Also known as a "psychographic" profile.

5. You may hear or see these referred to as "tactical" recommendations.

6. K. Goldman, "Poor Payoffs Push Agencies to Drop Clients, *Wall Street Journal,* 17 November 1992, B1.

7. Ibid.

8. Levels of authority differ from agency to agency. Know the structural organization of your media house: who's who, who does what, and to whom you're directly responsible. The same homework task applies to journalists.

Writing the Media Proposal II

Content and Style

There's no mystery about what content belongs in which component. Once you've identified and set up your units of information, you'll see what items in your body of knowledge belong where. You'll recognize them readily because all points of information specific to a particular component are filed away in both your memory and your records.

SELECTION CRITERIA

Trust the preparation you've done for your project. You already know that your information is *relevant* to the problem and is thorough, reliable, and timely. You also know that you have many items that are *unique,* interesting, previously unknown. And you know that the program you recommend is *feasible* because you have the facts to substantiate that position.

Because you've studied your problem and body of knowledge well, you'll find that certain facts, figures, and details related to each component will stand out above all others. Those items remain at the forefront of your mind and tell you where to put them and what to say about them. Everything else will fall into place. Test your selections by asking yourself: *Does the item reflect any characteristics of the following criteria?*

Relevance

These are items that inform through definition, description, or backgrounding. They consider not just one point of view but all sides of the problem. They mark both confirmations and contradictions, advantages and disadvantages, corrections and errors, strengths and weaknesses, facts on record as opposed to those overlooked by authorities. In short, these elements inform all dimensions of the component in question. They're in your body of knowledge—even overlooked items because they're obvious by their absence. You can't help noticing them. If you don't notice them, they'll pop out at you. Incidentally, none of this noticing suffers from that cognitive quirk, biased selection, because you took necessary precautions against falling into that trap when you "cleaned" your data.

Uniqueness

This is of interest to decision makers because it represents new information, facts never known before, or is an attribute of items so unusual they surprise and remain in memory or engage attention, sustain interest, and encourage action. Look for these features in your body of information for any given component. They'll stand out from the record because of their particular nature and because you have the evidence to substantiate their validity.

Timeliness

Timeliness means different things in journalism and in public relations and advertising. In journalism, it's a matter of currency; that is, your decision maker will want to know: *What evidence supports your claim that this issue is of current interest, concern, and in need of attention now? Why do you think it's important enough at this time for publication?* You have answers to these questions in your body of knowledge. Use them in your "Rationale" or in a unit listing reasons why this project is ripe for publication now.

In public relations and advertising, timeliness is more closely related to the component labeled "Time Line," or whatever you choose to call this unit of information. The time line is of special interest to clients because they don't want to pay for any more of the agency's hourly fee than they have to. So, tell the client when you're going to do what and when they can expect to see completion of the project in time for an audience-ready marketplace. In this instance, do yourself and the client a favor. Map the time line either in chart form, along a horizontal line, or as a list. A narrative description would be too time-consuming for decision makers to absorb at a single glance.

Feasibility

This concept, too, means different things in journalism and in public relations and advertising. In journalism, the main questions are: *Can you get the story? Are your sources willing to be identified and quoted? How much travel will be involved? What will this cost? How long will you be away? What personnel and equipment will you need? For how long?* You have the answers to these questions, too. Some could be part of your rationale or under a unit called "Facts and Feasibility" and others under "Sources." Answers to cost questions would fit nicely under "Budget."

In public relations and advertising, a feasible project is one the client is willing to pay for and the agency is willing to take on for that price. It has much less to do with "getting" the job done. You and your agency are the experts. If your agency is willing to take on the job, as a team member you're expected to help complete the assignment to the client's satisfaction. So, your proposal needs to show that you and your agency have the ability and resources to carry out the recommended program.

All the above represent basic criteria for content selection, but you should remain open to any factor that might strike you as vital to any one of the components in your proposal. The task now is to give expression to the content and in a style that's easily read and understood.

WHAT TO SAY

Afraid of writer's block? Dismiss the thought. Remember, you've just finished internalizing a mass of reliable information about a specific problem embedded with all its own particular facts, figures, and details. The necessary words are in your mind eagerly waiting expression. A comment attributed to the late Washington columnist Walter Lippmann makes that quite clear. Equating ready expression to a mind prepared for the task, Lippmann remarked, "The truth is that anyone who knows what he is doing can say what he is doing and anyone who knows what he thinks can say what he thinks. Those who cannot speak for themselves are, with very rare exceptions, not sure what they are doing and what they mean."

Still wary? Stimulate your memory bank by making some critical self-inquiries. Trust your knowledge and understanding of the content because once you phrase the question the words for content will come. You may want to rewrite and refine the content, but what you need now are those first words. So ask yourself the following:

- *What is the perceived problem(s)?* Demonstrate that you're aware of the perceived problem. Articulate it and write it down as it was stated.
- *Is this the precise and true problem?* If not, then . . .
- *What is the precise and true problem?* Articulate it and write it down clearly and succinctly.
- *What evidence is in the data that supports this finding?* Show why the perceived problem is not the true problem and why the identified one is the situation that requires attention. If you find more support than you can use in a paragraph, prioritize the major points of evidence.

- *Why is it important to attend to this problem and to do so now?* Demonstrate justification for carrying out the project. Provide verifiable reasons why it calls for attention at this time.
- *What facts best describe the audience? What is its relationship to the problem? What evidence supports identification of this group as the audience of concern or interest?* Show that you know precisely who will bring decision makers the best return on their investment in your project and for what reasons. No matter what media division it's for or how clever it is, an execution plan will make few waves if it's aimed at an unconcerned, disinterested audience. In fact, the very design of the execution plan depends on identification of the correct audience.
- *What do the data indicate is the answer to the real problem? What evidence supports that conclusion? Can the evidence be described briefly in narrative form? Would a bulleted listing facilitate review? Will charts, tables, graphs, and the like add or detract from the given information? Which ones would be most persuasive?*
- *What is your solution strategy? What evidence or personal experience with a similar problem suggests that this strategy is an effective plan?*
- *Exactly how will you execute this plan? Is it audience directed? Does it speak to the problem, the objectives/goals?*
- *What is the estimated total cost of this project? Can I, a house expert, experienced colleague, or an outside authority supply a detailed account of the total cost?* The detail of cost in specific dollar amounts applies in some cases to journalism projects. Journalists might need funds for a survey, services, or equipment supplied by an outside source. If that happens to be the case, they might make an estimate based on past experience, seek the aid of an experienced colleague or in-house expert, or research the costs themselves. Usually, cost estimates for public relations and advertising projects are done by office personnel practiced in this kind of calculation.
- *Will there be a statistical measure or general audit evaluating the results of this project? If so, what exactly will be done? If not, why not?* This applies more to public relations and advertising proposals. A newspaper or broadcast station may conduct an "audit"—for example, a poll of consumer reaction to a published or broadcast story would indicate the numbers who read, heard, and perhaps acted on the communicated message.
- *When can you begin this project? When will it be completed? What exactly will be done when?*

- *Who among staff members will be involved? Who will do what when? What are their qualifications for this particular project?*

Use questions like these to help remind you about content for each component. It's all in your body of knowledge. For brevity's sake, keep in mind the criteria given above when it becomes necessary to select only a few items from among many possibilities.

HOW TO SAY IT

The rule for composing content for components in a media proposal is a commonsense one that applies to any written communication designed to inform and, in certain instances, to influence. A media proposal especially should demonstrate clarity, precision, brevity, directness, and confidence.

Clarity .

Webster's defines clarity as "directness, orderliness and precision of thought or expression." Another dictionary defines it as "lucidity as to perception or understanding, freedom from indistinctness; intelligibility, exactness, simplicity." In other words, to be clear means leaving no room for questions or confusion. Begin by using words familiar to the majority of English-language users. Avoid jargon and abstract words. If you use any of these, explain your use of the terms. Rely on the S-V-O (subject, verb, object) formula as a basis for structuring sentences. That doesn't mean your sentences need to be sterile or that you can't begin with an introductory phrase or use modifiers. It does mean that the formula is the backbone of a sentence clarifying who (or what) is doing something to whom (or what).

Precision

Clarity also means being exact. That is, use specific, concrete words so that decision makers grasp the meaning you intend. A general reference misses the mark. A specific reference makes a direct hit. That's because a generality refers to a broad class of things, whereas the specific identifies a concrete object within that class. For example, here's how two generalities, "book" and "industry," break down to a specific:

- Book—fiction—historic novel about the Civil War—American—*Gone With the Wind.*
- Industry—clothing manufacturer—blue jeans—western jeans—women's western jeans.

Notice what the breakdown does? It removes questions and confusion. The first generality raises questions like: *What kind of book? What kind of fiction? Which civil war? Which historical novel about the American Civil War?* The second one raises questions like: *What kind of industry? What kind of clothing? What type of blue jeans? For whom—men, women, children?*

Make your action words precise. A specific action word has descriptive energy and carries much more vigor than an action word that shares a similar meaning. For example, which of the two sentences below strikes you as more effective?

(1) Our sales volume reached a new high this month.
(2) Our sales volume hit a new high this month.

If you chose (2), you made the right choice. "Reached" fails to impress as forceful an image on the mind as the action verb "hit." Proposal language is much like business language, which Theodore O. Yntema, former vice president of Ford Motor Company, defined this way: "The first requisite to effective communication is clarity and organization of your own thoughts. The second is understanding of your audience. The third is just plain hard work to achieve a good job."[1]

Brevity

Brevity stands with equal importance alongside clarity and precision. You can achieve brevity by various means. Begin by trying to limit the number of words in your sentences. That restraint moves your sentence directly to the point and, at the same time, achieves conciseness and simplicity. Sometimes, you need to write lengthy sentences or sentences embedded with several modifying words or phrases. When you do, ask yourself: *What words, phrases can I eliminate without obscuring my meaning? Can I break up this lengthy sentence into two sentences? What punctuation would simplify and clarify a lengthy sentence?*

Eliminating just a few words helps. For example, why say "In the event that you do not prefer the . . ." when "If you do not prefer the . . ." will do? Why say "If you would kindly respond to . . ." when "Please respond to . . ." will do? The point is to simplify without obscuring meaning; otherwise, decision makers lose concentration, miss your intended meaning, and you lose your audience.

Also, avoid exaggeration and excessive use of adjectives and adverbs. Some modifiers produce appropriate emphasis, some make your meaning more clear and precise, others overstate or detract from the true substance of the statement and often invite dispute.

Brevity is essential in proposal writing, a principle that applies to the length of paragraphs and units of information and to the sentences in them. As few as three or four sentences can make up a paragraph. A unit of information needs only the most relevant information included in it. Any more and you run the risk of inviting indifference or boredom. Don't overkill the evidence, either. Pages and pages of tables, charts, and graphs probably will not be read. Use only those that illustrate the issue under scrutiny and can be understood at a glance.

Incidentally, when you trim away the unnecessary you not only achieve brevity, you also create "orderliness," one of the features of clarity as *Webster's* defines it. A clean, lean body of copy makes a quick review possible and saves decision makers time, something they appreciate.

As for how much to say in a proposal, Armand Lauffer, University of Michigan professor of social work, believes that "no proposal should be expected to say everything that could be said. It only needs to say as much as is necessary at a particular point in the exchange or communication process."[2]

Directness

Directness means to arrive at an end point in a straightforward line. Applied to composition, it means getting to the point of your statement directly and avoiding detours. You can make detours in conversational communication, but in the context of composing a proposal the object is brevity and conciseness. Detours only throw decision makers off track. It helps to use specific nouns and active verbs, avoid superfluous modifiers, and clear away obstacles to the direct object.

Using bulleted lists of telegraphic phrases also helps. These are phrases that drop parts of a complete sentence—the article, subject, verb, or object—but still make sense. They may appear under an introductory paragraph, a single sentence, or a specific heading. A telegraphic phrase may look like any one of the following: "Five witnesses questioned," "Poll conducted by XYZ Research, Chicago," "Maintains flexibility yet sustains holding power," "Reduces cost," "Improves taste."

Use of direct voice, that is, electing to use active over passive voice, helps as well. Judge for yourself: Which sentence has the strongest sense of direct movement?

(1)   The meeting was postponed by the chairman.
(2)   The chairman agreed to postpone the meeting.

Both sentences have the same number of words, but in the second sentence, the subject is doing the action (active voice), whereas in the first, the subject is being acted upon (passive voice). That doesn't mean you have to write all sentences in active voice. That becomes monotonous. Besides, there are times when the passive voice is appropriate, particularly when you choose to emphasize something other than the doer of the action. The point is to use active voice wherever it performs more effectively than the passive. Again, passive voice appears more frequently in conversational communication, but active voice works well in proposal composition.

Confidence

Confidence comes with knowing your statements stand up to question and having the feeling that you're prepared to answer even unanticipated questions and challenges. It's the kind of confidence that raises belief in your project and infuses a tone of enthusiasm in your proposal and oral presentation. That kind of tone, in turn, assures decision makers that you're the right person for the job, that they'll get what they need and expect.

Enough has been said in this and previous chapters about justifying your claims and statements, but perhaps the danger of making assumptions needs a brief mention. Avoid statements like "It is assumed . . .", "We believe this . . .", "We feel that . . .", "We think we can do . . .", or "It should be obvious. . . ."

Never assume anything. The first of these statements pretends that the decision maker knows what you know. You can't be absolutely sure what the decision maker knows or doesn't know. Find out what the facts are and provide them along with the evidence that establishes their validity. It's what decision makers are paying you to do. You need to reassure them that you have the information and that it's complete and accurate.

The next two statements, "We believe this . . ." and "We feel that . . .", are just as troublesome. They assume that the decision maker is supposed to accept what you believe on its face. Neither statement is convincing. Make sure you have the evidence and then say "We know this . . . because . . ." or "We are certain that . . . because . . ."

The third statement, "We think we can do . . ." falls in the same wishy-washy class. Demonstrate confidence in your knowledge and expertise—say "We can do A, B, and C because . . ." or "A, B, and C are exciting possibilities because . . ."

Notice that the above examples are written in the third person. That form speaks for the strength of the media house and its project team. Use the first-person "I" only if you're the lone researcher and writer, which is not a frequent occurrence.

The assumptions that can creep into proposals are infinite. You'll know when you make one because it will sound wimpy, appear vague, and communicate the sense that you lack the knowledge to establish certainty. Remember, a proposal is supposed to demonstrate your expertise, knowledge, and leadership. If you've got it, show it. In a televised discussion of *Silent Spring*, Rachel Carson's heralded book about environmental pollution, one of her researchers quoted her as having said, "When the book is written it will have been based on an unshakable foundation."[3] That ethical and leadership stance is no less a product standard for journalists and public relations and advertising writers.

Above all, never assume that something "should be obvious" or that decision makers will agree with you. Such assumptions insult decision makers and suggest they're incapable of drawing their own conclusions from the given presentation. Decision makers look for expertise, evidence of it, and the promise of a good return on their investment. They can get opinion, uncertainty, or trial and error from anyone on any street corner any time for free. Write clearly with precision, brevity, directness, and confidence and the "obvious" will take care of itself—so will judgment about your abilities and leadership.

PRESENTATION STYLE:
RECOMMENDATIONS

As for style of presentation, it's akin to the rule for brevity. If your decision maker wants to see all components on as few pages as possible, then follow suit, using some white space around units to make the divisions clear and the whole piece easy on the eyes. Try not to jam everything together in the effort to get it all on one or two pages. Better it should be three or four pages with white space between key units. As you learned earlier, journalistic proposals can run more than a few pages, but generally there's an effort to be complete but as succinct as possible.

The rule of brevity holds also in public relations and advertising. If you recall, internal documents describing the content for one or two components may be as compressed as the journalistic proposal, but the final proposal delivered to the client has generous amounts of white space between and within components and runs many more pages.

For example, the petitioner may choose to confine main points of a single component to one point per page, especially if that point calls for extended elaboration. Another choice is to list all main points of a component double-spaced on a single page and then allot each main point a separate page for its elaboration. If an elaboration extends into extensive subpoints of information, these are better handled on a separate page or pages. When information is less detailed, not so complex, devote a single page to each component. In any case, try not to add more pages to the document than is absolutely necessary. Stick to the measure that the presentation must be complete, easy to follow, easy to read and understand, and easy on the eyes.

Brevity also applies to content style—that is, whether information is written out in full sentences through several paragraphs or in running lists of telegraphic phrases—and how that content appears on a page. Blocks and blocks of copy on a page suit the novel or textbook but not a proposal, not even the journalistic proposal.

Proposal style also calls for short paragraphs, sometimes no more than five to six sentences in each paragraph on a page. They may run longer, particularly if the complexity of the component requires extended explanation. If the main point of the subject on a page runs into subpoints, start a new paragraph for each one. Indent the subpoints or subtexts at both the left and right margins so they stand out from the main point text. Center main points and subtexts and use as much white space between as you can spare.

Use a transition to carry the reader's eye into the next point—for example, "In addition, three other factors must be considered. These are. . . ." List these in telegraphic form prefaced by a bullet or similar symbol. The technique eliminates words and calls attention to their significance. Where necessary, elaborate on a point and its impact on the issue in a few brief sentences.

Both narrative and telegraphic styles, or a combination of the two, appear in proposals across all divisions of media, but the telegraphic, bulleted style is preferred, especially for lengthy proposals. The telegraphic format creates a staccato tone which lends itself to quick review by decision makers who have little time to study lengthy explanations.

Even with a normal number of components and limited content, the narrative mode tends to increase the number of pages. The combined style reduces the volume somewhat, but use of the telegraphic, bulleted style throughout produces the least number of pages. It's used more often where the petitioner and decision maker have lived with the problem over a period of time, or have worked together on previous occasions and know each other's preferences, or the petitioner has learned that this is the style the decision maker prefers.

No matter which format style you use, the object is to sustain a narrative tone. The full-telegraphic style can tell a story just as well as the all-narrative format. The former almost takes on the characteristics of a children's book—a main point of information on each page, brief sentences or bulleted items under it, perhaps a graph or other visual on a following page, a transitional device such as a phrase ending with three dots or a symbol directing attention to the next page, and so on. This doesn't trivialize the formal style of a serious proposal or demean the nature of children's books. The telegraphic format is simply a way of illustrating facts and other information that is easy to read and quickly absorbed.

As for the number of paragraphs or telegraphic phrases on a page, no set standard prevails. The number depends on the main points that need to be displayed to inform or convince the reviewer of your proposed intention. Ideally, these may number as few as three but no more than six. Brief subtext sometimes elaborates on these.

The aim across all media divisions is to cover all bases yet present the argument succinctly so that you avoid burdening your readers with more information and verbiage than they want to see or need to have. You might take the advice of the King in

Lewis Carroll's *Alice in Wonderland:* "Begin at the beginning and go on till you come to the end: then stop."[4]

WHY SOME MEDIA PROPOSALS
SUCCEED AND OTHERS FAIL

A successful media proposal identifies the true problem, shows evidence for it, demonstrates an understanding of the problem and decision makers' needs, provides a solution to the problem, and outlines a plan that meets expectations within agreed-on boundaries. The inclusion of these basics indicates an understanding of the effect that proposals should project—realization that it is a reciprocal affair. Decision makers have certain needs and expectations that they communicate to experts whom they expect will set things right. The experts communicate what decision makers really need and, in turn, expect certain recognition for their expertise.

The lack of reciprocity in the communication process is often the factor that leads to proposal failure. Armand Lauffer notes the reciprocity factor in his definition of proposal writing that he says is the

> professional process of communication. Communication implies bringing together; it requires what we have or could have in common. Communication, in its fullest sense, is a reciprocal process. A well-written proposal is based on an understanding of this reciprocity. It presumes that the party or parties being communicated with have a set of interests and concerns. The proposal speaks to those interests. It further presumes a response. If the proposal is properly phrased and targeted, the response is likely to be positive.[5]

Aside from honoring the reciprocity factor, there are certain unspoken needs that enter into the picture. Sensitivity to these is the petitioner's best defense, that is, tuning in on silent expectations that the petitioner feels could enter into decision makers' determinations. As pointed out in Chapter 4, the way to develop that sensitivity is to study each decision maker by observing them in and out of their environments, noting their idiosyncracies, likes and dislikes, and listening carefully, very carefully, to what they say and, especially, what they fail to say.

In the main, expressed and unexpressed expectations differ for decision makers in journalism and decision makers in public relations and advertising, but sometimes they're the same. The object is to be as well informed as possible about your particular decision makers so you pick up on unexpressed expectations, even personality quirks that call for respectful management. There are no guarantees, of course, that such efforts will ensure success, but being aware of hidden obstacles puts you on the alert to prepare for such unknowns. Above all, know your material. Nothing works better than a demonstration of your knowledge about the decision maker's problem(s) and what has to be done about it. Take some precautions. Use a checklist like the one below.

REINFORCING THE APPROVAL FACTOR: A CHECKLIST

Print and Broadcast Journalism

What counts in journalism is the timeliness, audience interest, and feasibility of your proposed project. Test the approval factor of your proposal by asking yourself a few critical questions:

- *Is my project a timely one? If so, how? If not, to what past, current, or impending event can it be linked? How else can I demonstrate the timeliness of my enterprise project?* If you can't demonstrate audience interest, or that the time is now for your project, keep it in your reserve file until the climate out there is just right.
- *Does my information provide my audience some advantage, value, or interest? What?*
- *Is there some long-term public concern, issue, or violation of public trust they should know about?*
- *Does my project idea offer my audience something new, or unique, or previously unknown?*
- *Have I demonstrated that I can get the job done according to my decision maker's expectations?* If you haven't, it's not too late to plug in your justifications.

- *Have I identified my information sources fully, explained what I learned from them clearly and concisely? Have I indicated what information I can put on record?*

- *Have I identified documents researched and described what I learned from them clearly and concisely? Have I referenced other documents to be reviewed and for what purpose?*

- *Have I included what I've collected and know so far and what questions I intend to answer?*

- *Have I described the types of staff personnel I'll need for what purpose and how long they'll be on the project?*

- *Have I anticipated and detailed the cost of necessary outside equipment or services I'll need and why they're needed?*

- *How much of this am I willing to give up if editors like my project but want to reduce the cost? Can I get the job done effectively anyway? Do I have an alternate implementation plan that will cost less, yet achieve the same end?*

- *Have I presented my information accurately? Have I been thorough, yet concise?*

- *Decision makers don't know me or have probably forgotten about the work I've done here and elsewhere. Aside from evidence justifying the merit of my project, what information can I provide to prove my capability in terms of this project and similar past projects?*

- *Is my presentation easy to read, with wide page margins, easy-to-notice points and groups of information, and some white space between units, or is it jammed up in solid blocks of information?*

Don't count on this list as a guarantee against rejection. Your project may be timely and its rationale sound, but rejection always lurks behind the scenes for whatever reason. Editors may not agree with your perception of the project's value, or believe it's too controversial, or decide this month's budget is so tight that approval at this time is out of the question. Don't junk the project—file it and wait for the next appropriate time. Some new event will break and make your project an imperative.

It's unrealistic to expect approval for every proposal you submit. The reasons for rejection run the gamut from external pressures to budget limitations to editorial whim. Don't be discouraged. The way to overcome these amorphous presences is to put the proposal in your reserve file. In the meanwhile, keep collecting data to support your interest and timeliness argument and to strengthen the feasibility factor. If you've guessed right about the merit of your project, your time will come.

Public Relations and Advertising

Timeliness and feasibility also figure in public relations and advertising, but other considerations predominate—accurate problem and audience definition, objectives that address the problem, factual presentation, format style, and unexpected influences.

Timeliness counts in instances where it's important to get implementation under way to reach a ready market. Feasibility becomes a crucial factor when a client holds certain expectations but then restricts the budget necessary to effect them.

It's not uncommon for an agency representative to pose the question of budget up front. Early knowledge of what the client is willing to spend allows quick judgment about whether a project can be done for what the client expects and before the agency's team starts jumping through in-house hoops.

If the client's budget is low, and if the agency determines the project would not be compromised, the agency may cut back on some of its recommendations. If the idea is too good to give away, the agency has the option to refuse to continue with a client who holds a tight purse. If, however, a solution idea that has passed through in-house hoops after the fact and the client has approved all recommendations made, the agency team simply finds a way to get the proposed job done. They might eliminate certain of its implementation features, substitute less costly options, use fewer agency resources, personnel or delivery channels, anything to reduce cost but not their reputation as an effective media house.

Such issues are the responsibility of the client contact person. Your responsibility is to never lose sight of the importance of accurate problem and audience definition. Without that base of assurance, nothing that follows will fly. Also, be sure your objectives address the problem, that you present fact and not fiction, meaning the evidence ought to follow facts and claims.

Ask yourself questions. If you don't know where to begin, use the following as starters, then shape additional questions that meet your particular needs. Again, begin with the problem statement:

- *Have I stated the perceived problem(s) accurately and clearly?*
- *Have I made a clear distinction between it and the true problem(s)?*
- *Is the evidence for the true problem(s) presented so that it can be quickly reviewed and understood?*
- *Is my rationale for attention to this matter at this time convincing? What should I include or eliminate to improve it?*
- *Does my evidence-based description of the audience(s) add insight to client knowledge of their particular audience and/or market?*
- *Is the solution strategy outlined clearly?*
- *Is my argument for its validity convincing, positive, and reassuring?*
- *What questions might the client raise about our plan?*
- *Do we have the evidence to support our responses to these issues? Where in the body of knowledge do these points of evidence appear?*
- *Has anyone double-checked the cost estimate?*
- *What questions can we anticipate about checks on our strategy plan?* (the auditing design)
- *Do we have correct and adequate responses available? What are they?*
- *Is our time line realistic? If not, what modifications are necessary?*
- *Is our agency talent identified and presented fully and clearly so that their ability to do the job creates confidence in the minds of decision makers?*

Raise questions like these to test every portion of your proposal. Review the document with others and ask them for their input. Ask if something is missing, unclear, or unconvincing. Ask what questions they might raise if they were the decision maker. The crafting of a media proposal can use the mind of more than a party of one. There may be differences of opinion, but remember you know the background of this problem. Rely on that if you disagree with another's opinion.

There's one dimension on which all pros agree: the use of clear, precise, concise, and direct language. In their view, you either follow the principles of good English usage and evidence or you don't. And if you don't, the result will be a less effective proposal, very often a failed one. Style, they agree, is flexible, an act of creative presentation directed by the specific nature of the information at hand. If your media house follows a standard format design, then by all means abide by that style. In the next section, media pros explain what they do to increase the chances of a successful outcome.

HOW THE PROS DO IT

Print and Broadcast Journalism

With principles of good writing as a given in proposal composition, pros concern themselves with proposal features discussed earlier and a few others. For journalists, it's mainly timeliness, interest, uniqueness, and feasibility. Notice the pre-thinking they practice to avoid deterrents to their proposition. Here's how one reporter tests the merit of his project idea (see case introduction, Chapter 4):

> I always ask myself questions like: *Is it a ground-breaking idea? Is it innovative? Does it expose a wrongdoing that ought to be corrected? Does it explain something to editors that helps them understand the issue? Does it tell them something they didn't know? How do we know this? Can it be done? Is this person in a position to know? Is there some written documentation?* If I wanted to go down and cover the aftermath of Hurricane Andrew, for instance, that'll probably get rejected because the editor might say "Let's not put our resources into that" or "Travel funds are limited for this month." So you have to examine what you're asking editors to support.
>
> **Jeff Taylor,** national correspondent,
> *Kansas City Star*

Another feels it's a good idea to submit an alternative plan, just in case (see case introduction, Chapter 3):

Even when you know you have a story idea that will register with them [the editors], I always like to explain a worst-case scenario along with a best-case scenario—you know, what's the best story you can get out of this, what's the least story you can expect to get out of the time and energy you're going to expend working on it.

David Hanners, special projects writer,
Dallas Morning News

The next two journalists knew they had subjects of recurring concern because public frustration with certain events had increased over a short period of time and called for still another look by the media (first case introduced in Chapter 5, second in Chapter 4).

There was a lot of public attention focused on drive-by shootings, innocent children caught in the crossfire, especially through the summer. In one case, three children were killed in the same incident. We knew we had to get this story out now before school started.

Jane Daugherty, projects associate editor,
Detroit Free Press

Several polls showed high voter dissatisfaction with their elected officials in recent months. Local elections were not too far away, so we knew this was the right time to propose our story idea: If you're dissatisfied, then run for office, and here's how to do it. We had to get that information out now for it to do any good for anyone who aspired to public office [in the coming election].

Ronald D. Dzwonkowski, projects editor,
Detroit Free Press

Besides testing the project idea, especially one that's fairly complex, this journalist advises testing its "doability," that is, its feasibility (see case introduction, Chapter 3):

I brought five or six of our people together and asked them: *Is this something we can do?* There was kind of an intuitive sense that we could, but they said, "Yes, we think so, but let's give it a month or so to really look into it." I think you have to do that with a big story idea. It was probably a little over a month when we could finally say "Here's what we can do." The military would call it reconnaissance.

John A. Costa, deputy managing editor,
St. Petersburg Times

Broadcast journalists take similar precautions, realizing full well the resistance factor and the competitive arena in which they work (see case introduction, Chapter 3, also in Chapter 6).

Before I propose a story idea to my editor, I critically examine my purpose and intentions: *Will this be good enough to sell? What's this story about? Why is it important? Why should it be aired? Will it appeal to an American audience?* You have to answer each of those questions and others in detail. The rejection rate for the stories I do is much higher than the acceptance because you're pitching for a very limited amount of air time, and you're competing against everybody stationed around the world. So your proposal has to be very strong, very specific, very unique, and has to be very well thought out because when your editor asks about something in these proposals, if you're not prepared to answer, or you haven't done your homework, you end up looking rather foolish, which makes it harder to sell.

I wanted to do a story about the World's Fair in Seville, but it was rejected because it wasn't of interest to the American people. So in that sense, it wasn't well defined. I should have taken it one step further and made a connection between the American public and the Fair, that is: *Why would somebody in Cincinnati, Ohio, be interested?* Timeliness, too—for example, if I wanted to do a story about the economy in Baghdad and how they're recuperating, editors would say "Well, let's make it timely. Let's do it on the first anniversay of the [Persian Gulf] war." If you do that first, it helps.

Victor D. Solis, producer,
NBC News, Europe

Narrow the boundaries of a complex project idea, this broad-caster advises. It reduces the amount of needed air time and cuts execution costs, savings that will sit well with decision makers (see case introduction, Chapter 3).

> I wanted to do a piece on how minorities were treated not just in department stores but in other businesses like restaurants and banks. But the management felt we had to narrow our focus because it would have a lot more impact with a single business, especially the retail stores where everybody goes. You also have to give managers a clear idea [of your plan]. I always call it a "Plan of Action." If I say "Here's the problem: Retail security guards are discriminating against minorities," they want to know very clearly how we're going about documenting that. So I say "Here's what we need: I need three professionals, freelancers, to work as security guards." We have a standard rate for freelancers. And I did that with other needed personnel, people to pose as shoppers, and I set a three-month time frame to do the project; also, how we'd put one freelancer on as a security guard at one mall just to see if it would work. It did, and so we went ahead with it.
>
> **Joel Grover,** investigative reporter,
> KSTP-TV, St. Paul-Minneapolis

The predominate operative in all these defenses against failure is asking the right questions not only to test the problem's merit but to define it clearly in order to set solution strategies on track. Researchers Gerald Nadler and William C. Bozeman have found that poorly defined problems occur because the petitioner failed to raise the right questions and that the way a problem is defined determines the approach to problem solution and the quality of the solution strategy itself.[6] These are concepts proposal writers in public relations and advertising also respect. Here's how they manage those concerns.

Public Relations and Advertising

As Nadler and Bozeman make clear, without accurate identification and articulation of the real problem the rest of the proposal project collapses like a dead balloon. This public relations executive is well aware of that reality. Experience with a similar problem on former occasions primed him for this one. Nevertheless, he verified his understanding of client needs with those involved because planning the objectives and identifying the appropriate audience depends on a clear understanding of the problem at hand. With that established, he knew what had to follow (see case introduction, Chapter 3).

> Two things are critical: the objectives and the audiences by which you will achieve those objectives. Because I've handled this type of problem before [community outreach programs for hospitals], I knew pretty much what the client expected. However, no two clients are alike, so you have to listen closely, check back with their rep to make sure you're both on the same song sheet, and take note of every nuance. On this one, I did a ton of research on audience because, like clients, no two audience environments are exactly alike. If the objectives don't fit the environment, the program is way off the mark. I always test my program with questions like: *What does it do? Does it address the objectives? Does it suit the objectives? Will it produce results?* I could use formal testing methods, but who's going to pay for that? However, if I have an untried idea that looks like it'll work but I'm not sure about it, we'll investigate the feasibility of "X" just so the client knows there's a chance it might work. So you argue your point, justify the program, point to some parallel program where certain of the ideas have worked. That's why they hire you as an expert.
>
> **Gerald Lundy,** executive vice president,
> Southfield, Michigan

Audience also looms large for this public relations expert but for a different reason (see case introduction, Chapter 3):

> Language is a key factor in our work for Bosch because we work with people who are engaged in highly technical operations. So it's our job to first understand this complex technology so that we can then translate it into understandable terminology. Otherwise, we wouldn't be reaching the audi-

ence our client expects us to reach. You can still use all the important factoids related to the product, but you need to explain them in user-friendly language. Try them out on a colleague or a friend. *Do they understand your terminology? Do they know what you're talking about?* An accuracy check on your translation with the technicians wouldn't hurt either.

James A. Bianchi, vice president,
Eisbrenner Public Relations, Troy, Michigan

A proposal may be well received, but other influences sometimes interfere. This public relations executive knows something about that (see case introduction, Chapter 4):

> I've never had a proposal that flat-out failed, but I have done a lot of proposals that have never been implemented—sometimes because the project was too expensive for the client, sometimes there's a need but the proposal just dies because of apathy. A lot of proposals never make it because someone misfired on identifying the problem, and that's usually because no one was really listening to the client from the start and then failed to raise the questions necessary to verify client perceptions. Everything proceeds from accurate problem identification.

Jim Little, president,
First Communications Group, Inc., Findlay, Ohio

For clients who are uncertain about the nature of their problem or what their objectives ought to be, agency initiative must take charge and fill in the blanks for the client. Like other media pros, this advertising executive believes that's the way it should be in any case (see case introduction, Chapter 3, also in Chapter 5).

> Even after querying the client, we still may not have a clear idea of what they're looking for because they're not sure where the problem lies. Actually, it's not up to the client. It's up to us to find out. That's why they've come to us. So once you've covered all the questions you asked at the initial meeting, came up with the answers, and identified the problem, your proposal must make the client understand, not necessarily what they want to say, but what the research says,

what the audience is currently hearing from competitors, what the audience expects to hear, and what the client will need to hear if their message is to provoke a direct response from their audience.

Philip Smith, creative director,
NKH&W, Kansas City, Missouri

In the process of defining the problem and presenting the evidence, experienced proposal writers, including this advertising executive, advise petitioners to

strive for simplicity. That's the magic. I think some clients and agencies try to complicate the business instead of playing it straightforwardly. Complexity doesn't impress and it definitely obscures the overall purpose of the proposal—to convince. The only thing complexity achieves is boredom, even rejection. Successful presentations are succinct. They provide insight without over-verbalizing, over-charting, and a simple, direct approach allows those insights to come through.

Steven S. Swanson, senior vice president
and management supervisor,
Ross Roy Communications, Inc.,
Bloomfield Hills, Michigan

The concept of simplicity applies to presentation form as much as it applies to keeping the verbiage and visuals to a minimum. The style described by this advertising executive is a popular form in both public relations and advertising. In this instance, the proposal was completed for the California Raisin Advisory Board.

Our proposal covered no more than ten pages, ten pages of one to a few lines on each page. First we had a "Business Situation" [statement of the real problem] which just said consumption [of raisins] was off. We had a page that answered the question: *What is the challenge?* Another page described what we learned from our research and itemized the reasons they were having a problem. Another page focused on a list of [focus] group perceptions of the product. We had a page that said "Here's what the strategy is." Then we had a page describing what the campaign idea was. In the following pages we presented the creative idea, and following that, a page with information about executing the campaign. Most of the details about the research were discussed in some depth at the oral presentation because that's a pretty important part of the proposal.

Veronica Buxton, senior vice president
and group management supervisor,
Foote, Cone & Belding, San Francisco

If you've determined that writing a proposal is a methodical, functional, yet creative work of architecture, you've made the right decision and achieved an understanding of not only its science but also its artistry. Now you need to understand how a conclusion statement about the problem translates into still another form of artistry—creative ideas for communication to the general public.

NOTES

1. In M. C. Bromage, *Writing for Business* (Ann Arbor: University of Michigan Press, 1965), 20.

2. A. Lauffer, "Foreword," in S. M. Coley and C. A. Scheinberg, *Proposal Writing in the Human Sciences* (Newbury Park, CA: Sage, 1990), 10.

3. Aired on a weekly literary program titled *Imprint,* 22 April 1991, 8 p.m. EST over TV Ontario during which a panel of writers and authors discuss various published works of interest. This particular panel discussion, titled "Green Books," concerned books published about the problems and preservation of the environment. Panelists included Pat Potter, Lorraine Johnson, and Patrick Carson.

4. L. Carroll, *Alice in Wonderland* (New York: Holt, Rinehart & Winston, 1961), 118.

5. Lauffer, "Foreword," 10.

6. G. Nadler and W. C. Bozeman, "Relationship of Planning and Knowledge Synthesis," in S. Ward and L. J. Reed, eds., *Knowledge Structure and Use: Implications for Synthesis and Interpretation* (Philadelphia: Temple University Press, 1983).

8

The Creative Factor
Cues and Insights

Typically, the final version of a media proposal includes a creative manifestation of the preparatory work. It may appear within the proposal as a communication idea for mass distribution or as a supplement, that is, a stand-alone creative product. The source of these creative manifestations, more often than not, resides in the problem/conclusion statement. The statement's creative power comes from the fact that it represents a synthesis of all the substantiated information accumulated in previous stages of the problem-solving process. Because the statement is a sum of the relevant facts, it serves as a reminder of all the details embedded in it, in themselves "nuggets" of creative inspiration.

Together the statement and its "nuggets" helped you compose the proposal. That's the role they play here, as well. However, the types of creative inspiration they generate vary according to the need required by the problem and the solution strategy it demands. Let's look at some types of creative manifestations.

PRINT AND BROADCAST JOURNALISM

A creative inclusion for an enterprise proposal in this environment can be any number of things: a synopsis of the planned story topped with a catchy headline, a unique phrase that heads a series of feature stories on a topic or issue, section heads for divisions in the narration, and ideas for sidebars, graphics, tables, and charts illustrating the story's high points of evidence. In broadcast journalism, the creative inclusion may be an intriguing opening and dramatic closing over a background of appropriate music or sound effects, suggestions for visuals that might come from stock tape or on-site shoots, and ideas for graphics that illustrate quantitative details in the form of diagrams or pie charts, perhaps illustrated with cartoon characters that move the numbers about. Radio writers can do the same even without the visuals. Descriptions, music, and sound effects help listeners envision what's being said, even quantitative measures. For example, one might use an analogy to describe the increases and decreases in school subsidies for certain student services or broadcast the sounds of schoolchildren to mark reaction to the same situation. The possibilities are endless, and they're always directed by the facts in the case.

PUBLIC RELATIONS AND ADVERTISING

The creative possibilities are even more numerous in these settings. When creative ideas appear in the proposal, they may be no more than a written representation of a head-turning theme phrase, headline, or campaign slogan. Or the creative manifestation may be just a list of ideas for delivering the public message, that is, "devices" such as press releases, sales information packages, pickup flyers, brochures, radio/TV/magazine/ newspaper ads, direct mail, and the like. Other ideas for "getting out the word" might include product information pamphlets, catalogs, sales training films, videos, canned speeches for client executives, an employee seminar or skills program, meeting guidelines, product demonstrations in retail stores, community promotions in cooperation with churches, organizations, schools, and sports events, or any combination of these devices, plus others not mentioned here.

Market researchers at PR and advertising agencies may play a role in the selection and choice of delivery channels and devices. However, that doesn't negate your responsibility. You're expected to demonstrate some familiarity with them and voice what you feel is the most effective means of delivering your particular message.

Some of these creative manifestations may also appear as a stand-alone product—for example, a sample layout of a brochure carrying the campaign slogan or theme phrase, a sample layout of a magazine ad showing the campaign slogan and an inviting illustration, a recording of a catchy jingle for a TV ad along with a storyboard showing the planned visuals and voice-over narrative.

Creative inclusions are expected and can enhance a petitioner's chance of winning project approval. However, aside from desired effect or need, a great deal depends on available time, resources, money, and how many creative ideas you or the team decides ought to be "given away" before getting approval.

CHOICES AND POSSIBILITIES

Time and money may be available, but one or both may be limited. In that case, decide what choices can be made from the field of creative inclusions. Beyond visual representations of creative ideas, that field includes visuals for insertion in your written proposal. These might be graphics of some of the facts, numbers, or recommendations in your proposal, and the cost of producing these ought to be considered as well. Let the purpose of your project, the solution to the problem, and the importance of the project to you or your agency determine how large your investment ought to be. If you decide on including some graphics, first determine where your proposal could be strengthened with a visual representation. Ask yourself these questions:

- *Are any of my facts in any one of my units of information so complex that an illustration might tell the story at a glance?* This could be a pictograph, diagram, map, table, pie chart—anything that takes the place of words yet tells the story.
- *Does my conclusion statement constitute an accurate summary and description of the body of knowledge?*
- *Is my list of recommendations or creative ideas too sterile?*
- *Which item in that list would enhance my argument and generate interest and enthusiasm in visual form? Which one would be less costly and still do the job?*
- *How many visuals are really necessary? How many is too many?* Remember, don't overload the proposal with graphics. Illustrate the complex, not everything. Keep pages to a minimum. The aim is to present a quick, precise, and easy-to-review proposition.
- *If I choose to produce a sample product, can we afford to produce it?*

Whether you opt for one or several, the possibilities for translating them into persuasive visual representations are numerous. But, again, selection is directed by the purpose and needs of the problem and cost.

It's not likely that editors and producers expect a visual representation. However, journalists these days are taking the lead in this regard mainly because so many computer programs now provide capabilities for drawing up page formats, choosing symbols, making sketches, pie charts, tables, handwritten inserts, and the like. If you have those program capabilities, have the time, and believe it would help sell your proposed project, then give decision makers a few visuals. Use them to illustrate a quantitative fact, or how you would like to see your project represented in print or illustrated on the air. Decision makers may modify your ideas or junk them and do it their way, but at least they'll know you've been thinking about this project creatively as well as methodically. Visual representations in public relations or advertising proposals are far more common. But here, too, don't overload the proposal with visuals. Again, brevity is the rule.

You might also decide that a listing of creative ideas coupled with a few graphic inserts in the proposal would be sufficiently persuasive and that any remaining dollars should be reserved for the stand-alone product.

In public relations and advertising especially, reserving the creative product for the stand-alone piece is a precautionary measure. Cost has a lot to do with it, as does the risk involved, that is, giving away creative ideas too soon. The creative sample takes a good deal of agency time and high-paid talent to complete satisfactorily, and either the client or the agency has to pick up the bill. So account executives test the waters on all other components of the proposal before investing any agency dollars on an undecided client. In fact, many executives try to get a signature before revealing the agency's creative ideas or products. At the very least, a meeting of the minds ought to be preliminary to producing a sample of a creative idea.

STRATEGY FOR CREATIVE THINKING

To give expression to your ideas, to create a visual representation or product, call on your innate creative abilities. Start with the knowledge base you've worked hard to accumulate and substantiate, keep your conclusion statement in mind, and rely on your habit of self-inquiry. For journalists and public relations and advertising writers, those self-inquiries generate inspirations for delivering your public message in a dramatic, inviting way.

Try the following self-inquiries for starters and add any of your own as your particular project and its purpose demand:

- *What is the problem?*
- *What does the conclusion statement say about the problem? What, therefore, is our purpose or objective?*
- *Who is our audience(s)? What do they need to know and see?*
- *Does the conclusion statement suggest a title, headline, theme, phrase, or slogan for a public communication that is relevant and inviting for this audience? What is it?*
- *What detail embedded in the conclusion statement suggests a title, headline, or theme? What would that be? Is it more clearly evident in the body of knowledge? If you can't answer this or the previous*

question, you need to review your body of knowledge once more.

- *Is my title, headline, theme, phrase, or slogan punchy enough?* If not, try translating the statement into more concise, precise terms, try eliminating words, or use an S-V-O construction or telegraphic phrase (for examples of headlines, theme phrases, and slogans, review those given in this and preceding chapters' "How the Pros Do It" sections).
- *Is it an accurate and fair representation of the conclusion statement?*

Supported by a wealth of knowledge concerning the problem at hand, relevant self-inquiry clears the way of obstacles and directs the way to creativity. However, the question remains about how that happens. How does one generate a creative idea from a summarized statement? How does the conclusion statement, that is, the outcome of the analyzed body of knowledge, translate into a publicly appealing message?

The answer is a mystery of the mind veiled from view, and perhaps that shroud will forever stay in place. But like all mysteries, one is drawn to this one and compelled to try and understand it. As you will see, that's exactly what so many researchers have tried to help us do.

PART SCIENCE, PART ART, PART MYSTERY

Ordinarily, the creative product alone is seen as the off-spring of a fertile mind. It is, of course, but that doesn't mean that up to this point preparation has not been creative. In fact, many researchers have noted the mix of creativity with systematic method in their own work and in the work of others.[1] Cognitive scientist Morris Stein characterizes the overall function of problem solving as a creative act made up of a series of nested activities, each with its own set of problems requiring creative solutions.[2]

The series of nested activities constitutes an observable order; however, the creative demand that its various activities pose can be frustrating, often requiring modification, even redoing a previously completed task. The sequential order is upset, and the expected linear progression becomes, instead, more recursive and therefore regarded as chaotic rather than systematic. Still, the orderly progression toward creative award is there if one cares to see it.

But even as the preparatory work ends and the calm of closure sets in, the need to translate the closure into an objective form in reality sets off the panic button. Set aside your fears. Whether you realize it or not, the sources of inspiration reside in you. Focus on your conclusion statement, review the body of knowledge, your records. Either the conclusion statement, something in it, or some piece of information in the body of knowledge or your records will trigger an inspiring thought.

Driven by the power of other mental functions we know very little about, images of creative possibilities begin to somehow emerge from these reminders. Sometimes, it's association with past sights, sounds, odors, sensations, or a similar or contrasting experience. Sometimes, it's so spontaneous you can't identify how the connection was made. But believe it, your immersion in the knowledge of your project problem, your background and personal experiences, fired those hidden connections.

You can appreciate the creative paradox between orderly process and random exploration if you reconsider the material covered in previous chapters. From the start, you learned that the next step in the problem-solving process cannot be undertaken unless a previous or parallel activity provided the information necessary to proceed. You also learned that you had to think about and develop productive questions concerning every need at each point in the sequence in order to find the ways and means of obtaining relevant answers and advancing to the next step.

For example, you learned how to raise questions in order to research the perceived problem, identify the true problem(s), understand the audience(s) you had to address, and heighten your sensitivity to decision makers' needs and personal quirks. You also learned that you had to develop critical-thinking questions in order to evaluate the collected knowledge base, organize and analyze it, and draw a fair and informed conclusion/solution statement from the substantiated evidence, guarding against personal biases as well as the biases of others. Finally, you learned how to think systematically and creatively about the design and content for your particular proposal.

The presence of disciplined application in this progression can be characterized as its discipline or order, or as others see it, its "science."[3] The other side of that coin, seen as its "art,"[4] reflects the order acquired from its "science." F. C. Bartlett might refer to the latter as thinking within a "closed system" and the former as "open system" thinking.[5]

Part of that "open system" thinking in media includes the search for cogent questions and self-inquiries at every step of the problem-solving process, the drive for inspired closure to a problem, the formulation of a conclusion/solution statement that stands up to question, developing ideas for implementing a solution strategy, and producing a creative representation of the conclusion statement.

The clash of seemingly opposing forces residing in the same environment may suggest disharmony. In truth, it is the tension between these two opposites that somehow operates harmoniously in the mind to allow for creative freedom—the freedom to formulate productive ideas that withstand challenge.

DISCOVERY IN UNITY

The discoveries this union releases are what make the "chaos" worthwhile and the reward of creative discovery so exciting not just at the point of idea generation for a visual representation or sample product but at each task point throughout the problem-solving and proposal composition process.

Make no mistake, the coexistence of science and art is not exclusive to mass media work. It's present in most areas of human activity, a presence not lost on a number of keen observers. In fact, some have found that the ability to function in both worlds marks the nature of the creative person.[6] For example, Jacob Bronowski, himself skilled in several disciplines, among them philosophy, science, psychology, and education, says the following about this phenomenon of the human mind:

The exploration of the artist is no less truthful and strenuous
than that of the scientist. If science seems to carry conviction
and recognition more immediately, this is because here the
critics are also those who work at the matter. There is not, as
in the arts, a gap between the functions (and therefore
between the fashions), of those who comment and those who
do. Nevertheless, the great artist works as devotedly to uncover the implications of his vision as does the great scientist. . . . Whether our work is art or science or the daily work
of society, it is only the form in which we explore our
experience which is different; the need to explore remains
the same.[7]

James Webb Young shared this view of similarities between
artist and scientist. He was vice president and creative director
at J. Walter Thompson for many years until he retired in 1928.
Shortly thereafter and on invitation from the president of the
University of Chicago, he spent the next five years as the university's first and only professor of business history and advertising.
In his popular text, *A Technique for Producing Ideas,* which is still
in print, Young focuses on the concept that a solid knowledge
base is essential to the process of creative thinking. But he also
makes the point that this knowledge must be so internalized that
its significance is explored again and again in memory until it
emerges as new combinations, relationships, patterns, trends,
and productive ideas.[8]

The mystery of that process is believed to involve hidden
mental functions which psychologist and educator J. Paul Guilford identified during studies conducted at the University of
Southern California in the 1950s and 1960s. Guilford named
three of those principal performers "association," "transformation," and "ideation."[9]

Although it is not yet clear exactly how the triumvirate
performs its magic, the mystery intrigued not only Young and
Guilford but such scientific giants as Bertrand Russell and Albert
Einstein, all of whom wrote in a similar vein about the phenomenon. Einstein defined creativity as "intuition," and Brewster
Ghiselin, author of *The Creative Process,* documents in Einstein's
own words how "intuition" occurred in his work.[10]

In the interest of trying to understand the vigor of our creative resources, it's helpful to understand the meaning of terms attached to creativity.

TERMS, DEFINITIONS, AND CREATIVE GYMNASTICS

Words such as association, transformation, and ideation appear more often in scientific studies, whereas other terms attached to creativity are far more common—for example, inspiration, imagination, creativity, and intuition—but because they're used interchangeably and arbitrarily in reference to creative work, they invite the question: Is there a difference in meaning between them? Some, but because the differences are quite subtle and because they produce much the same result, the differing connotations go unnoticed and, consequently, the terms are used interchangeably. Still, the subtle differences should be noted.

According to dictionary definitions, *inspiration* refers to any stimulus to creative thought or action. In terms of problem solving, it happens when something you recall from past or current knowledge stimulates an association or link to something concerning the situation at hand.

Imagination is an impulse to act on the inspiration, that is, forming a mental image of what is not actually present or creating new images or ideas by combining previous experiences (process of association followed by transformation).

Ideation is similar except that the outlines of the new form or course of action take on a more defined shape.

Creativity may be seen as the mature stage of ideation, where the mind directs manifestation of one's mental imaginings.

Intuition is a state of "knowing," or the direct knowing that something rings true apart from the aid of an external influence. However, as scholars point out, one cannot "know" without first having stored some past or recent knowledge or experience in memory.

When the associative mechanism acts on the memory, all this stored data mysteriously operates to produce an answer or image relevant to the creative problem at hand. Assured that the creative solution evolved from the context of substantiated data and actual experience, intuition tells you it's "right." It can also tell you if it's wrong. If the latter, it means your imagination has missed something or injected something that doesn't fit, and so the engine of your imagination is off the track. You need to go over the facts again and reset your engine in the right direction so it will go the distance to the correct decision.

As for *association* and *transformation,* the former means recognizing a link between items in new knowledge (in this case, the conclusion statement or knowledge base) and something in old knowledge that remains in memory—a phrase, person, object, event, scene, experience, or the like. Recognition then mysteriously transforms (the act of transformation) that link into a viable idea (ideation) that can be supported and manifested. That transformation doesn't have to be an exact parallel of the original; it can be "like" something else. It also can be something unlike the original—a scent, teapot, song title, children at play, a happy or embarrassing event. Still, the association more often than not begins with some word or phrase in the new knowledge or an image those words may ignite. One way or the other, the association-transformation functions operate together to generate an idea related to your creative need that fits the situation and stands up to challenge.

This mental gymnastic of association-transformation-ideation can happen in unison, or there may be a lag between, each waiting on the other, as it were, to convene and produce an idea. Then, at an unexpected moment, the gaps between the trio close, everything falls together, and the idea takes shape in your mind and insists on being taken seriously in manifest form. If the terms related to this mental mystery are used interchangeably, it's because the particular term used is appropriate to its particular context.

Even though the cognitive processes of association-transformation-ideation reside in a place hidden from view, researchers and observers sustain our interest in this phenomenon and, along the way, have uncovered some intriguing insights and clues to the mystery.

WHAT IT TAKES

Investigation of the creative personality conducted in the 1950s by Calvin W. Taylor for the National Science Foundation, University of Utah, prompted numerous studies based on his original framework.[11] Taylor identified units of intellectual, motivational, and personality characteristics that delineated the creative individual.

According to Taylor's findings, creatives are those persons able to sense problems, develop hypotheses, pursue them, and "toy" with solutions. They are persons motivated by curiosity and an inquiring disposition, who need variety, demonstrate preference for the complex, have a tolerance for ambiguity, show resistance to premature closure, yet possess a strong need for ultimate closure, and have a high energy level for vast work output through disciplined work habits. Such people demonstrate a personality that thrives on autonomy, is self-sufficient, sensitive, and more open to the irrational, yet they show stability and control in their own behavior.[12]

Other studies in more recent years mirror Taylor's investigations of the creative individual and one adds yet another dimension to his profile—possession of a sense of humor. In a study of 63 male and female undergraduates, aged 28-61, William Hampes found a relationship between a sense of humor and the ability to generate ideas.[13] Investigations into the makeup of the creative individual continue and no doubt will add even more dimensions to Taylor's original profile.

Due to the work of dedicated researchers, we are tentatively assured that certain preconditions must be present for creative generation. These include acquiring a relevant knowledge base, responding to your natural sense of curiosity by asking others and yourself questions, and cultivating a personality that, above all, demonstrates drive, persistence, and a passion for the problematic. We also know that a high IQ is not a requisite (see Chapter 1), but that a high energy level is desirable, that a sense of humor helps, and that a period of mental incubation of what is known (see Chapter 2), perhaps mistakenly seen as "mental blocks," is to be expected and is necessary.

But the nagging question still remains: What goes on during the incubation period? How does transformation from cold fact to a hot idea occur? Does one just hope for the best? Or does one start with something? If so, what is this "something," and what does one do with it?

We've only had an uncertain glimpse at how the mind operates, what it takes to be creative. Although certainty may be out of reach, we at least have some assurance that creativity is there for the asking, particularly if one knows how to nurture that resource and to labor for its rewards. Make no mistake, even the most creative among us employ various devices and methods to activate nature's endowment. Here are a few.

TRICKS OF THE TRADE

Earlier, you learned how the problem/conclusion statement can work for you. Its words, the knowledge base that produced it, often generate the seed idea for a needed creative product. One or the other becomes, as Calvin W. Taylor puts it, the "toy" the mind plays with in search of ideas for creative transformations that reflect the essence contained in those sources. In previous chapters, you also learned that the play involved a persistent series of self-inquiries. Even though you've already asked yourself some of these questions, ask them again:

- *What is our purpose or objective?*
- *Who is the audience I need to reach? What are their needs, preferences?*
- *What is the current status of thought about this problem with this audience? What audience trends or patterns of habit, attitude, need, or preference are evident?*
- *What does the conclusion statement say? What does it suggest to me in terms of implementation ideas, creative representations?*

- *What is in the conclusion/solution statement or knowledge base that reminds me of something similar in my own experience or someone else's, something from a different context that I've seen, heard, felt, or read about and applies in this case, or something unrelated in memory that applies?*
- *What is in the statement or knowledge base that suggests something entirely new, an anomaly, contradiction, another possibility, yet fits the creative need in this case?*

Remember, the habit of questioning opens the mind to opportunities for associative thinking. Once the questions are posed, they sit in the mind and incubate, merging the statement and elements in the knowledge base with everything you've stored away in your mind from past and present experience. Ask yourself more thought-provoking questions. If the "Eureka!" moment is slow in coming, engage in some physical activity: jogging, walking, working out, bowling, shooting baskets, playing softball, cleaning off your desk, straightening up your office, cooking a meal—whatever works.

During physical activity, whether you realize it or not you'll find yourself preoccupied with your creative problem. In fact, you may be unconsciously dealing with it even in your dreams. Remember what newscaster Scott Lewis said in Chapter 6? He becomes so engrossed in his projects that at times he barely hears what his wife is saying to him. That's a mental state that Dr. John Kabat-Zinn, associate professor of medicine and director of the Stress Reduction Clinic, University of Massachusetts Medical Center, says is the mind's continuous chatter just below the level of consciousness, a state of mind that drives our activities throughout the day and weaves through our thoughts at night. It's a preoccupation that continues until the creative problem is resolved. So get away from the task for a while. Let the mind work for you. Self-inquiry operates even then and without you even being aware of it. You've prepared for the "Eureka!" moment. It will happen.

If getting away from the task doesn't work, try visualization. Studies by Rudoph Arnheim and Jacob Getzels mark its value and recommend it as a means of achieving creative closure.[14]

Their studies apply mainly to artists who work with brush and stone, but you're an artist who works with words and the technique will work for you just as it has for other wordsmiths.[15]

First, write down the conclusion statement. That's what you need to think about. Take in each word. Look at the whole. Understand what it says. Ask: *What does the statement mean to me? How do I see it operating in the real world? How does it relate or apply, and what does it mean to people and their day-to-day lives?* Then, visualize whatever comes to mind about that statement. Write down whatever the statement makes you think of. Do you see a link between it and the creative problem? Does it trigger an idea for a catchy title, a campaign theme, an implementation idea, a visual? If so, that's the image to develop and work with.

If that doesn't help, review the facts in the knowledge base. Toy with them. Write them down, look at them, prioritize them, push them around, look at them again, then look at these as a whole. Ask questions to envision something about those facts, the whole. Or write down words that come to mind as you review the facts, then look at them, and let word association kick in. Or write down whatever provocative headlines or theme phrases you can think of. Keep writing these until you get one that fits the creative problem. You'll know when you hit the right one.

If you're still stumped, try these mental stimulators. Draw doodles or whatever comes to mind. Make sketches of related or unrelated objects, people, symbols, signs—whatever the creative problem makes you think of. Do any of these trigger an image that relates to what is in the solution statement or in the knowledge base? Do you see a relationship between that image and what you need to do?

Sketch a series of pictures that tell a story, one that reveals a beginning, middle, and end. The pictures don't have to be a work of art. Angular lines and circles will do. For each picture, write in a slug line, a sentence, or a line of dialogue, whichever one applies. Or group the series of sketches in sections and give each group a slug line, then see what the total tells you. Does that total call up an image in your mind that relates to the creative problem? Does that image suggest a headline or overriding theme for your project, some implementation ideas, visuals?

Flip through magazines looking for illustrations that link what you see to your creative problem. Even looking through yearbooks, photo albums, or catalogs of sports equipment, historic locations, and antiques can help.

Another helpful activity is to talk about the creative task with friends or colleagues. Even if they fail you, just talking about it helps you straighten out your thinking. Besides, they may say something, related or not, that could plant the seed of an idea in your mind.

The point in all this is to find some device that turns on your imagination and ignites the momentum necessary to arrive at ideation for whatever the creative task requires. No one device always works for everyone in every case. You may have to go through the whole repertoire before spontaneous reaction occurs.

But once you reach that point, everything else concerning the creative problem falls into place. The subheads for units of information in the print article become clear, the content for each broadcast story in a progressive series becomes delineated, the public relations theme suggests the information required for each of its public messages, and the advertising theme or slogan suggests both the visual and accompanying copy needed in its various public communications.

HOW THE PROS DO IT

The creative journey is not an easy one, and practiced media pros know this better than anyone. Understandably, some of them were not able to explain how they achieved their creative ideas, but all of them pointed to reliance on both their knowledge base and its outcome, recalling what they learned and that their "intuition" told them they had hit on an idea that fit the bill. But notice that their "intuition" speaks to them mainly because *they* push the "on" button with their own self-directed inquiries.

As you now know, and what researchers Guilford and Taylor and many others keep reminding us, recall relies mainly on a knowledge base so well internalized and considered that its bits and pieces can be pulled from memory at will. Novelist Pete Hamill characterizes this incubation period in a similar manner but in a more dramatic way. Writers produce creative ideas, he says, because they are "rememberers." Those remembrances are then "marinated in memory and when writers need them, they recall them and make associations and see the connections between them."[16] Journalists and public relations and advertising writers are not novelists, but they are "rememberers" and also rely on a knowledge base grounded in substantiated information that informs, often persuades, and sometimes entertains. Here's how pros describe their experience with the creative task, the result of which may be partially or fully disclosed in the proposal or reserved for later presentation. Notice their reliance on the knowledge base and on self-inquiry to reach the coveted point of "spontaneous" ideation.

Print and Broadcast Journalism

The series that won Jeff Taylor and Mike McGraw a 1991 Pulitzer carried a main title, "Failing the Grade," and a subtitle identifying the source of the failure, "Betrayals and Blunders at the Department of Agriculture." For six days thereafter in the series, the main title was sustained, but subtitles reflected the theme represented in each day's presentation of information relevant to the overall theme (see Chapters 4, 6, and 7 for other details concerning their proposal).

> I can't adequately tell you how we hit upon the themes and titles for our series. We were so immersed in all of it that at first we couldn't see the forest for the trees, not until we got all the information together, saw it as a whole. I guess the gist of it is that the information told us what the themes had to be.
>
> I like the idea of treating this in a very workmanlike fashion, maybe the way a prosecutor would put together a case. I want to go step by step, document things along the way and pull back at some point and say: *What have we got? Where are we now? Is this the same story now that we thought it*

was going to be? How has it changed? You deal with the facts.
That's what tells your story.

Jeff Taylor, national correspondent,
Kansas City Star

Taylor's partner agreed:

> After 16 months of gathering every stick of information we
> could on an agency as big as the U.S. Department of Agricul-
> ture, the collected mass compels an editorial function—that
> is, reducing the checked-out information down to a sentence
> or two that sums up the story. And unless you have a clear
> idea of the problem you're working on, you can't do that or
> tell the real story for the reader.

William M. (Mike) McGraw, projects reporter
and reporting coach, *Kansas City Star*

The creative product that won David Hanners and the *Dallas
Morning News* the 1989 Pulitzer was another team effort. But the
dramatic effect of the 12-page layout for the special section insert was made possible mainly because of Hanners' knowledge
base and conclusion about its relevant content (see Chapters 3
and 7).

> This story was like following clues in a mystery case. That's
> true in any news story, but it seemed more so in this instance.
> The story broke down easily into four parts because that's
> how the investigation problem evolved toward its solution.
> The parts and their final outcome allowed the graphics
> people to come up with page designs and experiment with
> how the pages would look laid out and how the photos would
> be placed. One of the things they wanted was a theme title
> to cover the four parts. That rose naturally out of the sum of
> the information in the four parts. We came up with this
> banner strip that ran across the top of each page in the
> section: "Anatomy of an Air Crash." The story carried itself,
> but the presentation made it noticeable.

David Hanners, special projects writer,
Dallas Morning News

Like the previous journalists, Candy Cooper was guided by the knowledge base she had collected to understand the story she wanted to write. But unlike their enterprise projects, hers was a completely independent, almost secretive effort because she wanted a solid body of evidence before proposing her story to decision makers (see Chapters 4, 5, and 6 for other details). That independence extended into offering suggestions on how she felt the story should be presented.

> You have to get rather specific with the editor. You have to say, "I envision a two-day series, three stories each day, one main story that would be 100 inches long and two sidebars, each 30 inches long, plus a 10-inch graphic and photos." Once you've sold them on the idea, you have to be quite specific as far as what the package will look like, which doesn't happen until the end and when editors are certain you have adequate information to back up what you've learned is the situation. In this case, that situation and the information about it turned out to be my summary statement and the "lead" [the opening statement]: "Nearly one in four women who reported a rape or attempted rape to the Oakland Police Department last year was told, in essence, that she was lying, even before her case was investigated."
>
> **Candy Cooper,** investigative reporter,
> *San Francisco Examiner*

The extent of a reporter's role in the visual presentation of a proposed enterprise varies from newsroom to newsroom. But if you're asked, have a plan in mind and an engaging statement and/or title for it. Cooper was able to detail her vision of the presentation format and that's the way it appeared, except those who handle headline composition gave the series its summary title, "A Question of Rape." Have a plan, but remain flexible to other inputs. If they fit, accept them. If they don't, be prepared to explain why. That doesn't mean you'll get your way every time, but you should be able to justify your objections.

Arrival at the creative end point in broadcast work takes a route not unlike the one in print journalism. Here, too, it's a solid knowledge base that gets the broadcaster there.

Vince Wade delivered his enterprise idea verbally but not before arming himself with answers to challenging questions he knew he'd be asked. He also relied on his knowledge base for creative ideas. Wade's enterprise story rose out of a court trial he and other staff members had been covering about a former Detroit chief of police, now serving time for misuse of drug investigation funds. Having covered the story, he knew that the source of the problem could be traced back to the lack of oversight by supervisors and the absence of accountability to anyone in authority, including then Mayor Coleman Young and the City Council, and that the city's $1 million deficit was in large part due to equally loose management.

> I knew that there was a lot of squandering of money either through larceny or incompetence, or bungling, missed deadlines, bad judgments, bus drivers pocketing dollar bills because they didn't have a mechanism to accept dollars—things like that. The evidence we had added up to a single conclusion—sloppy city management. So the theme statement and visual for this story was a natural: "taxpayer money down the drain." That came out of the readings [news clips] and research. The visual just occurred to me. "Down the drain" just lent itself visually to the theme.
>
> **Vince Wade,** reporter, WJBK-TV, Detroit

For the thematic opening, Wade suggested a visual showing a sink faucet, but instead of water flowing down the drain, the visual showed a sink full of play dollar bills being electronically swirled down the drain. Wade also showed a montage of what he called "financial screwups," and the series included excerpts from interviews with Detroiters talking about expected but missing public services. Investigations into city management problems were ongoing, so Wade's series proved to be both timely and informative for local taxpayers.

Timeliness and new information also characterized Scott Lewis's project (see Chapters 4 and 6). After an intensive three-month investigation, Lewis had gathered a massive amount of

material on previously unknown information about white su-
premacy groups in Michigan. Here's how he handled it to arrive
at *ideation:*

> I always joke that you usually have 25 pounds of stuff to fit
> in a 5-pound bag. Then what becomes the most difficult job
> of all is sorting through it, organizing it, and putting it into
> nice little packages so people can hear it the first time and
> understand it. It has to be written in such a way that people
> who did not hear parts 1 and 2 will understand the other
> parts, which have to stand on their own. So what I try to do
> first of all is find out: *What is the bottom line on this story? What
> is this all about?* The bottom line always goes to the top. In
> this case, it was "There is a rising tide of hatred in Michigan
> and an increasing number of white supremacy and neo-Nazi
> groups are becoming more and more active." We had a title
> for each part, but the title for the series had to cover the
> whole. That turned out to be "Nazi Neighbors."
>
> **Scott Lewis,** investigative reporter, WJBK-TV, Detroit

The series ran in 3-minute segments over five nights during
the evening news hour. Lewis, an Emmy award-winner, won awards
from the Michigan Association of Broadcasters and the Anti-
Defamation League for this project.

Public Relations and Advertising

The knowledge base is no less a source of creative inspiration for public relations and advertising writers than it is for print
and broadcast journalists. Notice that the key to generating ideas
is again the habit of self-inquiry, as well as familiarity with the
knowledge base.

This public relations executive had a crisis management
problem to resolve for her client and its product, Hygrade's Ball
Park Franks. Several consumers claimed they injured their
mouths on sharp objects when they bit into a frank. After a
thorough police investigation, the charge turned out to be a
hoax. But sales had dropped and still another problem had to be
resolved—image repair. The executive attributes ideas for resolv-

ing that problem to "logic," determinations made possible because she and her staff had done their homework and raised questions that inspired the ideas they put forth to the client. There was no time to submit written proposals. This was a crisis situation. Immediate action was necessary. So, the research, solutions, implementation strategy, and promotional ideas were delivered verbally within the span of a few weeks.

> We had explored the city [Livonia, MI, a suburb of Detroit] where Hygrade has some of its largest plants, the area around its headquarters there, and became familiar with places where people go to eat hot dogs. *Where do people gather in greatest numbers to eat hot dogs?* The ball park, of course! *And what would be the most logical city to work with us?* Livonia, of course, which they did. Their cooperation [client's informative inputs and community cooperation] gave us the signal to head up our promotions with "Livonia Loves Hygrade." We told the media what we planned on doing: Ball Park Hot Dog Day at the ball park, a 25-cent day at a local restuarant for a Ball Park hot dog, a party, various types of events, and free hot dogs at a rally to kick off these and other promotions. We got a lot of local coverage, which then attracted national media attention, including coverage by *Fortune* magazine. Consumer faith in Ball Park hot dogs was restored and so was the company's image.
>
> **Beverly Beltaire,** president,
> PR Associates, Inc., Detroit

Where the situation is one other than a crisis, it takes time and an elaborate proposal to win a new client or sustain a house account. The latter was the case for public relations executive Hud Englehart (see Chapters 4 and 6). His agency's effort for a standing client, United Airlines, passed through a two-year process of research, discussions, and proposal documents, including one with promotion ideas for the proposed implementation strategy.

> Our creative team was well versed in information concerning the product, the consumer, the market, the required media

channels, what the client wanted, the whole thing. They knew our thematic, "Communication Is Service," and that the client had failed to communicate their policy of consumer service to employees and so employees had failed to convey that behavior to consumers. The team also had information about the consequences: dissatisfaction with all aspects of airline travel such as delayed departures, fears about safety, flight attendance failings, etc. So the issue here was: *How are we going package the thematic to convince the client that we can change perceptions out there?*

That was answered by translating the thematic into eight ideas which instilled the service concept in the minds of both employee and consumer groups. The employee program was backed up with a consumer strategy that included a radio infomercial concerning maintenance delivery on UA planes, a newspaper ad showing an airline pilot talking about on-time arrivals and departures, a television commercial demonstrating flight attendant courtesy and talking about UA's quality food, etc. The attracting intro for each was different, of course, but service delivered was the gist of each.

Hud Englehart, executive managing director,
Hill and Knowlton, Chicago

The transformation from the "scientific" mode to its flip side, the creative mode, is as much a mystery to advertisers as it is to other media pros and creatives. However, attempts at explanation always end on the importance of the knowledge base and self-inquiry. Here's how one creative director described development of the "waterfall" TV commercial for Chrysler's Jeep vehicle, the Grand Cherokee (see Chapters 3 and 6):

The new Cherokee model had been launched within the past 12 months and its brand, the Jeep, was well known for its quality, its technology, its sports utility. We knew from the research we had that consumers still expected all that, but now they wanted, as well, passenger-car features along with Jeep durability. That was our creative track. But in advertising you have to talk about quality and all the rest in a more interesting and entertaining way. For one thing, you make it simple. If you talk about how quiet the car is, which translates into whatever quality aspect there is, you don't talk about how the rivets fit together, you talk about a quiet-riding car. So the question was: *How do you do that in a Jeep-like way?* You don't necessarily use traffic noise. That's not where the Jeep lives. The Jeep lives out there in the wilderness, which raises the question: *Well, how do you do that?* So the next question had to be: *What makes noise in nature that we can use that translates the difference between the intrusions of outside noise and insulation against them?*

We talked about things, outdoor things, mountains, avalanches, but waterfalls kept coming up because most of us had had that experience on road trips, camp trips. So we decided that was more universal and might work. We gave the viewer a sense of driving up a steep road toward a waterfall, seeing it but not hearing it because, like the driver in the Cherokee shown in the commercial, the viewer was inside the vehicle. Then the driver opens the door, and the roar of the waterfall makes the point without words: Here's a tough sports utility vehicle, well insulated against outdoor road noise, yet it drives and looks like a quality passenger car. No voice-over, no signature slogan was needed. The silent visual was more effective without it. The waterfall commercial evolved from an analysis of the research, and the outcome of that analysis was what the commercial had to convey—the new Cherokee Jeep model is built with a quality that, among other advantages, sealed its interior against outdoor noise, yet was designed to give the look of a fine passenger automobile.

Gary Topolewski, managing partner
and executive creative director,
Bozell Worldwide, Inc., Southfield, Michigan

The waterfall commercial aired nationally over both cable and major networks from April 1993 to August 1994 and proved to be a winning sales mover for the Jeep Cherokee. The TV commercial was supported by other media promotions informing consumers about the model's other quality features.

Because the need in advertising is to be informative in a more entertaining way, the research thematic has to have an identifiable factor, or as Topolewski put it, a "universal" flavor.

That's what happened in the next case—the California Raisin account (see Chapter 7). Research revealed that the product had an image problem. People surveyed characterized raisins as wimpy, dull, and boring, and "not the sort of person that you'd want at a party." The attribution of human characteristics to an inanimate object by those surveyed was an important clue.

However, the first creative attempt to give the raisin human physical characteristics was junked by the creative group not because it didn't receive high marks in quantitative testing but because earlier research indicated there had to be a way of "beefing up the [humanized] figure" and making it entertaining to watch. The agency's group manager explained that the "beefing up" turned out to be an image most people take to easily, the animated cartoon figure.

> The test public liked our initial creation, but we had to ask: *What more can we do to make it very hip, very cool, very contemporary?*—just the opposite of the way people in focus groups had perceived raisins. "Hip, cool, contemporary" was our thematic directive. We didn't do anything revolutionary. We just worked with the sort of things that mainly came out of our focus group research, things people associated with being hip and cool, being a fun person to know. The image kept its human qualities, but in the second raisin figure it took on exaggerated features—tennis shoes on oversized feet, gloves on oversized hands, oversized sunglasses, etc., dancing to the rhythm of a contemporary tune written especially for the commercial.

> **Veronica Buxton,** senior vice president
> and group management supervisor,
> Foote, Cone & Belding, San Francisco

The research gave Buxton's team direction, but initial interpretations were set aside in favor of what Buxton called an "instinctive" need for refinements. They didn't do anything "revolutionary," as Buxton points out, but note what they did do: "We just worked with the sort of things that mainly came out of our focus group research, things people associated with being hip and cool, being a fun person to know." Clearly, those instincts were motivated by the need to link research findings to familiar experiences with which people could identify—in this case, a Mickey Mouse type cartoon figure common in almost everyone's life experience. Recall of those pleasant memories gave the raisin life in the image of something more universally familiar and amusing than the humanized creation that originally passed audience approval. The new figure became an animated happy-faced cartoon image, something that works for raisin eaters of all ages. The agency has licensed the dancing raisins to dozens of companies since the TV commercial first aired in 1987 for its client, the California Raisin Advisory Board.

At Wunderman Cato Johnson creatives were looking for a memorable way to tell the complex story of their client's product, Du Pont NDT Systems. NDT stands for nondestructive testing, a technological method of testing the tensile strength of industrial materials at the job site. Testing materials for their tensile strength and other qualities was costly and often environmentally dangerous, but Du Pont had developed various cost-efficient testing methods in ways that were safe environmentally and safe for the tester. The client wanted the manufacturing industry to know this and to choose Du Pont's NDT systems. James Turnbull and Mary Grams participated together in this explanation of their creative effort for Du Pont.

> We established criteria and raised questions based on the research given to us. In the best conditions, you also have all the competitive advertising stuck on the walls so that you can say, "Yes, but we've also got this, this, and this." Then you ask: *Would I have done that campaign that way? If not, why not? What do we have that goes one better on competitors?* Then you need to say: *What's a dramatic way to say and show that?* You have to think like an investigative reporter.
>
> **Mary Grams,** vice president
> and creative director-art,
> Wunderman Cato Johnson, Detroit[17]

The research information, Turnbull explained, showed that Du Pont had a broad offering of solutions to a variety of testing needs for manufacturers in diversified industries. To deliver that message, the creative team developed a series of ads all of which carried the same thematic head: "Think what Du Pont can do for you." Turnbull then explained how that conclusion statement translated into an appropriate illustration, subhead, and text copy explaining what each one of NDT's several systems could do for a prospect's particular testing problem.

One ad in the series showed an illustration of a familiar twelfth-century structure, the leaning tower of Pisa, displayed the main head, and then the subhead, which read "With Du Pont's Skan 'N' Stor, you can keep all your data straight, so that critical structural changes don't go undetected." Another with the main head showed the wooden horse of Troy and Grecian troops pouring out of its hollow center from a side trapdoor to defeat the enemy and conquer Troy. The subhead read "Du Pont NDTRapid could have warned the Trojans about the trapdoor while in the field in just 10 seconds." Here, Turnbull explains how these creatively rendered messages of highly technical information came to be.

> We thought of analogies and parables from the classics that would take a technical experience and tie it into a story, one that was totally understandable and interesting. In this instance, we used both an analogy and a familiar parable—the leaning tower of Pisa and the wooden horse of Troy. In the first, the copy focused on one of Du Pont's on-site systems that recorded structural changes that needed attention. In the second, the copy explained the testing device available that would have made it possible to figure out where the cracks were in its structure [the outline of the trapdoor] and how they [the Trojans] would have gotten them all [the Greeks] if they had Du Pont's testing system.
>
> **James Turnbull,** senior vice president,
> group creative director,
> Wunderman Cato Johnson, Detroit

Clearly, translating technical data into the familiar language of a story was an inspired touch. So were the images of the tower and the wooden horse. But notice that these were triggered by past experiences with those images, perhaps seeing a picture of the tower in a travelogue or having read Homer's epic poem *The Iliad.* In each case, the connection seen between new knowledge and old knowledge triggered an association to one of Du Pont's featured systems and generated a brilliant idea for communicating a complex topic in a form that both a general audience and an audience of industrialists could understand.

Media creatives transform substantiated research into catchy heads, slogans, and products in much the same way. The examples above illustrate that the creative exploration moves from a base of substantiated research and moves through a process of association-transformation-ideation by the same device that drove preparation of the written proposal—self-inquiry. What goes on in the secret corridors of the mind still remains unknown to us. But along with the insights of scholars and researchers, these pros have given us some clues about the passageway to an idea, one that produces closure to a media problem in the form of a message quickly and easily understood, a summarizing and familiar visual, and an overall unity of information carrying a distinctive appeal, preferably a universal one.

This doesn't mean the passageway leads everyone to the same idea. Not at all. Minds store different pieces of information, experiences, and memories. These produce different associations. That's the magic of creativity. Its test in media, however, depends on its relationship to the creative problem. One must always ask: *Among all ideas placed on the table, which one is most representative of the substantiated knowledge base and, at the same time, demonstrates high potential as a solution to the creative problem at hand, greatest promise of audience impact?*

All your preparation up to this point should give you the answer to this question, and if you can explain why one particular idea is better than the other, then you can be fairly sure you're on the right track.

If transformations turn on the momentum directed by the facts linking them to relevant images in memory that then lead to an idea that fits the creative need, then hitting on a workable idea is rarely, if ever, accidental, spontaneous, or even miraculous. It only seems so because one cannot see, feel, or hear the evolving process of creativity rising to the surface to express itself as an idea.

Moreover, it's easy to forget about the investment of hard work and deep thought that preceded the moment of discovery. Nor is one aware of that disciplined process during periods of self-inquiries that churn around in the wondering mind. Suddenly, this "continuous chatter," as Dr. Kabat-Zinn puts it, surprises the thinker with a solution that fits the creative end and brings closure to the problem as well as peace of mind for the creative explorer.

To be sure, this remarkable "talent," this "stroke of genius," is an exhilarating moment, but the point now is to sell decision makers on the fact that your creative solution does, in fact, fit what decision makers now know is their need, their ultimate purpose. That task is what the next chapter is all about.

NOTES

1. For example, see R. Arnheim, *Visual Thinking* (Berkeley: University of California Press, 1969); F. C. Bartlett, *Thinking: An Experimental and Social Study* (London: Allen & Unwin, 1958); and J. S. Bruner, "On Perceptual Readiness," in J. C. Harper, C. C. Anderson, C. M. Christensen, and S. M. Hunka, eds., *The Cognitive Processes* (Englewood Cliffs, NJ: Prentice Hall, 1964), 225-27.

2. M. I. Stein, "The Creative Process and the Synthesis and Dissemination of Knowledge," in S. A. Ward and L. J. Reed, eds., *Knowledge Structure and Use: Implications for Synthesis and Interpretation* (Philadelphia: Temple University Press, 1983), 363-96.

3. C. E. Moustakas, *Heuristic Research* (Newbury Park, CA: Sage, 1990); and W. R. Shea, "The Mainspring of the Arts and Sciences," in W. R. Shea and A. Spadafora, eds., *Creativity in the Arts and Sciences* (Canton, MA: Science History Publications, 1990), xiii-xviii.

4. Shea, "The Mainspring of the Arts and Sciences"; and R. Weisberg, *Creativity: Beyond the Myth of Genius* (New York: Freeman, 1993). Also see R. Grudin, *The Grace of Great Things: Creativity and Innovation* (New York: Ticknor & Fields, 1990).

5. Bartlett, *Thinking*.

6. For example, see M. Antebi, *The Art of Creative Advertising: A Visual/Verbal Problem-Solving Approach* (New York: Reinhold, 1968); Stein, "The Creative Process"; and K. Strike and G. Posner, "Types of Synthesis and Their Criteria," in Ward and Reed, eds., *Knowledge Structure and Use.*

7. J. Bronowski, *Science and Human Values* (New York: Julian Messner, 1956), 92.

8. J. W. Young, *A Technique for Producing Ideas* (Chicago: Crain, 1977). Young's book was first published in 1940 and reissued through five editions and at least seventeen printings.

9. J. P. Guilford, "Creativity: Its Measurements and Development," in S. J. Parnes and H. F. Harding, eds., *A Source Book for Creative Thinking* (New York: Scribner's, 1962), 151-68.

10. B. Ghiselin, *The Creative Process* (Berkeley: University of California Press, 1952).

11. C. W. Taylor, "A Tentative Description of the Creative Individual," in Parnes and Harding, eds., *A Source Book.*

12. For other investigations describing the creative individual, see I. A. Taylor and J. W. Getzels, *Perspectives in Creativity* (Chicago: Aldine, 1975).

13. W. P. Hampes, "The Relation Between Human and Generativity," *Psychological Reports* 73, no. 1 (1993): 131-6.

14. For example, see Arnheim, *Visual Thinking;* and J. W. Getzels and M. Csikszentmihalyi, *The Creative Vision: A Longitudinal Study of Problem Solving in Art* (New York: John Wiley, 1976).

15. See E. K. Parsigian, *Mass Media Writing* (Hillsdale, NJ: Lawrence Erlbaum, 1992).

16. A comment made by Pete Hamill during a January 27, 1994 interview with Charlie Rose, host of his own weeknight PBS program *Charlie Rose.*

17. Mr. Grams is now principal owner of Grams' Group, Grosse Pointe, Michigan.

9

Getting to "Yes"

The Art of Proposal Delivery

Your proposal is written, packaged, and ready for presentation. Think your work is done? Think again. Now you have to argue for it before an audience of decision makers—not before just one set of decision makers but several. In journalism, the rite of passage begins with the supervising editor and moves on through one or more levels of upper management. In public relations and advertising, the creative director may be your first judge and jury, then the account executive or supervisor, and then a group of agency personnel involved in the project. Once it's been decided that your oral argument passes muster, it then moves on to the final set of decision makers, the client.

It's true that a supervising editor or account executive usually delivers the oral argument, but not always. Editors and account executives like a show of competent personnel around them. Decision makers like it, too. The appearance of a team demonstrates joint participation in and agreement with a well-thought-out strategy. It's a confidence booster for decision makers and could well speed final approval. So, although you may not be the principal presenter, you along with other team members must be prepared to participate.

The presenting team always includes a project director and usually members having the type of expertise the project requires. In journalism, that always means the reporter(s)/writer(s), sometimes the artist, and perhaps a production representative. In public relations and advertising, the presenting team includes the account executive and other top agency personnel such as the director of research, director of marketing, the creative director, sometimes the artist, and frequently the writer(s). You may be called on to deliver a portion or portions of the oral presentation or answer questions, particularly regarding that portion in which you were heavily involved. That's because any proposition presented to those in authority is rarely an exclusive responsibility. A solid proposal requires solid thinkers at each stage of its development, and you can expect to be involved in all of them, including the organization and presentation of the oral argument.

CUES AND CLUES

Can the writer rely on the written presentation for the oral argument? Yes, of course, but only on its most important and persuasive points. Communication consultants recommend three major points and no more than five subpoints per major point. Why this limitation? Because studies have shown that information overload tires receivers and interferes with efficient processing and recall.

In fact, they recommend brevity throughout the course of any oral presentation. Kevin R. Daley, president and chief executive of public speaking advisers at Communispond, Inc., New York, says "If you can do it in 20 minutes, you have the best shot at the minds of the people present."[1]

Listener attention is elusive. It tends to fade in and out, often losing itself to fantasy after the first few minutes. That doesn't mean you can't lure listeners back from Wonderland. You can.

There are ways to do that, which you'll learn about later in this chapter.

As for selecting the important points and pulling together data that supports them, it's not a daunting task. Remember, you've lived with this project for weeks, months, maybe years. You know everything there is to know about the problem. You have a firm grasp on its background information. You've discovered how the problem can be solved, hit upon an idea around which you've designed a solid solution strategy, checked out the strategy and maybe even tested it. You're confident the strategy will sell because it answers decision makers' needs and expectations and even takes into account their personal quirks, likes, and dislikes. Besides, you have the data to substantiate the main points of your argument. Every generality and detail in the proposal is in your head, in every bone and sinew of your body. You know what must be said.

Furthermore, you've had time to get to know the decision maker(s) through either personal contact or your project director (see Chapter 4). You've had several opportunities since the beginning of the project to demonstrate your reliability and expertise, maybe even to "pre-sell" your project. You've won their confidence and trust that you can do the job. Don't underestimate the rapport factor. It's the chemical ingredient in the stew of opposing forces that often seals an agreement to the advantage of all concerned.

So, no need to panic—you're *prepared* to verbalize your proposition. Now you need to know how to deliver it in order to win that final seal of approval. In this chapter, you'll learn how to organize a persuasive face-to-face presentation and deliver it convincingly.

ORGANIZE FOR UNDERSTANDING

The goal of any presentation is to persuade someone or a group of persons to act on your suggestions because those recommendations respond to *their* needs and *their* expectations. So what you want your print or broadcast editor to *say* is "Sounds solid. It's timely. Go ahead, do it." What you want the client to *do* is sign on the dotted line.

To get to "yes," first take a few steps back and think about how *you* would like to hear this presentation, what information you'd like to hear at the start, next, and so on. It will probably fit the protocol commonly followed; that is, identify yourself, recognize your audience, articulate succinctly what the problem is, why it should receive attention (the rationale), what you discovered about it, and how, based on the evidence, you plan on resolving the issue.

Then review your written document, information in your files, and all the notes you've taken throughout the various phases of preparation. That review will remind you of statements and nonverbal messages communicated by decision makers during preliminary considerations of your proposal.

Why this exercise after having labored through the process of researching and writing the final document? Because the written proposal can help you shape the auditory message. It also can prevent possible blunders at the crucial moment of delivery. Reviewing files and notes will remind you about certain notations made during the preparation process: notes on decision makers' personalities, preferences, and dislikes, their attitudes about their environment, product, and limitations, all the little subtleties that are not in the written document but could influence whether you'll get a final "yes" or a surprise "thanks, but no thanks."

Maybe all those influencing factors are already ingrained in your mind, maybe not. Basking in the euphoria of making it to the final stage, it's easy to forget about them, and the written document won't remind you of all those influencing factors. Better to be on the safe side and perform the complete review exercise.

Just as important, the review helps you decide what points in the written document respond most persuasively to decision makers' needs and expectations, what they'll accept at face value, and what statements will need visuals to illustrate or emphasize a point of information (for how visuals can be used, see the examples given below and a more detailed account in Chapter 10). Make a list of those points under columns headed "Include" and "Set Aside." The latter may not be as important as other points, boring to hear, or too detailed for an audience to tolerate. Nevertheless, they may serve their purpose as alternatives. Include a brief note on why you chose each "include" item, what needs to be said about it, and whether a visual would amplify its significance. Set the chart aside and refer to it as you begin drafting your oral argument.

THE THREE-PART PLAN

No single organizational pattern fits all projects. However, a very basic one is the three-part format. Similar to narrative design, it has a beginning, middle, and ending, sometimes with subsections in the middle. A close cousin is one that some speech consultants recommend: Tell 'em what you're going to tell 'em, tell 'em, then tell 'em what you told 'em. However, in media proposals the latter model may not always apply as strictly as its three-part plan suggests.

To avoid tiring an audience, most media presenters try to keep within the three-part minimum. There will be occasions when the nature of the data commands more breakdowns than just three units, but even so the narrative model with its subsets is the one most frequently adopted. The important thing is to become so familiar with your file notes and the contents of the leave-behind document that the data speak to you, telling you the number of parts the information falls into and what needs to be said in each part. The following demonstrate how the narrative model plays out for oral presentations in the mass media.

Print and Broadcast Journalism

Suppose you're a print or broadcast journalist and have been called upon to give a summary report of your proposal before a final group of editorial judges. You might open with the following *beginning:*

> I'd like to begin by saying that Joe and I appreciate all the guidance our supervisors, Mac Smith and Ernie Fisher, have given us on this project. And we appreciate the time you've taken from your busy schedules to hear what we believe will make an informative and timely story.

Journalistic settings are informal, and usually everyone knows who the main players are. Still, it's a good idea to establish who you are and, as a matter of courtesy, to name your teammate(s). It's also important to thank key people for their presence, and it doesn't hurt to arouse their curiosity about your project or to express faith in its value:

> Some months ago, Joe and I raised the question: Why has the city's Department of _____ failed to realize its purpose? Established over two years ago, it has yet to show taxpayers any tangible results. As you know, the department was organized to _____ .

Explain the department's mission and purpose and state the total tax dollars allocated to it since its inception. Next, introduce the problem and its background. Then explain what you've learned about it. For example,

> But we've since learned that's not what our tax dollars are doing. Instead, the department has been involved in activities outside its given mandate, throwing money into self-promotion, unnecessary out-of-state trips, and chauffered transportation, which I'll detail later on. But first let me explain why Joe and I pursued this story.

Then present your rationale, the reason why this story deserves attention and why it's important to go with it at this time:

> We feel very strongly that citizens have a right to know where their dollars are going. It's our job to be their advocate, and

that's especially important at this time because elections are coming up. Not surprisingly, one of the proposals on the ballot calls for an allocations increase for this department.

The *middle:* Tell them what they'll see and hear and the evidence substantiating your discoveries. This is a good place to show a visual.

So today we want to show you how the department has mis-handled its current funds. First, let me show you the amount of funds received and the expenditures made in the past year. Notice that 85% has gone to underwrite _____ , _____ , _____ , and only 15% to _____ , leaving at least half a dozen promised services shown here unfulfilled.

To establish the legitimacy of your data, show the date they were collected, the sources used, and explain by what means the information was checked and corroborated, then move to the next issue:

The question is, why was this extravagance allowed and by whom? After some investigation, here's what we learned _____ .

Explain what you found, who told you what, the verifications obtained, and the opposing views obtained. Then, state that a series of three daily stories would be sufficient: a 35- to 40-inch story on the first day and a full page with graphics on the next two days, each detailing the thematic evidence for that day's presentation. If you intend to use sidebars, say how many on what days and for what reason. Indicate what visuals—that is, photos, artwork, graphs, charts, chronology of events, and so on—are planned, and finally, what personnel you might need for how long to help you and your teammate(s) do the job.

Having introduced the problem, given a rationale for pur-suing it and your strategy for dealing with it, notice that you've set it up in such a way that you now have material for an *ending.*

Avoid repeating everything you've told them. It's boring and keeps decision makers captive longer than they need to be. The supervising editor has called this session and most likely given senior editors some basis for the request, so decision makers have a fairly good picture about your proposition and what they expect to hear. You've given them your principal points of information, the evidence you have behind them, the sources you've used thus far, and how you intend to handle the project. They don't need a full-length summary. Instead, be brief and close with something like this:

> The mishandling of funds by the Department of _____ is a quiet secret known to most personnel at City Hall. Our readers are the ones who are in the dark. We sincerely believe this story needs to reach them now, particularly in view of upcoming elections. Are there any questions we can answer for you?

Avoid ending with a "thank you." It's too patronizing, and you've already thanked them for being there and listening. It's better to end with a statement that reiterates your belief in the importance and timeliness of the story and sells your product, the proposal. Even if questions have been raised during your presentation, end by asking for additional questions. It's another show of how well you've prepared for this appearance, including its Q&A portion.

You can see how obtained data determine what additional parts will be necessary. In this case, they happen to be subsets of the middle. In other cases, it might be separate and unrelated units with their own subsets of information and visual evidence of that data. Of course, added units increase the length of the presentation, but if that's what the situation demands, bend to the demand of the data.

However, if you've been given a time limit to present, stick to that limitation and talk about only what is most important to decision makers. If they want to know about something you may have left out, they'll ask about it during or after your presentation.

In the section on "How the Pros Do It," you'll see how opinions about presentation length can differ across various types of projects. Just be *brief* and to the point, no matter how many units you have to deal with. Everything that's been said thus far about the number of units and presentation time allotted also holds true for public relations and advertising as well as for journalistic presentations.

The use of visuals, however, plays a much larger role in public relations and advertising than it does in journalism. Generally, journalists use visuals only on rare occasions. Still, they can't hurt. In fact, if you have the time and if your data suggest a good pictorial representation, you might want to do more than one graphic. In this case, your second visual could show the specific services and $$$ value that taxpayers failed to receive because of departmental misuse of funds.

Public Relations

For a public relations presentation, *begin* the same way. Introduce yourself, recognize your audience, present the problem, why it is a problem, and so on. For example,

> _____ (name your agency) appreciates the opportunity to meet with you today to show you how we can offset concerns about a possible strike. As you know, during one of our visits to the North City plant recently, we learned that production rates had slipped to below ___% of the quarter-year quota. Supervisors believed the "slow down" represented signs of an upcoming strike. When we brought this possibility to your attention, you asked us to look into it.

Again, there's an arousal of curiosity and an invitation to attend to information important to decision makers. Incidentally, the client is an established account with the agency, and in this case, the agency is doing its job in terms of monitoring the health and welfare of its client. Now the *middle*—your findings:

> We now know the reason why Acme Manufacturing is experiencing a decreased rate of production at this plant. Supervisors attributed it to low morale and deliberate absenteeism, signs of a pending strike call.

What we discovered, however, was that no strike is planned nor is morale low or the absenteeism deliberate. Rather, production fell below established quotas because of worker fatigue. Overtime and double-shift assignments are simply too wearing. So workers take more rest breaks while on the job—or they stay home a day or so to rest up.

In fact, we found high morale and job satisfaction. However, extra hours hampered strict adherence to time on the production line and created the condition of high absenteeism.

Initiate the plan we've designed for you and you'll find production will rise and absenteeism will fall. Here's our goal plan, simple yet it has worked before for several of our clients in manufacturing and it will work for you.

Provide the main points of strategic action. Put them down as bulleted heads on a graphic, for example:

<u>Goals</u>

- Improve _____
- Increase _____
- Decrease _____

Three points cover the problem. Begin each goal with action words like the ones shown. Then put each of the goals on separate graphics and explain what you intend to do to achieve each one. Use three bulleted one-line explanations under each point. These visuals can be done on a flip chart or posterboard, or projected onto a screen from a transparency or from slides, or shown on a monitor using a computer program.

If the proposed plan has worked elsewhere, say so, but avoid naming the company unless they've given you permission to do so. Usually, they prefer to remain anonymous and you must honor that. Without mentioning the company's name, you can explain that after implementation of your strategy your agency was able to improve the company's production rate ___% over the projected estimate. Then explain that, based on your data concerning this client's problem, you can do the same or better for them. On a pictorial visual or a line graph, demonstrate and explain what your agency is prepared to do to increase North City's production rate.

Another visual might show how the new schedule will now permit workers to meet production quotas under less stressful conditions. The narration might run something like this: "We've learned that this _____ plan" (name the plan type, e.g., "rotation") and then call out the production quotas achieved over a period of several months. The point is to provide proof of or the potential of your strategy. You want to reassure the client that your statements are based on fact or a reasoned estimate, not fiction. Again, save everyone's time and *end* by inviting questions:

> We've had repeated success with this corrective plan in the past, and we feel certain it will resolve your problem in this case. Can we answer any questions for you?

Is the presentation different in an advertising setting? It depends on the problem and client expectation. In earlier chapters, you learned that the nature of the problem in journalism, public relations, and advertising determines how the written document is handled. That also holds true for the oral argument.

Advertising

One of the differences in advertising is whether a creative product is part of the solution and oral presentation. This also can be true in public relations; for example, the client may request creation of a brochure, manual, or trade ad, sometimes a giveaway souvenir for certain publics. But the need in advertising may include all these and more—that is, creative promotions designed for the public at large rather than a certain public such as product manufacturers, industrialists, trade journal editors, or journalists. So the advertising presentation with a creative product designed for distribution to a mass audience might *begin* like this:

> Members of our staff at _____ (name your agency) have
> enjoyed working on this project and thank _____ (name
> the company) for the opportunity to participate in this crea-
> tive effort.

Again, you identify the agency, recognize the client, introduce
any new faces on your team unknown to the client, and thank
members of the client group for their faith in your agency's
expertise. This is a new business effort with a new client and this
agency is competing with other agencies for the account. Continue along these lines:

> Recently, Mr. Charles Smith and Ms. Ann Neal of your
> company asked us to develop a new campaign theme for your
> product, _____ (give the name of the product).

Let's say, in this case, it's a line of cosmetic products. If
you're on a first-name basis with the people mentioned, use their
first names; otherwise, use the formal address form. Again, you
need to articulate the problem and what the company expects
the agency to do. Indicate verification, modification, or correction of the client's stated problem and the mutual goal:

> We know your products have an established position in the
> marketplace. We've also learned that you are quite correct in
> believing you could reach a still wider market with a new idea,
> one that will sustain present customers and draw in the new
> crop of teenagers filling the marketplace.

Now move into the *middle,* the findings. Tell the client what the
research revealed about the available market and what's important about the current marketplace:

> We found that regular customers are pleased with your
> products, also that a good portion of the market knew about
> your line but had never tried it. What was most interesting
> was that current customers said they would like to know for
> sure whether introductions of new makeup shades were right
> for them. They felt they could not rely on salespersons'

selections and chose not to make a change. Prospective buyers, including teenagers, said they would try the line if given assurance the colors suited them before making an investment. That told us that consumers are becoming more cautious about the cosmetics they buy and that we have to respond to that trend.

Continue with an example, but use examples sparingly. One from a large survey should do it:

> For example, in a test case conducted at Central City, we learned that the "need to know prior to purchase" proved to be of paramount importance above all other factors. When respondents were asked what feature in a cosmetics line they would most like to see made, here's what our research revealed.

Display a pictorial visual indicating the number of women surveyed and a comparison between the "need to know" comment and three or four other variables in the class of "preferences." Avoid numerics. Instead, use small head silhouettes of women to represent numbers. Present them in an aggregate of 20 or more in a column or horizontal line to demonstrate their majority number over variables in the same class. Pictorial visuals are more memorable than a visual loaded with lines of copy or nothing but numbers.

In another visual, show a breakdown of the respondents: their age, occupation, economic status, and so on. An artist should be able to translate either one or both visuals into one that has some graphic relief in it. Accompany these visuals with appropriate narration. For example,

> Notice that the "need to know" factor far outweighs all other issues for the majority of women surveyed. And here you'll see how that sentiment was shared across the range of characteristics represented in that population. Ages ranged from _____ to _____ , occupations from _____ to _____ , incomes from _____ to _____ . Notice the similarity of numbers concerning the "need to know" factor across that range (show these in color so they stand out from the rest).

And as our proposal document indicates, that similarity repeated itself in all of the two dozen metropolitan cities and outlying areas we surveyed.

Bring audience attention back to you by saying,

Now let me show you how a model of the idea we've created responds to consumers' "need to know" and how we intend to reach this ready market.

Uncover your creative product, a prototype model of a machine that measures a customer's hair color and skin tone and condition and identifies the appropriate products for that customer. If the machine is developed so that it's operable, the presenter can then use a live model to demonstrate how the measuring device on the machine works to coordinate her hair color and skin tone and texture to the client's various cosmetic and skin care products. Let's assume that's the case in this instance.[2]

Give the client an indication of how this creative idea will be used in the promotional campaign you've planned—perhaps magazine ads, TV commercials, pickup brochures in retail stores, direct mail, and others. Ready a sample of at least one or two of these, perhaps a storyboard for the TV ad and a mockup of the magazine ad. Samples should show the campaign theme line and the intended artwork, ideally in color. For the ad, sections for copy may be represented by lines sketched in at certain places, or filled in with the first word, phrase, or sentence. Narration for the TV commercial can be abbreviated inside a balloon above a sketch of the speaker or appear in an outlined script.

The campaign strategy may have several phases. The first phase might have a series of TV commercials to introduce the device and its technological accuracy by using live models with different skin tones and hair color. Another phase might emphasize the elimination of trial and error for all age groups in magazine ads and other print media. Another phase might feature testimonials from professional models, seniors, teenagers, and housewives, which could be placed in any of several different types of delivery channels. Convey your enthusiasm for the product:

> We're calling the machine the _____ (give the machine a
> jazzy name). We're very excited about it because we've tested
> it in our labs and with focus groups. It was enthusiastically
> received and here's how that response looks on paper:

Show the results on a self-explanatory visual and let the data
dictate the nature of the display. Now go into a selling mode:

> The machine is unique, one of a kind. There's not another
> like it on the market. That's a tremendous marketing advan-
> tage for your product. So as soon as you give us the signal to
> move ahead, we're prepared to assist you so that the machine
> remains one of a kind.
>
> You can appreciate the impact this creative device will have
> on market demand. It responds to consumer need, is a novel
> idea, assures customer satisfaction, and provides a competi-
> tive edge beyond the quality of the product line itself.
>
> As importantly, our marketing strategy is media comprehen-
> sive, yet feasible because it falls within your budget quote and
> because each phase can be done within the time period
> specified.

Show a self-explanatory visual that dispenses with the need for
narration, one indicating the budget quote and cost estimate
over a client-specified time period for completion of each campaign phase. Move into the *ending*. There's no need to cover
everything you've talked about. By this time, your audience is
tired and doesn't want a repetition of the whole. Make it simple
and brief. Close with something like this:

> For these reasons we're quite confident our marketing plan
> will put _____ (name the company or product line) way
> ahead of its competitors for some time. If you have any
> questions, we'll be happy to answer them for you.

You've aroused the client's appetite for your ideas, now allow
time for questions.

CHALLENGES AND QUESTIONS

Reassure yourself about challenges and questions from the audience and anticipate them. No need to panic. No need to agonize about what questions will be raised. Remember, you've prepared for this meeting and you know your material intimately. Just think about what you might challenge or question if you were a decision maker.

First, think about what you didn't cover in your presentation because brevity was your guide. Formulate an anticipated question and prepare an answer. Don't be tempted to insert answers to all anticipated queries in your presentation. Give your audience a chance to participate. It allows them to become part of the effort, perhaps even an advocate for it.

Then think about other challenges and questions you might raise. For instance, regarding the journalism project above:

- *How did you arrive at the conclusion that funds had been mishandled?*
- *How did you find out about it? Who told you? What's their interest in this?*
- *Are they willing to be identified and go on record?*
- *Who (or what) do you intend to use as additional sources of information?*
- *What's your justification for a three-day series instead of a two-day series or a single story feature? Why can't you do this with fewer personnel?*
- *Why can't you use fewer graphics/photos?*

The questions will differ from one journalistic project to another, so let the project tell you what the challenges might be. That applies also to public relations and advertising projects. However, in regard to the public relations issue above, decision makers might raise these questions:

- *How did you learn about high morale and job satisfaction?*
- *Why does your information differ so much from what supervisors believed was the case?*
- *How many workers did you interview in what areas of the plant?*

For the advertising example given above, these questions might be raised:

- *Have you ever used a technological device before to promote a product?*
- *What was customer reaction to its use on them?*
- *Exactly how much will production of the device cost?*
- *How do you plan to prevent its duplication?*

If decision makers eliminate parts of your promotion plan due to additional costs such as producing a cosmetic machine, be flexible. Show them what you can do to comply, or have solid reasons why you disagree. Don't insist on having your way on everything. It's better to leave with something rather than nothing. You want to make this a win-win negotiation, not a win-lose one either for you or for the decision makers. Besides, it keeps the climate pleasant and the doors open for another negotiation.

Don't depend solely on an easy-to-follow presentation. Depend, as well, on other factors that facilitate clarity and comprehension. If you're a novice, you might want to begin by writing out your presentation (more about this in a later section headed "Write It Out? Rehearse?"). Seasoned presenters usually work from an outline of bulleted line items for each part in the message and use these as reminders of key points. But novices need to know some of the features that go into a "listenable" and persuasive presentation. Some of these are described below.

LANGUAGE, STYLE, AND PACE

Review Chapter 7 because the precautions named there about writing a proposal also hold true for the oral argument. Here are a few: Use everyday language, avoid jargon, seven-syllable words, and unfamiliar terms such as "vacuous" ("senseless" does just as well). Besides, multisyllabic and rarely used words are hard to say and you're likely to stumble all over them and end up speaking nothing but mush. It's not smart to compromise clarity for impression. Remember, unlike the written word, the receiver has nothing to return to for another reading of your meaning. If the receiver doesn't get it on first delivery, that's it.

You also want to avoid combining words that create an alliterative blowing or hissing sound: "Beaches built by bulwarks binding bow-breaking boundaries" or "She saw shiny snow sheets sweep swiftly southward." Admittedly, these examples are forced and make little sense. Nevertheless, they make the point that repetitive sounds fall unpleasantly on the ear; besides, they're hard to say. Keep your meaning but change the words.

As for style, try to sustain a friendly and personalized climate. Project a conversational tone and manner. Talk to your audience like you would talk to a friend—confidentially and sincerely—because what you know is something you want to share with your friend. You create an air of exclusivity that secures the relationship you and your friend have built and you want to keep it that way. Do the same in this media setting.

If conversational style bends the rules of English, don't be concerned. That's the way people talk to one another. The rules of English facilitate understanding of the written word, but you're not reading in isolation, you're speaking to a group of people. Punctuation rules can be violated, and it's OK to start a new sentence with "and."

One criterion for delivering an oral presentation that doesn't change from the written one is the length of its sentences. Varied pacing and a comfortable rhythm are just as important in oral form as they are in written form. So vary the length of your sentences. Mix some short ones in among the longer ones, but in oral delivery, especially, shorten lengthy sentences wherever possible.

A fair number is 17-25 words maximum for long sentences and 3-15 words for shorter ones. Remember, although long sentences in written form can be reread, that's not possible here. So, less is better. Sometimes, however, you can't avoid going beyond the maximum length.

As for short sentences, injecting these among the longer ones helps keep receivers awake. After processing a certain amount of information, they begin to wander off and fantasize.

Mixing short sentences with longer sentences is a pacing device that aids comprehension and provides a rhythm to keep audiences attentive. A short sentence (3-15 words) brings them back and sets them up for the next body of information.

However, avoid placing a short sentence in a predictable pattern among the longer ones. The rhythm can become so regular that the beat itself will sing-song an audience to sleep. One way to avoid the lullaby effect is to inject a few short sentences one after the other before getting into the next long sentence. Or use short sentences of varying lengths between the longer ones. Test your narrative: Say it out loud and listen for a predictable rhythm. If you hear one, make adjustments.

Above all, aim for attentiveness. Ordinary language, conversational style, pleasant sounds, and varied pacing all work together to keep listeners on the alert. Continue testing and adjusting until your ear tells you the narrative delivers well and sustains interest. Then try it again on others. Ask what they didn't understand, what interfered with their reception. Let clarity of sound as well as meaning be your guide because this may be your only chance to deliver your message to this audience.

TIMING FOR EFFECT

In the entertainment industry, timing can either make or break the comedian's joke or the singer's effect on an audience. Phrasing is like that. A close cousin to pace, a phrase creates a pause, a slight hesitation in the right places. A phrase at the beginning of a line prepares reception for the rest. A phrase in the middle of a line allows the audience a chance to absorb what's been said before attending to the rest of the line. A phrase at the end of the line adds emphasis to what has been said before moving on. Some say knowing where those pauses belong is a matter of talent. Perhaps, but it's also a sensitivity that can be developed with practice and experience.

See if this works for you. Look at your narrative and find where the commas fall, not the ones in a series because hesitations between each item would amount to overkill. Look for possibilities within sentences, especially the long ones. Look for places at the end of a sentence that need separation because they seem to summarize or emphasize what's gone before. Look for places at the beginning of a sentence that need separation from the rest of the sentence before moving into it. A few trials before an audience and you'll soon get the feel for placing and timing your hesitations.

TRANSITIONS

A transition is an introductory phrase or sentence that performs several functions. It acts as a mini-review of a point just made as well as a mini-preview of a point or body of information about to be made. Transitions also act as links connecting one main thought with another, connecting one section of the narrative to another. They're critical to the smooth delivery of the whole. Transitions are also close cousins to pace and timing. They facilitate comprehension and, with appropriate pauses or emphases, retrieve listeners' wandering concentration.

Transitions can be snippets, like the words *but, however, so,* or phrases, like *in fact, on the other hand, in this case,* or full statements that head into the next section—for example, *After examining the causes and reviewing the situation, one would think the causes had little merit at all. However, let's look at this case a little more closely.*

Transitions are not difficult to devise. Don't overlook using them. Without a transition, you risk losing your audience as they try to follow you from one point or unit of information to another. You may be far into your next point while your audience is still wondering what connection that point has to do with the one you just made. What's worse, they lose track of an otherwise well-organized message and leave with the impression that your oral argument was disorganized and unclear. They might conclude that your written document must be the same and therefore not worth their additional time.

You'll find examples of transitions in the preceding examples and throughout this text. The following paragraph is a transition into the next unit.

Language, style, pace, timing, transitions—all figure large in the organization of an oral argument, but efforts to enhance delivery depend on still another dimension, its sensual effect on an audience, the topic of discussion in the next section.

APPEAL TO THE SENSES

How you sound and look as you deliver your presentation can influence the effectiveness of your message no matter how well it's put together. That may seem frivolous, even artificial, after the serious attention you've given to composing your presentation. But UCLA psychology professor Albert Mehrabian has found that nonverbal behaviors can overpower, even diminish verbal impact.[3] For example, if one has likes or dislikes about whatever one is talking about, those feelings come through in the form of facial, hand, and body movements.

The sins of nonverbal communication are exclusive to the sinner and come in many and varied forms. But usually they stem from face, head, hands, and body movements inconsistent with the verbal message. The effect is that the nonverbal rather than the verbal cues take over. According to some studies, of the three channels in oral delivery, visual perception (the effect of the speaker's appearance on the audience), vocal quality (pitch and tone), and verbal content (the message), the first makes the greatest impression on an audience (55%), followed by the second (38%); the message itself has the least impact on the affective senses (7%).[4]

You might ask: If that's the case, why bother working on a verbal presentation when you can say what you know as long as you look good and appear enthusiastic and agreeable all the time? Because that's not the way oral communication works. It's not its separate features that sell, it's the unity of the whole package—the message, your gestures, voice, and appearance.

If you truly believe in what you're talking about, that attitude will come through naturally in your face, hands, body, and voice. Every gesture, every movement should have a purpose that is consistent with the content of the verbal message and should come only where it counts. Let the word, phrase, sentence, or point of information find its own natural union with a gesture or movement. Just be aware of any mismatch.

Some Inconsistent Nonverbal Messages

Ever see speakers make an inappropriate gesture at a point when they want you to believe or agree? For example, they narrow their eyes, or slip into speaking from the side of their mouths, or strain their faces into forced smiles. If those inconsistent facial gestures produce distrust in you, it's likely they'll do the same in others.

Ever hear speakers punctuate a point of information or conclusion so explosively that it loses its importance for you? Give your audience the courtesy of being kind to their eardrums. Does a hand pull on the nose distract you from what's being said? Does nervous handling of pens, pencils, markers, or objects of any kind do the same? Avoid committing unseemly gestures. Grasp objects firmly in hand or set them aside.

What to do with your hands is a common problem. Nervous presenters will slip them in jacket or trouser pockets. That's okay during a relaxed moment. But keep in mind, there aren't too many of those moments for media petitioners. When you're trying to win approval of your project, slipping hands into your pockets can be inferred as indifference or relinquishing control. Besides, you need your hands to make gestures consistent with what you're saying. If you're nervous and can't avoid calling attention to it, hold a pen or marker in one of them and try not to grasp it so firmly that your knuckles turn white.

Keep in mind that gestures must not be so similar that their repetition reduces the significance of all points made. Any gesture should be used sparingly. Ever notice speakers constantly churning their hands around and around in the air? Were you listening or watching? Most likely the latter.

A prominent network broadcaster has the habit of waving his shoulders like a go-go dancer or swaying his body in a manner incompatible with the message. Another has the habit of constantly nodding her head as if agreeing with herself or shaking it from side to side in response to a variety of emotions. Still another cocks his head to one side and never sets it upright again until his sign-off.

None of those habits serve the objective message, and if they distract or annoy you, they're likely to do the same for others. Practice in front of a full-length mirror, or if you have the equipment, make a "before" and "after" videotape of your delivery. Identify and correct unattractive gestures or those inconsistent with your message. Notice which gestures enhance your message. Rehearse using those gestures only. Keep this in mind: *Less is better.* That doesn't mean you have to look like a statue. If you're seated, keep your hands away from your face, control inappropriate facial movements, and use appropriate head and hand gestures sparingly. If you're standing, do the same and move about, not frenetically but almost imperceptibly.

Since the Mehrabian experiments, several studies have reflected, in different ways, the importance of nonverbal consistency with verbal communication. For example, one study conducted with 135 university students determined that speeches consistent with speaker attitude were relatively more fluent, had superior content, and fewer nonverbal clues.[5] Another published in 1990 found that greater perceived persuasiveness was related to facial and vocal pleasantness.[6] Two other researchers found that nonverbal behavior can influence the behavior of others.[7]

Dress

How you put yourself together for the occasion is as important as how you put your oral argument together. It's another dimension of delivery effect. You want your audience to see you in the best possible light. Without intending to, you may do just the opposite. Avoid making a serious error in judgment. Abide by the general rule and choose garments in keeping with the environment you'll be entering. Learn beforehand what level of apparel is worn at such meetings in that environment. Do they wear formal or informal attire? Your clothing should be similar in kind.

As to the level of formality, some speech consultants advise that speakers dress to a level of formality that is at or slightly above that of the group.[8] When in doubt about formal versus informal, counselors advise conservative dress rather than casual wear, that is, women in suits and blouses, preferably solid colors, and men in conservative business suits, shirts, and ties, which means the plaid pants and wild ties belong elsewhere.[9]

As always, knowledge is better than doubt. Ask those who have been at similar meetings. Journalists usually dress informally on the job, but they may need to find out how senior editors dress in decision-making situations. If you haven't been to one before in your media house, better ask your supervising editor. When dress is informal, blouse and skirt or trousers do just fine for women; open shirt, pullover sweater and dress trousers or jeans work for men.

Public relations and advertising settings usually permit informal dress in-house, but conservative is the rule for all team members when meeting with clients on their turf. Formal or informal, after you've left the room the audience should have forgotten what you were wearing, yet when asked can say you were dressed neatly and appropriately.

Whatever the level of attire, remember that good grooming and careful dressing are part of the total visual impression. Women should avoid outlandish hairstyles, excessive makeup, and seductive clothing. Men should avoid haircuts commonly characterized as "weird" or the appearance of indifference—unpressed suit, unkempt nails, worn down or unpolished shoes.

Posture and Status

Another given in terms of visual impression is posture. If you're accustomed to thrusting out your chin or slouching when you walk or stand, draw in the chin, throw back your shoulders, and straighten up. If you're in the habit of slouching in your chair, straighten up. Nothing is more telling than a posture that spells defeat. It creates doubt in decision makers' minds that you have either the energy or enthusiasm to get the job done. The impression you need to make is that you're a "together" person, competent in your field, sure of your project, and able to deliver.

When you stand before an audience, stand proud, straight, and firmly on both feet. If seated, sit upright. When called on to speak, remain in your chair until the introduction is completed, then rise from your chair quickly and walk confidently to a position where everyone can see and hear you. Project authority. If you want to win their trust, demonstrate you've earned it.

Good posture also sends positive signals about your professional status. You may not be a senior editor, producer, creative director, or vice-president, but as a writer you're a vital part of the media project. Executives can't do without the writer. You carry an exclusivity the titled cannot share. Decision makers in media know that. So let good posture demonstrate the importance of your status.

Speech consultants and researchers agree that status is just another one of several positive messages you want to send. In one recent study conducted with 80 Australian and 80 American university students, researchers found that status was the most important source characteristic for determining the effect of persuasive delivery.[10] Over and above status by title, there's no better way to project your status as a writer than to show it in the way you carry yourself.

Eye Contact

Connecting with your audience is still another way those present make judgments about you. If you fail to look decision makers in the eye, it's a nonverbal signal that you're unsure of yourself, or indifferent about selling your argument, or cavalier about audience interest in it. You're there to make a positive impression, not to create a wimpy image or a "take it or leave it" attitude. So project a sense of mastery and earnest confidence in your proposition.

One of the ways to do that is to make eye contact with each member of the decision-making group and speak directly to each one. No need to give any one person more than a few moments' attention. Extended eye contact with one person could prove embarrassing for both of you. One sentence's worth is sufficient; a phrase or two will do.

Try to avoid a predictable round of contact, that is, first talking to those on the left and then to those on the right. The pattern becomes so mechanical that the message, no matter how powerful, loses believability and attention is distracted from the message and rests, instead, on the rhythm of your eye and head movements. Let what you say direct your delivery to whomever your eyes light upon.

A warning: Don't make the mistake of playing favorites, that is, focusing on someone you've identified as the principal decision maker. Sometimes, without previous knowledge or introduction, the real decision makers show up for the first time. Unaware of their importance, you wonder why they're present so you talk mainly to familiar faces. That's a mistake. The strange faces are as important as the familiar ones, otherwise they wouldn't be there. Play no favorites—give everyone present the courtesy of equal recognition.

Eye-to-eye contact and direct address give everyone the feeling that what you have to say is intended solely for their personal benefit. What's more, they'll almost feel obliged to attend to you more carefully and not wander off so easily. Consider this: How do you feel when a speaker looks away, up, or down but never at you? You might feel indifferent about what the speaker is saying, doubt its veracity, and even look away at something else. In contrast, how do you feel when a speaker meets your glance and addresses you directly? You perk up, listen attentively, and conclude, "This person has something to say, is serious about it, and is sharing that message with me."

Voice Quality

Several factors influence quality of voice: pitch, volume, rate, and tone. In general, the guiding rule is a midrange pitch at moderate volume and rate and in modulated tones, which means that if you have a shrill, grating, high- or low-pitched voice, work at it until you hit a midrange level. Tone, volume, and rate will then neutralize into a pleasant effect—but not so neutral that you put everyone to sleep. Allow for some variety. Let the meaning you intend for a word or phrase tell you when to raise or lower your tone or increase or reduce the volume and rate. Just make sure the pattern of change doesn't fall into a predictable drone and rock your audience into dreamland.

Another precaution: Emphasizing a point doesn't give you license to deliver an insistent tone or to shout at your audience. This is a sales effort, not a political speech. High vocal intensity is akin to pounding the table or podium—it's offensive and doesn't work. People don't like being pushed, even in a persuasive "sales" situation. Using small, not excessive, increases in the intensity of your voice and tone work better and leave a more favorable impression. A number of early studies with hundreds of undergraduate students showed that low-intensity delivery proved more effective than moderate and high-intensity delivery modes.[11]

In fact, even the rate of speech can leave a negative effect. In a study with over 100 undergraduates, researchers found that a faster than normal speech rate inhibits favorable elaboration of a message and thus undermines its persuasive impact.[12] Earlier studies found that people tend to believe fast talkers more than those who speak slowly and deliberately; however, those same people were unable to recall what they had heard.[13] So try to deliver your message at a rate that gives your audience a chance to take in and comprehend the content—but not so slowly that it puts them to sleep. Delivering a comprehensible message is why you're there and why they've come to listen to it. So, take some precautions about the quality of your voice as well as attending to eye contact, gestures, and personal appearance.

WRITE IT OUT? REHEARSE?

Opinions among speakers and consultants vary from "Yes, do write out the oral presentation" to "No, absolutely not"[14] They vary as much about rehearsals versus no rehearsals. So, what should you do? First, understand your situation. It's a media setting and you're addressing a group of decision makers. That's not quite the same as addressing a large audience. Your setting is intimate, and the numbers present are few. Yes, you're selling a product, but it isn't a consumer product or service. Rather, you're selling an idea. You're also selling your research and writing skill, reasoning power, and creative recommendations. Your purpose is to persuade decision makers that your solution to their needs is the best they can get.

Then understand yourself. Know what you as an individual can do. Can you deliver what you know without first writing it down word for word? Can you keep all the major points in mind and develop each one without missing a beat? If so, then take that route. If not, then by all means write down what you need to say.

Can you then deliver what you know from an outline? Can you fill in the details just by glancing at the main heads and subheads or some bulleted items of relevant information? Experienced speakers can; novices need a lot of practice. If you're uncertain about what you're capable of doing, begin by writing out your presentation and becoming very, very familiar with its content. That doesn't mean reading from it. Rather, it means knowing the message so well that just an occasional glance at your notes will carry you through. After some experience before audiences, try the outline approach. Avoid notes on file cards. They're too cryptic, can get mixed up, and there's always a chance of dropping the whole bunch on the floor. It's embarrassing and hard to get back on track. Then there's the added embarrassment of having to pick them up yourself—doesn't leave a positive impression.

In any case, master the facts. That doesn't mean memorizing them. You'll be spending so much energy recalling, you won't be able to think about what you're saying and whether you're really relating to your audience. Internalize what you need to say until it becomes second nature; then set your notes and outlines aside and practice without them.

Practice out loud in front of a full-length mirror or video-tape yourself, watching for weak points. Practice until your nonverbal cues demonstrate consistency with your verbal message, eye contact becomes an honest gesture, good posture reassures, a pleasant voice engages, and confidence in yourself and your recommendations instills trust. If you tend to suffer from stage fright, you'll be surprised how much this practicing reduces your fears. If you need a security blanket, rely on your outline, prompt sheet, or whatever type of summary guide of your oral presentation works for you.

How long and how many times should you practice? One speech consultant recommends one hour for every minute you talk. Another suggests multiplying the length of your talk by the number of people in the audience. Both seem a little extreme, considering you've been working on this project for some time. A better rule is to practice until you feel so confident you can feel the words and where they belong in every corner of your mind, in every bone in your body. Practice until you get rid of all the "ahhhhs" and "uhmmms." Listen to yourself and think about your message as you practice; otherwise, the exercise becomes mechanical, just talking out loud, and makes only weak traces on your memory.

As for a dress rehearsal, it's a little different from a practice session. Dress rehearsals are valuable for a number of reasons. If you're displaying visuals or models or working with props, you need to practice smooth movement from your speaking position to whatever type of display you're using. You need to achieve a compatible flow between what you say and what you show. Moreover, if you're part of a team, you need to see how your part fits into the whole, and you need to hear the reactions of your teammates so you can modify and correct both your argument and the way you deliver it.

A FINAL CUE

In the process of understanding decision makers, problem solvers in public relations and advertising may learn that an informal rather than a full-blown formal presentation is the client's preference. That is, they may want just a brief presentation of your solution strategy—no visuals, displays, or samples—and have their questions answered. Honor their preference, but if you're in a competitive situation with other agencies for the account, take some precautions. Try to find out who your competitors are and whether a formal or informal presentation is their style. If that's not possible, consider what might happen. If you follow an expressed preference and the competition comes in with a dog-and-pony show, their luster could bury you. Then again, they may overdo it to such an extent that they'll lose the business anyway. Nevertheless, some of their glitter might still be too stark a contrast to your low-key presentation. In such an uncertain situation, rely on your own good judgment, that is, critical thinking/self-inquiry. Do what's necessary, what the problem, evidence, and solution to the problem absolutely require. The prospective client likes an informal atmosphere? Fine. You can create that and still manifest your skills with careful selection of a few very relevant and illustrative visuals and/or samples. Decision makers who prefer an informal climate usually are the kind who like to do the talking, so tell your story briefly and give them a chance to ask questions, listen carefully, respond courteously, and always remain in control. After all, you have all the answers and that advantage belongs to you. Use it with good judgment.

HOW THE PROS DO IT

Variety characterizes the preparation of an oral proposal in the media. That doesn't mean that standards don't exist; they do. As you will see in the comments that follow, the predominating requirement is preparedness. All other standards flow from that single precautionary measure. Earlier, you learned that having command of a body of relevant data was not only a requisite of proposal composition but was also a defense against resistance to your written presentation. The same holds true for the oral argument.

Memos or discussions may be exchanged between petitioner and immediate supervisor before facing primary decision makers, but in the final showing what counts is preparation, which also includes paying attention to your physical appearance and delivery style. The bottom line is this: Final approval depends entirely on your grasp of the data and how effectively you project what you know to a group of judges.

Print and Broadcast Journalism

Seasoned reporters like Robert Capers leave nothing to chance. He had won his editor's confidence many times over. Yet he spent two years researching his story idea before proposing it (see Chapter 6). He was well prepared to deliver an oral presentation if necessary, but his reputation as a reliable and trustworthy reporter preceded him, so his enterprise project required no more than a verbal suggestion. Novices, however, must work for that advantage and need to deliver a persuasive "sell."

> My editor and I have a good rapport and we talked from time to time about what was going on and what I knew. I think, too, as a younger reporter, I probably would have been questioned about projects more closely than I am now, but I guess I've established some respect or something so that when I suggest there's a story there, the odds are pretty good it's there. It may not be exactly what we thought going in, but there's something there and probably deserves to be written about. In other words, I don't have to sell the stories very hard in most cases.
>
> **Robert S. Capers,** staff writer,
> *Hartford Courant*

Earlier, you learned that timeliness of a proposed story is one criterion that judges consider seriously. Knowing the time wasn't quite ripe for his proposal, this next writer put together a draft of a proposal and then left it alone for a year (see Chapter 3). Over several months of research, he collected enough data to believe that African American organizations were not reflective of their members' concerns. He wanted to go a step further and query African Americans about their observations. He also knew that respondents would resist such a poll. The time wasn't ripe. So he set the draft aside and waited. The event that finally brought undercurrents to the surface was the nomination of Clarence Thomas to the Supreme Court. Disagreements within and between representative groups and their memberships became known. A poll of African Americans about their organizations now seemed feasible. With a one-page document containing an expanded rationale, evidence gathered up to the time of Thomas's nomination, and a request for funds to conduct a poll, this reporter appeared before decision makers.

> Basically, I was just prepared for any type of questions they asked. If they asked "Why would you have to do a poll?," I was able to say "This is why you have to do a poll." A presentation can last a few minutes or longer. You just outline what you're going to say [to decision makers]. Then you give them the written proposal and say, "Look, this is why we should do this." Then they'll be able almost immediately to ask you questions and react. Some of the other questions they asked were "How long will it take?" and "Why should your story be national and not just statewide?" You just have to make sure you know everything about the story [you propose] and how to go about getting it and be able to prove what you know about the issue.
>
> **Everett J. Mitchell II,** assistant city editor,
> *Detroit News*

Others go in with a more formal written document, which contains all the necessary components and details. As explained earlier, you can't put everything in your oral argument that's in your written document, just its most persuasive points, but as this reporter cautions, preparation is a prerequisite to a pitch for acceptance (also see Chapter 6).

> Either you have enough information to predicate a decision at the time it's proposed and the information has already been checked to sufficient depth, or it's so inchoate that it's

too soon to even submit to the editors for their consideration. You have to have achieved that threshold of confidence
that the project's going to pan out by the time you reach the
presentation stage. Before going in I spend a lot of time with
it, looking at it, examining it, inquiring about what it is I
have—looking at the information and making sure I understand it sufficiently to make authoritative statements about
it to the editors.

John Wark, investigative reporter,
Detroit News

Approaches vary in broadcasting as well but not the standard of
preparedness and display of reliable evidence. Like Capers,
Vince Wade had earned a trusted working relationship with his
editors. Initially, approval of his proposal came after a few
informal meetings with his immediate editor (see Chapter 8). He
sometimes presents from a written proposal. Other times, he
goes in without one. He characterizes his oral arguments as
conversational, "like friends talking things out" and exchanging
ideas on how the facts could be visualized on videotape.

Because of the volume of major stories breaking in Detroit
at the time, none of us [writers, editors] had the time to write
memos to each other on paper or even on the in-house
message system for this story. So I did this [story proposal]
in brief, verbal presentations. We [Wade and his editor] also
know each other well enough to know how the other one
works, what the other one wants. I pitch a concept, and he's
bright enough to visualize what the concept will look like on
television and he either accepts it or rejects it.

Vince Wade, reporter,
WJBK-TV, Detroit

The pressure of time often disallows a written proposal or a
prepared oral presentation. Nevertheless, the success of any
friendly discussion about a proposed story requires a solid grasp
of all the facts involved. Full knowledge also assists other factors
involved in the oral presentation: relevancy of the project, its

timeliness, and the time needed to complete it (see case introduction, Chapter 5).

> I knew my editor would ask me why people would watch this
> story, what news value it had, or how relevant this story was
> to Detroiters. I also knew I had to say how much time it would
> take to get the story, why this story was worth the time it
> needed, and how much air time it would take. This story was
> not an easy one to sell [about Detroit firefighters and how
> they face constant danger of injury and death to save the lives
> of others]. But it was a good story, and my producer and I
> felt these firefighters had a tremendous story to tell. They
> put their lives on the line every day for total strangers and
> they're not becoming wealthy doing it. We just knew their
> story had to be told, so we argued for a real-life story behind
> the movie *Backdraft,* which was showing in theaters at the
> time. That tie-in made it timely, and that was our argument.
>
> **Ann Thompson,** reporter,
> WDIV-TV, Detroit

Rapport with decision makers, substantial evidence to support a
proposed story, meeting expected criteria for approval—these all
count in terms of content presentation. How one delivers the
message verbally is still another aspect of a presentation. Delivery
style may not be as important in print and broadcast settings as
it is in public relations and advertising, but there's always an
occasion when the effect of an oral presentation enters the
equation. The equation in this case included a pitch for supple-
mental state funds to underwrite a television series on teen
pregnancy. This TV director's written proposal received quick
internal approval and station funding (see Chapter 3). Then, with
the help of teammates and the state's department of health, the
argument was taken before state legislators.

> There were certain themes we knew we had to push, espe-
> cially male responsibility, also parental and taxpayer respon-
> sibility. In my judgment, the principal winning characteristic
> of a verbal presentation is preparedness, being able to ver-

balize the problem and being specific in your solutions, demonstrating how your campaign is going to significantly impact on the problem. We had to assure them [legislators] that the results would be available to them. That was important because we knew the money would be well spent and that we could prove that. My station manager, Tom Bonner, gave the actual presentation before legislators with Dr. Elders [former secretary of the U.S. Department of Health and Welfare, but at the time a state welfare department official]. Tom is an excellent speaker, an on-air person whose voice projects confidence and invites trust. Together he and Dr. Elders exhibited informed responses when legislators raised questions. He and Dr. Elders made a lasting impression, and our campaign proposal for state funds was approved.

Anne Wright, community relations director,
KARK-TV, Little Rock, Arkansas

Public Relations and Advertising

A more formal setting differentiates oral presentations in public relations from those in journalism, but preparedness still stands high on the list. Preparedness counts even in a crisis situation. There's little time to do anything but research and act quickly. But if on previous occasions you have obtained a body of knowledge about your client, the product, its competitors, and your sources of cooperation, with some additional research you're prepared to respond to the crisis situation. Of course, not all public relations projects are quite that hectic. In fact, there will be occasions when you bring client attention to a situation that has escaped their notice, needs attention, and on which you've accumulated some advance information.

That was the case for this public relations executive with a client of record. After verbally presenting the problem and winning approval to pursue the issue, an extensive research program, several meetings, and a series of written documents followed, then an oral presentation of the problem and its solution strategy. This executive and his team relied on their preliminary and final written documents as a basis for their oral presentation (also see Chapters 3 and 7).

We used all the little "factoids" we had collected along with overheads and a leave-behind document. The overheads ran through the basic program and the traditional formula: the situation, research results, analysis, our objectives, the audiences, publics we want to reach, the key messages we'd like to communicate, media channels we'd like to use, an overview of the strategies and tactics, how we'll evaluate the program. We try to have a number of people see, sometimes hear, everything that goes out. We work pretty hard at being sure of our facts. We believe in what we're doing for the client. That comes through, and I think clients find that reassuring, perhaps even convincing.

James A. Bianchi, vice president,
Eisbrenner Public Relations, Troy, Michigan

A competitive situation is quite different. Unlike the situation involving a client of record, the limitations on oral presentation can be narrow and restrictive. This pro (also see Chapters 4 and 6) advises,

Be sure you clearly understand what the ground rules for the presentation are. In most cases, you will be limited by time. So you've got to be sure you're hitting the right buttons and saying the right thing. Basically, the presentation is similar to the [written] proposal. We thank the people for allowing us to be there; if they don't know anything about our company, we give about a 2-minute overview. We might say, "First let me tell you a little bit about us. We've been in business 25 years in North Carolina. Our staff includes 42 people in two offices, etc. We represent a wide array of clients, some of whom are companies similar to yours and have seen situations such as yours, for example, A, B, C, etc." We're in and out of that in less than $1\frac{1}{2}$ minutes. "But what we're here for is not to talk about us, but to talk about what your needs are. And with us is our account team . . . " I introduce them, and the person [who does the talking] gets up and says, "Here's how we understand your circumstances and what you need." We get that off very quickly, but it clearly demonstrates that we understand them, their problems, have empathy with them. Then, "Now here's how we're going to solve it." Each person on the team will participate and hit certain points.

We go through these very quickly and close with "The proposal is in front of you. It outlines our budget, timeliness, etc. [whatever else is relevant in the proposal]." Usually, we won't get into that in a presentation unless they start asking questions. If we're given an hour, we'll do 30 minutes for presentation and 30 minutes for questions and answers. I know when we're winning when the group [decision makers] goes beyond the time they allotted. If I go into a presentation that's 45 minutes, and it's $2\frac{1}{2}$ hours before we get out of there, I walk out feeling we've got the work. But if it's "Thank you very much, we appreciate it, we'll let you know" and you're right on the dot [within the time given], you walk out with an "iffy" situation.

It's like writing the proposal. You have to develop empathy and contact with the people. You avoid talking about yourself. You focus on just the bare basics, what the client's situation is, the way you're going to solve it for them. Every team member has to exude that level of confidence, experience, professionalism that everyone at that table can respect and recognize right off the bat. And you have to rehearse, rehearse, and rehearse, individually and together. It has to come off like clockwork, yet not seem like it. It's not memorized. Nobody's nervous. Everything's got to flow naturally, smoothly. And you work as a team. You don't have team members grandstanding each other. It's like an ensemble performance. We'll [during rehearsals] go through and be very critical of each other: "How can you do this better? You stumbled over this, you went off on a tangent on that." We make sure everyone stays within a given time frame. You cannot just go in there and shoot from the hip.

Joe S. Epley, chairman and CEO,
Epley Associates, Inc., Charlotte, North Carolina

Whether the situation is competitive or noncompetitive, restrictions may still be prescribed, but the standards for oral content and presentation remain the same. This public relations executive prepares for the oral presentation from the decision makers' point of view (also see Chapters 3 and 7).

If they [decision makers] walk out of the room with the feeling that four or five primary objectives have been addressed with a reasonable, logical program that makes sense, then that's an effective presentation. You're really missing the boat if you don't continually refer back to what your program does in terms of fulfilling the primary objectives, knowing the client and what is needed. I regard public relations as a social science. One has to know about human behavior, how you enhance human relationships. That requires method. You don't do it haphazardly.

I always prepare for a presentation. After the program is written, I set it aside. I don't look at it for at least 24 hours. Then I read it. Generally, I try to have a day or two before to prepare. I visualize the presentation, visualize the rough questions, the answers, how I feel. There may be a rehearsal internally [in house]. We don't do it cold. I want to see the room in advance because I don't take any of that lightly. As for the length of a presentation, it depends on the life of the program, but generally, an hour or hour-and-a-half. This program, including questions and answers, lasted two-and-a-half hours.

Gerald Lundy, executive vice president,
Southfield, Michigan

Like Lundy, this next advertising executive takes the client's point of view and explains what he does to keep the oral presentation brief and to the point.

It's like the written proposal, even an ad. You need to ask yourself: *What is reasonable to expect someone, a prospect or customer, to remember? If I didn't have this in the key communication idea, or this in the background, would the prospect or customer still have the right message? Does it meet the objective?* It's a paring away.

I think familiarity with the material and practice with it are among the most important things one can do. I never have a script or use notes. I just think about it a lot and review what I have, run through it four or five times, again in dress rehearsals. We always have samples of the work, and sometimes I get right to them. Depends on the client, how they like to operate. Some clients are tactile. They like having the work in their hands and react to it and don't want to hear a lot of words. You just have to know what your client likes and doesn't like. Another very important thing is pre-selling. That is, sharing your strategy, the creative ideas as they develop, with the client, preparing them for the end result. Sometimes, it steals thunder from the actual presentation, but I'd rather go in feeling I've sold the campaign.

Brian K. Nienhaus, senior account executive,
Young & Rubicam, Wilmington, Delaware

Rehearsals are not uncommon in either public relations or advertising, and visuals, too, are a more frequent by-product in these contexts than they are in journalism. Still, the precautions taken to achieve brevity, familiarity with the information, and smooth rather than mechanical delivery predominate across all media divisions. Knowing your decision maker is another precaution. As Nienhaus explained, some clients are tactile. Others are visual and like to see pictorial representations of an argument, including visuals of the product designed for mass distribution. Still others are auditory and want to hear rather than read a proposed TV script for a commercial. On occasion, all three channels of reception become necessary. Know your client's preferences but also do what illustrates your creative campaign ideas most effectively. Here's what this advertising executive took to his presentation (see case introduction, Chapter 7):

We took acetates [for overhead projection] and the creative work itself. These included television storyboards and actual radio demos. So we actually did the radio ad, recorded it, and did it in demonstration form instead of providing them [decision makers] with scripts. And then we had print ads, with completed copy and artwork.

Steven S. Swanson, senior vice president
and management supervisor,
Ross Roy Communications, Inc.,
Bloomfield Hills, Michigan

Knowing the client's preferred reception channels helps, but let the presentation content tell you what types of visuals are most appropriate for your particular presentation. Ask yourself these questions: *What facts, recommendations, and creative sugges-tions would I want to see illustrated? As the decision maker, how would I want to see these explained, hear them described, or reproduced in reality if they involved the sense of touch? If I were the prospective consumer, which channel of perception would receive the creative idea most effectively?*

There's more about augmenting an oral presentation with visuals, models, and props in Chapter 10.

NOTES

1. R. Susskind and J. S. Lublin, "Critics Are Succinct: Long Speeches Tend to Get Short Interest," *Wall Street Journal,* 27 January 1995, A1.

2. Based on an actual case drawn from the author's personal experience. The client developed the machine and patented it. Customer response was phenomenal, and the machine was used throughout the life of the patent in retail stores wherever the product line was sold. In the years that followed, the idea was imitated in modified forms by competitors.

3. A. Mehrabian, *Nonverbal Communication* (New York: Aldine-Atherton, 1972); also Mehrabian, *Silent Messages* (Belmont, CA: Wadsworth, 1971).

4. Mehrabian, *Nonverbal Communication.*

5. B. W. Batten and C. A. Insko, "Detection of Speaker's Attitude from Successive Pro and Con Advocacy," *Representative Research in Social Psychology* 16, no. 2 (1986): 28-37.

6. J. K. Burgoon, T. Birk, and M. Pfau, "Nonverbal Behaviors, Persuasion, and Credibility," *Human Communication Research* 17, no. 1 (1990): 140-69.

7. J. A. Edinger and M. L. Patterson, "Nonverbal Involvement and Social Control," *Psychological Bulletin* 93, no. 1 (1986): 30-56.

8. R. G. Plaveitch and B. H. Kleiner, "How to Be an Effective Public Speaker," *Training & Development* 46, no. 11 (1992): 17-20.

9. J. Kupsch and P. R. Groves, *How to Create High-Impact Business Presentations* (Lincolnwood, IL: NTC Publishing Group, 1993).

10. J. Pittam, "The Relationship Between Persuasiveness of Nasality and Source Characteristics for Australian and American Listeners," *Journal of Social Psychology* 130, no. 1 (1990): 81-7. Also see E. J. Wilson and D. L. Sherrell, "Source Effects in Communi-cation and Persuasion Research: A Meta-Analysis of Effect Size," *Journal of the Academy of Marketing Science* 21, no. 2 (1993): 101-12.

11. For example, see N. Miller, G. Maruyama, R. J. Beaber, and K. Valone, "Speed of Speech and Persuasion," *Journal of Personality and Social Psychology* 34, no. 4 (1976): 615-24; and W. B. Pearce and B. J. Brommel, "Vocalic Communication in Persuasion," *Quarterly Journal of Speech* 58, no. 3 (1972): 298-306.

12. S. M. Smith and D. R. Schaffer, "Celerity and Cajolery: Rapid Speech May Promote or Inhibit Persuasion Through Its Impact on Message Elaboration," *Personality and Social Psychology Bulletin* 17, no. 6 (1991): 663-9.

13. Miller et al., "Speed of Speech."

14. For example, see T. C. Smith, who recommends it in *Making Successful Presentations* (New York: John Wiley, 1991); and A. L. Schwartz, F. Bettger, T. Peters, and J. M. Wilson et al. who do not in "Tips for Successful Selling," *Agriculture Marketing* 31, no. 3 (1993): 66-7.

10

The Use and Display of Visuals

It's important to realize that visuals are not the presentation. You are. Visuals help lock the oral presentation in memory. They dramatize and support what you're saying. But they do not carry the presentation. You do. Some speech consultants say visuals are great reminders of what a speaker needs to say. Yes, they can be, but that's not their function. Your job is to know your material well enough so that you don't have to depend on visuals to recall your presentation. Let the visual do what it's supposed to do—lock a point of information in memory, dramatize and support what you say. In this chapter, you'll find cues and clues about visuals and some of the positives and negatives involved in their display.

VISUALS: TYPES, USE, AND SELECTION

The types of visuals available for display are wide and varied. A visual may be a chart, a line or bar graph, pie chart, photo, cartoon, sketch, illustration, storyboard, film, or video. In short, a visual is a picture, a pictorial representation of a series of facts, numbers, recommendations, or a creative idea. For example, pie charts and bar or line graphs are picture representations of facts and numbers. An illustration of an object rather than naming it on a visual is a pictorial representation; so is a sketch of a proposed creative idea.

All too often, speakers make the mistake of loading a visual with numbers or lines and lines of copy with no pictorial representation of the facts. That's boring. Your audience will neither remember all the numbers, follow the copy, or listen to you, because their attention is drawn in too many different directions. Instead, limit the numbers and words by substituting pictorials wherever possible. They must not be placed on the visual arbitrarily or just for the sake of pictorial relief. The pictorial must serve the purpose of illustrating the concept or fact intended.

Knowing what to visualize and when to display it is not a problem. Rely on the same principle of limited selection you used to organize your oral argument. Ask yourself these questions:

- *Which facts or numbers in my argument are complex and call for a visual, one that summarizes and simplifies and provides understanding at a glance?*
- *Which facts, statements, claims, or recommendations can be represented effectively with a visual?*
- *Which ones will ignite attention, dramatize the information, and lock its significance in memory?*

If the number of possibilities makes decisions difficult, then develop only those possibilities that promise strong persuasive impact, would be lost on the mind without a clarifying or dramatic representation, and cannot be carried by the oral delivery without a clarifying or summarizing display of the facts, numbers, recommendations, or creative ideas. The visual should not only wake up your audience and pique their interest, it should also answer challenges like "Oh yeah? You'll have to prove it to me" or "Show me, and who says so anyway?"

Don't overlook the available services in your art department. Artists can help translate words, statements, and numbers into pictorial representations, shape a series of facts and recommendations into a clarifying visual framework, and suggest ways of displaying a creative idea.

Above all, avoid throwing up one visual after another. Be selective, otherwise you'll become less a presenter and more a technician. If you have to fuss constantly with numerous visuals, perhaps frantically changing from one piece of display equipment to another, your audience will be preoccupied with all your movements and quickly lose track of your argument. Remember, your audience came to hear you, not to look at volumes of visuals.

DISPLAY EQUIPMENT:
ADVANTAGES AND DISADVANTAGES

Only you can determine which type of display device best suits your particular setting and purpose. You may need no more than a markerboard, flip chart, or posterboard. Some presentations may require more elaborate equipment such as an overhead projector, VCR, and video monitor. This section will help you choose the display equipment for your visual. First, know the equipment types available and the advantages and disadvantages of each.

Markerboard

Positives: Inexpensive and available. The visual can be done in advance and covered until you're ready to talk about it or it can be produced as you talk. Suitable for small groups.

Negatives: Slow moving, dull. Use colored markers and only those that erase because some don't. Requires good printing or handwriting. Poor visibility, subject to being blocked by speaker's body. If not part of room's facilities, is hard to transport. Unless set up securely, can wobble as you write on it.

Posterboard

Positives: Can be produced in advance. Best suited for small groups.

Negatives: Static, poor visibility, oversize ones hard to transport, requires easel for mounting, limits interaction between speaker and audience, and tends to be word dominated, which can be relieved by using colors or symbols.

Flip Chart

Positives: Can roll up for transport, easy to make and use, low cost, can be produced in advance, pads and markers readily available. Provides interaction between speaker and audience— you can roll up your shirt sleeves and dramatize your seriousness about the project at hand. Good for small groups.

Negatives: Subject to wear and tear, low impact capability, requires good print or handwriting if produced on scene, tends to be word dominated. Needs an easel. Colored markers bleed through several pages. Colored crayons can be used but risk spelling and other errors that can't be erased. Could end up with a messy chart page and leave the wrong impression.

Transparency

Positives: For some, the visual of choice. Easy to produce and inexpensive. Can be produced by hand or computer and copied, are easy to store and transport. Pictorials are possible. Suitable for large and small audiences.

Negatives: The overhead projector and screen should be available on request or rented. Otherwise, too difficult to transport. Requires several movements to obtain good focus, and placement of transparencies can be distracting. So can the mechanics of turning the projector on and off, and when left on draws attention away from you. Can face problem of burned-out bulb and no spare. Full-color transparencies take time and can be expensive.

Slide

Positives: Easy to store and carry, color slides economical to produce and have lasting quality. Projectors available on request, simple to operate. Suits large and small audiences.

Negatives: Projector hard to transport, requires a darkened room. Darkened room reduces advantage of eye contact and encourages audience tendency to doze. Artwork can be costly. Photographic processing takes extra time. Once machine is loaded, slides cannot be changed during presentation. Can face problems of jamming, focus, burned-out bulbs and no spares.

Videotape

Positives: Motion offers high interest level, no photographic processing necessary, easy and fast to produce. Suitable for large and small audiences.

Negatives: Audience focus falls on the visual rather than the presenter. Requires playback equipment that suits the recorded format of the tape. Expensive to produce professionally.

Model, Mockup, Prop, and Product

Positives: Each offers realism, high impact and memory value, versatility. All provide hands-on opportunities. Can introduce color, variety, texture, and feeling. Props and giveaways are available. Props can be symbolic of almost anything: a glove to illustrate a good fit, a sad clown mask to illustrate an attitude. Products can be reminders of almost anything: a miniature replica of a company's new logo or product attached to a key chain and shown as a sample of what can be distributed as a consumer giveaway. Models and mockups, too, can be a lively addition to a presentation—for example, a scale model of a machine such as the one described in the previous chapter to coordinate cosmetics to a woman's skin tone and hair color or a sketch of a new design for a bottled beverage.

Negatives: Must be appropriate to what's being said or will appear gimmicky and superfluous rather than serving as an illustration or recall link. Such representations take time and add to the cost of making the presentation.

Computer Presentation

Positives: The new wave in visuals. Charts, graphs, dia-grams, and other visuals made on a computer are shown on a monitor screen for small groups or projected on a large screen for larger groups. Offers smooth transition from visual to visual, can make changes easily. Shop around for the software program that best fits your needs. Your in-house computer technician or a technician at a reputable dealer can help you.[1]

Negatives: Initial cost of equipment. Not readily available and requires practiced facility with computer graphic techniques.

CREATING THE VISUAL

Using software packages to create visuals works for some; others prefer to leave the task of producing them to a profes-sional.

In the event you intend to use words only, it helps to know what to do to make the visual easy to see and take in with a glance. Raise these questions to test frames of information suitable mainly for such equipment as posterboards, transparencies, and slide or video projector:

- *Is the title of the frame at the very top and centered?*
- *Are the words underneath the title near the top?* Words near the bottom of the frame will not be seen.
- *Are the words centered under the title?* Center text right to left, not top to bottom.
- *Are there too many words for each idea?* Audience won't read them. Eliminate words wherever possible.
- *Are there too many ideas on the same visual frame?* Show three main ideas at a time, five at the most.
- *Are letters in upper and lower case?* Words in all upper case are hard to read.
- *Are the letters large enough for everyone to see?* 18 point is good, 20 is better.
- *Are letters sans serif?* Serif is standard in texts but harder to read on a visual.

- *Is the shape of my visual in a landscape or portrait frame?* Landscape is the standard and is wider than it is tall. Portrait is a narrow and tall frame. Landscape is preferred for transparencies and slides.
- *Would the use of color increase readability, or highlight a significant point of information?* Use color to set certain information apart from other matter or to direct attention to something.
- *Are borders overused?* Avoid using them. They take up valuable space, are distracting, and when projected are lost from view.
- *Is the style consistent?* Keep all visuals at the top two-thirds of the space and sustain typeface and font size. If heads are in bold or underlined, make that consistent throughout.
- *Can images replace some of the words, phrases, sentences?* Use images wherever possible. Just keep these to a minimum. Too much clutter muddies the visual's meaning and distracts. For example, if you wanted to illustrate the public services that were lost to taxpayers because funds were mismanaged, you could begin the visual with a word title such as "What Taxpayers Didn't Get." But instead of listing the services, a more effective means would be a clear image of each service with an "X" over it. If you still wanted to use the word list, another way to get in a visual is to set the title flush left, list the lost services under it and preface each item with a relevant symbol or bullet. This leaves some space in the upper right-hand corner to place a drawing of a kettle labeled with the total funds lost across it and dollar bills with wings flying out of it. Exchange ideas with your artist. You can be as creative as the next person. Precaution: Make certain that images and illustrations are relevant representations of the words.

THE PRESENTATION ENVIRONMENT

Journalists have the advantage of knowing where they have to present. They're on home ground and are familiar with their presentation environment.

That's not always the case for public relations and advertising presenters. Sometimes, their meetings are held on home ground, sometimes on the client's turf. If the latter, usually you can make a quick survey of the layout during a visit to the client's office. If it's not possible to examine the meeting room long before the presentation, ask for permission to make an inspection a day or so beforehand and during hours most convenient for the client. This gives you time to make room adjustments, test ordered equipment, or make replacements.

Whether it's on home ground or otherwise, familiarize yourself with the environment. Check the seating, facilities, acoustics, and room temperature. Go through the motions mentally on how you would work this room with decision makers in it. As always, the key word is *preparation.*

It's not possible to think of everything that might go wrong, but a check of what's there and not there helps. For example, consider the following:

- *Where should visual equipment be placed in relationship to the room's seating?* Be sure to test the equipment.
- *Are cords taped to the floor?*
- Is the bulb in the overhead projector working? Is there a spare, just in case?
- *Is the screen placed in the right position in relationship to the seating? Does the projector obstruct anyone's view?*
- *Are easels sturdy and properly placed? Are tables sturdy enough to hold equipment?*
- *Is the seating arrangement such that everyone can see me and everything on the visual?*
- *Is the monitor on a table or stand so that everyone has a full and clear view?*
- *Where are the light switches and plugs located, and do they work?*
- *Is the lighting appropriate?* You want less light over the screen and normal lighting in the rest of the room.
- *What about the acoustics? Is there an echo in the room? Will I have to moderate or raise my voice? Will noises from outside the room be heard and interfere?* If something interferes with your delivery, try to change the room. If you can't, be aware of what you need to do to improve conditions for delivery.
- *Is the room temperature too hot or too cold?* An overheated room induces sleepiness; a cold room subverts agreeability.

In short, find out if what you need is there, if everything works for your visuals, and if the room arrangement serves the purpose of your oral and visual presentation. Just keep in mind that media presentations occur before small groups. Seating is intimate but not cramped and is usually around a conference table, but the room itself may be cavernous, something you'd have to take into consideration.

If possible, try to avoid assignment to a small room simply because you'll need space to place your visual equipment, to rise from your chair easily, and to work with and from the visual without bumping into tables, chairs, or people or tripping over cords. Then, before leaving for the presentation, check yourself. *What do you need to take with you?* Make a checklist of those items. *Have you prepared all these in advance so they're packed and ready for transport?*

DISPLAYING THE VISUAL

One of the most common mistakes that presenters commit when introducing a visual is to stand in front it. The very persons who need to see it can't because the presenter is blocking their view. After investing so much time and effort on the visual, indeed on the whole project, frustrating a decision maker is the last thing a presenter should do.

Try to arrange the projector and screen so that you (or an assistant) can work the equipment and still stand away from the center and to the side edge of the screen. Placement should be such that neither you nor the equipment obstructs anyone's view of the visual.

Managing the Equipment

Working the equipment yourself as you present creates more movement than you want to create, but the activity has some advantages. Managing the equipment and dealing with the visual without obstructing it breaks the presenter's tendency to stand rigidly in one place, directs attention to the visual, then back to you. It also puts control of the equipment in your hands instead of another's.

However, there are some disadvantages. The activity can break the flow of the oral delivery and sometimes tries the patience of an audience. To avoid this athletic exercise, or the need to rely on an assistant, use equipment that you can operate remotely from the podium. Options include a slide projector, video presentation, or a portable computer coupled with equipment that displays the computer-generated image. If you do use a medium that requires movement, such as posterboards or transparencies, then be sure that the sequence of your materials matches that of your oral presentation. Check the order, arrange and load them in that order before you present. This avoids the embarrassment of displaying something that has nothing to do with what you're saying.

Make It Easy for Your Listening Audience

Another common mistake is failing to direct the audience's attention to where you want them to look. Don't expect the audience to look at you and the visual at the same time. Indicate when you want them to look at the visual and where they should look as you talk about whatever's on the visual. See how this works for you: Introduce the visual, display it, then stand aside facing the audience; use a pointer to direct attention to items on the visual and face the audience as you talk about each item from the edge of the screen. Restrain any gesture or movement that obstructs anyone's view. Just remember to hold the pointer in your hand nearest the screen; otherwise, you're inclined to twist your body away from the audience and block their view. Decide which side of the screen is easiest for you to manage and practice working with the visual until you feel comfortable about it.

Finally, don't read the visual word for word; the audience can do that. Besides, the visual is supposed to illustrate a point you're making, not a lesson in reading. If your visual is a list of items like the one shown in Chapter 9, simply display it, but don't read it verbatim. That's deadly. Instead, say something like this:

"By improving _____ we'll be able to _____ and succeed in doing _____ , _____ , and _____ . Those improvements, in turn, will increase _____ because _____ . The result will, therefore, bring about a notable decrease in _____ and _____ , and that's what all of us want to achieve." In that way you're not reading the words as much as you are providing the reasons why they're there.

OTHER CUES

Should a projected visual remain in view after you've talked about it? There's some disagreement about this. Some consultants say remove it and turn off the equipment. Others recommend leaving the visual and equipment on. It really depends on the visual. If the visual might divert attention away from the next presentation topic, remove it. If, however, the visual will not divert attention and gives the audience a chance to study it, leave it displayed until you introduce the next topic.

The disadvantage of leaving the visual and equipment on is not a small one. The projector light and constant whirr of electronic equipment may bother some people. Conversely, too much movement and constant clicking from "on" to "off" can be just as annoying. A reasonable alternative is to leave the visual and projector on and ready for the next illustration. In any case, the important thing to do is to direct attention back to yourself when you're finished with the visual. One way to do this is to move a slight distance away from the screen and return the pointer to either a horizontal hold across the center of your body or to a vertical position by your side. Then when you're ready for the next visual, move back to your former position at the side of the screen. Just remember to remove the final visual and turn off the projector when you're through showing visuals. It gives your closing a clean finish.

Your best defense against delivering a choppy presentation versus a smooth and well-coordinated verbal and visual one is to rehearse. Not everyone agrees with this precaution. Rehearsals, they say, interfere with a natural and spontaneous flow. This is probably true for practiced presenters. But it takes many presentations to get to that point. Until then, rehearse. After you feel you have the message anchored in your mind, rehearse again with the visuals in order to achieve the professional effect of a practiced presenter. That's what your decision makers expect to see and hear.

HANDLING INTERRUPTIONS

Usually, presenters ask for questions at the end of a presentation. However, those questions and other interruptions could come anywhere during your presentation. Interruptions can throw a presenter off track, but not you. You *know* your material. You know where and how to display the visuals, you know every detail in the written document, and you know everything there is to know about the problem, the strategy, and how it responds to the needs and expectations of decision makers. Questions or interruptions should be a breeze.

Handling them during your presentation is an opportunity to show you can keep your cool and get back on track with no trouble at all. Use transitions to return to the subject: *Now, in regard to . . . . That question, in fact, is directly related to my next point concerning . . . . Yes, that's true, but let me direct your attention again to . . . . You have a point, but let me remind you that . . . . Well, that's not quite the case anymore because things began to change about a year ago when . . . and now . . . .*

If the question is a good one, let the person know: *That's a very good question and I'm glad you brought it up.* If the question concerns something you've already covered, avoid saying *I've already said . . .* or *I've already explained . . . .* You don't want to insult the questioner. Simply go over the point again. If someone challenges your data, your conclusion, your approach or strategy, better be ready with an informative answer and substantiated data for these and other challenges. Anticipate them, because you'll get them. Ask yourself:

- *What questions and challenges would I raise if heard this petition?*
- *What was not covered in the oral argument that I might want to hear about?*
- *What more would I want to hear about a particular point that was discussed?*
- *If I were asked how I might handle the project differently than what I proposed, how would I answer that?*
- *How would I point out the weaknesses in the alternative and why the proposed strategy responds to the problem and need more effectively? What's my evidence?*

CONCLUSION

The process of solving the problem from start to finish proceeded from a base of systematic preparation facilitated by critical-creative thinking. Those habits are the ones professionals practice no matter what the problem may be, no matter what decision makers' special needs may be. Process and inquiry are your servants in this and all instances of media work. They will serve you well. Use them to your advantage to research the problem, manage the data, identify the solution, generate ideas for implementing the solution, compose the written proposal, and deliver the oral presentation. Together those functions help put your petition up front and decision makers in a supportive frame of mind.

NOTE

1. A number of software programs enable presenters to create their own graphics. Some recommendations are Aldus Persuasion, Lotus Freelance Graphics, Harvard Graphics for Windows, Microsoft's Powerpoint 4.0 for Windows, Vividus Cinemation, and Macromedia Magic. Ask yourself which program best fills your needs and purpose. Then seek the advice of your in-house technician, computer center, or retailer.

Index

About the Author

Elise K. Parsigian is Associate Director of the Center for Armenian Research, Studies, and Publication, the University of Michigan, Dearborn. She has taught journalism and mass media communication courses at the Department of Communication, University of Michigan, Ann Arbor and writing courses at Wayne State University and Eastern Michigan University.

A former journalist, public relations, advertising, and film writer with some 20 years of experience in the field, Dr. Parsigian also has her own consulting company, Communication Solutions. She serves clients with public relations, advertising, and general communication problems related to resolving research issues, producing ideas, planning strategies, and writing and presenting proposals and various types of mass communication products.

She is a frequent presenter at communication conferences, and professional journals have published her papers on issues concerning both national and international news communications. She is author of *Mass Media Writing*, which for the first time provides novices and pros with problem-solving, critical-creative thinking methodology that applies to general assignments and demystifies the practices common to producing media products whether the setting is journalistic, public relations, or advertising.

Dr. Parsigian holds a Ph.D. degree in communication studies from the University of Michigan, Ann Arbor, a master's degree in English language and literature from Wayne State University, and a bachelor of arts degree in English language and literature and psychology, also from Wayne State.